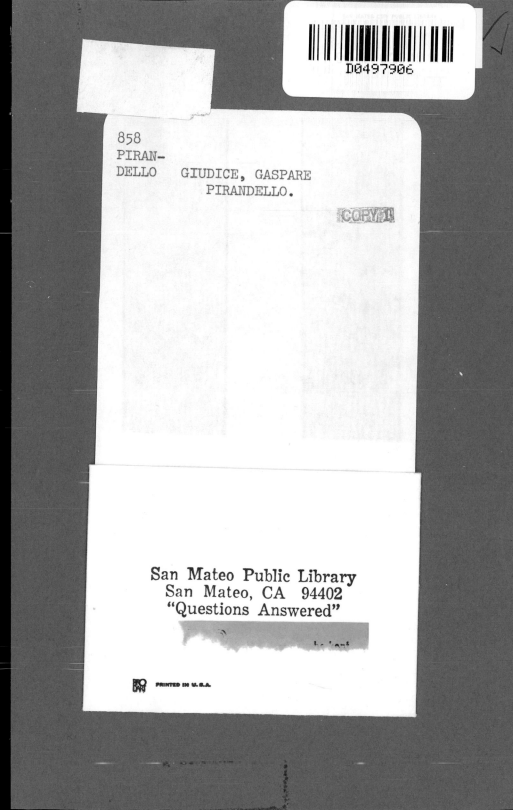

PIRANDELLO: A BIOGRAPHY

GASPARE GIUDICE

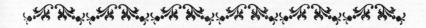

PIRANDELLO

A BIOGRAPHY

translated by
Alastair Hamilton

LONDON
OXFORD UNIVERSITY PRESS
NEW YORK TORONTO
1975

Oxford University Press, Ely House, London W1

GLASGOW   NEW YORK   TORONTO   MELBOURNE   WELLINGTON
CAPE TOWN   IBADAN   NAIROBI   DAR ES SALAAM   LUSAKA   ADDIS ABABA
DELHI   BOMBAY   CALCUTTA   MADRAS   KARACHI   LAHORE   DACCA
KUALA LUMPUR   SINGAPORE   HONG KONG   TOKYO

ISBN 0 19 212582 6

Printed in Great Britain by
Richard Clay (The Chaucer Press) Ltd
Bungay, Suffolk

CONTENTS

ILLUSTRATIONS

The photographs are reproduced by permission of Dr. Alfredo Zennaro, except for the portrait of d'Annunzio which appears by permission of Popperfoto.

SICILY

In a novel which Pirandello wrote when he was fifty, one of the characters says: 'What's the point of four generations of lights, four: oil, paraffin, gas, and electric lighting, all in sixty years? ... That's too many, you know. It harms one's eyes and it harms one's head. Yes, it harms one's head too.'[1] In a sense Pirandello himself was speaking. As a child he had been put to bed by the light of oil lamps and he and his family had dined in Agrigento by the light of paraffin lamps. He studied by gas light, and later, after his first volumes of poetry had been published, he started writing his prose works at the moment when electric lighting was being introduced.

Nearly everybody has forgotten that Luigi Pirandello was born in the heart of the nineteenth century. His critics have always projected him forwards, into modern times, yet the thirty-three years, almost half of his life, which he spent in the nineteenth century, were the years of the most decisive events of his childhood and of his cultural development. He was born in a period of conspiracy and political persecution, and he was born in Sicily, an island where, shortly before his birth, the political climate had been dominated by the conflict between an absolute monarch and provincial lawyers with the exuberant and generous temperament of, for example, Giovanni Ricci Gramitto, Pirandello's maternal grandfather.

Ever since the early nineteenth century the family of Pirandello's mother (unlike that of his father, who was descended from Genoese settlers) had lived a form of patriotism which was exclusively Sicilian.

Pirandello's grandfather had been a separatist. He had worked as a lawyer in Agrigento (Girgenti, as it was then called); he had violently opposed the Bourbon monarchy; and he had been one of the most influential organizers of the Palermo insurrection in 1848. He was consequently given a ministry in the provisional government set up by Ruggiero Settimo.

Settimo's programme was moderate. But, despite the letters he received from Giuseppe Mazzini in London, urging him and his followers to promote the idea of a united Italian republic, his policy also remained profoundly separatist. Indeed, this basic belief in autonomy was deeply imbedded in the nineteenth-century Sicilian mentality (particularly in that of Pirandello's family) and it was to play an important part in the playwright's Sicilian works, such as the novel *The Old and the Young* (*I vecchi e i giovani*). His mother and her brothers had all sworn allegiance to the political testament of Giovanni Ricci Gramitto and, after seeing through the 'illusion of unity', they called it to mind on every occasion—on the occasion of every 'betrayal' of Sicily, first by the Piedmontese and then by the successive unitary governments until the revolt of the *Fasci Siciliani*, the workers' movement which Pirandello was later to describe from a primarily Sicilian point of view.

In 1848, when Ruggiero Settimo was succeeded by the more democratic Filippo Cordova, Giovanni Ricci Gramitto left the government. He was no democrat. Owing to his profession and his clientele he frequented the class which monopolized the productive resources of Sicily, the landowners. The hatred this class had for the Bourbons was the consequence of a series of economic, political, and administrative provisions which the Neapolitan monarchy had promulgated at the expense of Sicily and, above all, at the expense of the Sicilian bourgeoisie, and the island was reduced to a semi-colonial status. The moderate bourgeois outlook which prevailed among Pirandello's ancestors should be noted, for as we shall see from Pirandello's own political opinions, he did not inherit any love for a democratic tradition.

Giovanni Ricci Gramitto's large family had both ideological and personal reasons for participating in the struggle against the Bourbons, and for opposing the clergy and the papacy. The Bourbon king, Ferdinand II, had approved the list of proscriptions himself and had excluded Giovanni Ricci Gramitto, together with Ruggiero Settimo and forty-one other men, from the amnesty. Consequently Ricci Gramitto died of a broken heart at the age of forty-six while his family, who had hitherto led a comfortable existence on income from their land, were now subjected to the humiliation of depending on the charity of an uncle who had the misfortune to be both pro-Bourbon and a priest.

The clerical uncle did what he could to re-educate his unruly nephews, to teach them common sense, and opportunism. He sent two of them, Vincenzo and Innocenzo, to a seminary, but Vincenzo, who got rid of his frock as soon as he could, was one of the few young men to resist the Bourbon troops from the garrison of Agrigento on 4 April 1860. Pursued by the police, he fled across Sicily and joined another of his brothers, Rocco, who had been one of the organizers of the unsuccessful revolt of the Gancia in Palermo. They both fought for Mazzini's former emissary Rosolino Pilo and accompanied Garibaldi's men as far as Naples. In 1862, at Aspromonte in Calabria, Rocco, Garibaldi's lieutenant, was taken prisoner by the government forces and sent first to La Spezia, then to Forte Ratti in Genoa, and finally to the barracks of San Benigno. Shortly before the battle of Aspromonte he had met Stefano Pirandello (Luigi's father), and when he was released and returned in triumph to Agrigento in October 1862 Stefano Pirandello was there on business. Stefano first set eyes on Rocco's sister Caterina in her brother's house. 'He was handsome, but she was not—except for her eyes,' Pirandello's son was to write later. 'Besides, aged nearly twenty-eight, she considered herself to be an old maid: she had given her youth to her country. When Stefano asked for her hand, there and then, she thought he was joking. It was a patriotic marriage . . .'[2]

Stefano Pirandello and Caterina Ricci Gramitto married in November 1863. Luigi, their second child, was born on 28 June 1867 in the Ricci Gramitto farmhouse, Il Caos, between Agrigento and Porto Empedocle. He was born a little prematurely since his mother had just had the shock of discovering that Stefano had been infected by the cholera epidemic which swept across Sicily from October 1866 to August 1867, killing some 53,000 people. But Stefano recovered and Caterina, together with her eldest child, Rosalina, was carried to Il Caos on a stretcher. There Caterina gave birth to Luigi six days later while one of her brothers was scouring the countryside in search of a midwife. In his old age Pirandello started an autobiographical novel which he never managed to finish, and in which he gave a poetic description of his birth:[3]

One night in June I dropped down like a firefly beneath a huge pine tree standing all on its own in an olive grove on the edge of a blue clay plateau overlooking the African sea. We know about fireflies. It's as if the blackness of night exists solely for their benefit, so that, as they fly this way and that, they can show off their pale green gleam. Every now and then one of them falls and, on the ground, gives a sigh of green light as if from very far away. That was how I dropped down on that June night while so many other yellow fireflies twinkled on a hill, near a city cursed by the plague. Out of fear of the plague my mother gave birth to me prematurely. An uncle of mine had gone out into the countryside, a lantern in his hand, in search of a peasant woman to help her give birth. But my mother managed on her own and I was born before my uncle returned. My birth was then registered in the little town on the hill. Because so many people died every day that year, one single birth was regarded as a form of compensation and was considered all the more important the more insignificant it actually was. But I believe people will think it inevitable that I should have been born there rather than anywhere else and at that moment rather than at any other, although I must admit that I myself have no views on the matter.

Little is known about the first years of Pirandello's life. He had two younger brothers, Innocenzo and Giovanni, and two younger sisters, Annetta and Adriana (who died at the age of four). He was a small, fragile child, constantly in need of more affection. His mother's love was not enough and his father was gruff, distant, and, although he loved his children, he never made any display of his affection. He was immensely tall; he was violent-tempered, and he liked to spend his time with other men, out of doors rather than at home.

Born in Palermo, the eighteenth son of a family of twenty-three, Stefano Pirandello had had to make his own way in life. He was only two years old when his father Andrea, the son of Ligurians from Pra who had emigrated to Sicily in the middle of the eighteenth century, died in the cholera epidemic of 1837 at the age of forty-six. By a series of truly Machiavellian manoeuvres the eldest brother, Felice, appropriated the entire inheritance and directed the family business, exporting sulphur and citrus fruits, with his other brothers working as his subordinates. When he was old enough Stefano too joined the business. But he had an adventurous temperament: he could be high-minded, hard, or contemptuous, according to the circumstances. He could even be ingenuous. When Garibaldi arrived in Palermo in 1860 Stefano was a youngster of twenty-five, capable of performing glorious deeds. He fought against the Bourbon troops for three days in Palermo and, at one point during the street fighting, was rescued by Garibaldi himself. Out of gratitude and admiration Stefano joined the Genoese carabineers and followed the general. He fought at Milazzo, Reggio, and the Volturno and, two years later, was with Garibaldi in Aspromonte. Here, with a more practical but less dutiful spirit than his future brother-in-law, Rocco Ricci Gramitto, he preferred to flee back to Sicily rather than be taken prisoner by the soldiers of the king.

Indeed, Stefano was very different from the Ricci Gramittos. The Ricci Gramittos, true Sicilians, liked to observe a rigid formality in their political activity, even when it came to positive and practical action. Thus Rocco, fully aware of his formal responsibilities, had chosen to spend six months in prison at San Benigno. Stefano, on the other hand, with his mixture of Sicilian and Genoese blood, chose a more instinctive and practical means of behaviour, and, when he returned home, Felice, his eldest brother, sent him to Agrigento to supervise the sulphur mines rented by the firm. Here he married Caterina Ricci Gramitto in 1863.

Pirandello grew up in the shadow of this enormous, indifferent, and overbearing man. And after fighting the Bourbons Stefano fought another victorious battle with the mafia of the sulphur trade.

'In 1867,' wrote F. V. Nardelli, Pirandello's official biographer,[4]

the year of Luigi's birth, Stefano had rented a sulphur mine called La Petrusa and had had the good fortune to find a vein full of the mineral. When the news got around a certain Cola Camizzi, the head and the terror of the mafia of Agrigento, accosted Stefano Pirandello in the hope of getting some money out of him and opened the conversation with a vulgar joke. 'Dear Pirandello, in order to succeed with sulphur mines you need. . . .' And, so saying, he touched his behind. But Pirandello reacted without further ado, and gave Cola such a slap that he spun round in his tracks. Cola must have been dazed more by surprise than by the blow and he said to himself, probably in order to convince himself that what had happened was true: 'A slap to Cola Camizzi. . . .'

'Not one but a hundred,' answered Stefano and proceeded to hit him in the face until he fell to the ground, his eyes, mouth, and cheeks swollen with bruises.

Then Stefano went his way. He entered a storehouse on the beach where he came across a prospector called Veronica. The two men were discussing the price of sulphur in the storehouse when they heard shots outside. Veronica displayed curiosity, but Stefano Pirandello said nothing. A servant who had gone out to see what was happening returned saying: 'It's Cola Camizzi trying out his gun.'

They thought he was preparing to go shooting. But, as he walked up and down with Veronica, Stefano Pirandello took his revolver from his belt and slipped it into the outer pocket of his jacket. Then they suddenly heard a shout: 'Out of the way! Out of the way!' And when they turned round they saw the gun pointing at them. Cola had crept up behind the sulphur stacks and was aiming at Pirandello. Veronica got out of the way while Pirandello, who did not have time to draw his revolver, watched the point of the gun and, as soon as it fired, jumped to one side, shielding his heart with his arm.

He was hit twice, and they say he went on shouting: 'Shoot, you swine!' One bullet injured his bone and tendons and he lost the use of a finger. The other went through his biceps into his chest and ended up against a rib. He fell to his knees and Cola, who had thrown down his gun, came towards him with his revolver to finish him off. But the servant who had thought he was trying out his gun picked it up and clubbed him over the head with it.

At this point Cola staggered away. Pirandello followed him for twenty paces, firing the six shots in his revolver, before he fainted for loss of blood. He was carried home to his wife. At first the doctors wanted to amputate his arm, but they subsequently changed their minds. Caterina, who was feeding Luigi, lost her milk as a result of the shock and Luigi had to be entrusted to a wet nurse. Cola Camizzi was sent to prison for seven years. When he was released he left Agrigento immediately, because Stefano Pirandello had sworn he would kill him, and he ended his days in a distant and obscure sulphur mine.

Stefano Pirandello, therefore, was a man to be reckoned with, and the barrier between Luigi and his father was never overcome. Indeed, it grew with the years and became insurmountable. Near the end of his life Luigi made a public confession:[5]

I remember that when I was a child I had absolute confidence that everybody would understand me. A form of ingenuousness which obviously caused me bitter disappointments. But it stimulated me to improve my faculties of expression and to study others in order to get an idea of the people I would be dealing with, firmly convinced as I was that I could communicate anything at any time to anyone. And this is why I can say that I started working then. When I was a child I had difficulties even with my mother, and as for my father, it appeared to be quite impossible to communicate with him, not just when I was preparing myself to do so but when I had actually tried and had failed abysmally. As an artist I owe a great deal to him for the agony of those moments.

Pirandello's childhood was marked by two episodes which are proof of the boy's exceptionally precocious moral standards, his uncompromising trust, and his sensitivity which was all too easily wounded and shocked. There was a maid-servant working in the Pirandello household called Maria Stella. Although she was of very humble origin she had spirit enough to want to share with the little boy some of her superstitious beliefs and some of her peasant mystical tendencies—especially since, in the Pirandello household, God was silent. She therefore felt herself to be something of a missionary; and Father Sparma, the priest at San Pietro, the near-by church, encouraged her.

It was from her that Pirandello learnt to believe in ghosts—in ghosts both concrete and abstract which could appear at any moment of the day or night and say what they have to say. And, once the superstitions had been exorcised by an aesthetic system rooted in idealist thought, these ghosts could be turned into characters. If ghosts as such, ghosts rattling their chains, pulling away the bed covers, shaking the furniture and ringing the bells, appear frequently in Pirandello's work this is probably due to Maria Stella. One night, when they had heard the scream of a man killed in front of the Pirandello house, and Pirandello's mother had closed all the windows in accordance with the conspiracy of silence, Maria Stella started to tell the boy about the dead man's damned soul and, a few days later, she said that she and others had seen his ghost stalking the street.

Maria Stella finally managed to take Pirandello to church. The priest did the rest. The little boy seems to have gone through a mystical crisis and he went to mass at dawn every morning, his mother closing her eyes to the fact, or perhaps even quite pleased about it. The religious atmosphere in the church and the celebration of the sacraments corresponded to an idea of perfection which he cherished. He believed in the precepts preached from the pulpit and listened earnestly to the Gospel, to its spirit and its commandments. One day he left his house dressed up in a sailor's suit just received from Palermo and returned home half naked after giving it to a child in rags. He wept and shouted when he had to take it back.[6] But the most important episode of that period is recounted by Pirandello himself in the short story 'The Wax Madonna' ('La Madonnina').

Father Fiorica (Father Sparma) is so pleased that a member of the Greli (Pirandello) family should come to church that he invites Guiduccio (Pirandello) into the sacristy and pampers him, until:

In this month of May, dedicated to the Virgin, in the church of San Pietro, after the sermon and the rosary, after the blessing and the hymns to the Virgin Mary accompanied by the organ, the faithful cast lots for a little wax madonna kept under a crystal dome. . . . The lottery tickets cost a *soldo* each. . . . [The priest] hoped that some miracle would allow his finger to pick the ticket with [Guiduccio's] name on it. And he was almost displeased at the boy's generosity for, instead of buying the ten tickets he could well have afforded with the half lira his mother gave him every Sunday, he only bought one so as not to have an advantage over the other boys for whom he even went so far as to buy nine other tickets with the change. . . . And so the devil tempted the priest . . . and told him to read Guiduccio Greli's name on the winning ticket. As the parishioners cried with joy Guiduccio, who had at first turned scarlet, suddenly went very pale, knitted his brows over his troubled eyes, started to tremble convulsively, hid his face in his arms, and, slipping from the crowd of women who wanted to kiss him and to congratulate him, rushed out of the church and ran home where he fell into his mother's arms and burst into tears. A little later, when he heard the roll of the drum in the lane and the chorus of parishioners who were carrying the madonna to his house, he started to stamp his feet, to twist and turn in the arms of his mother and sisters and to shout:

'It isn't true! It isn't true! I don't want her! Send her away! It isn't true! It isn't true!'

And indeed, why should he have the madonna if there was no ticket in his name that Sunday?

In order to calm her son Signora Greli ordered the madonna to be sent back to church and Father Fiorica never saw Guiduccio Greli again.

The discovery of hypocrisy and evil in Father Sparma who, because he was a priest, should have represented truth and goodness, was a catastrophe for Pirandello. He was searching for coherence and perfection but saw them being frustrated over and over again. But this time he fully understood the significance of his defeat and tried to shake himself free of it. The door slammed in the face of the madonna (and, for that matter, of the Father, the Son, and the Holy Ghost) is indicative enough. With very few exceptions the priest—and Pirandello's work is full of priests—was to become a symbol of falsity.

As an apostate child Pirandello needed something to be sure of; he wanted every truth to be absolutely pure and free of compromise; and he wanted his love to be requited fully, with no half-measures. His father and mother should love him because they were his father and mother. And so Pirandello's undemonstrative father became the enemy. Later, in his middle age, Pirandello modified his opinion whenever he spoke about his father in public. He said that he was a 'challenge to life', that he was a 'fine looking man' or that he had a magnanimous and patriotic spirit,[7] and he saw his merits and his qualities. But when he spoke about him to his friends, or with the alibi of the medium of art, he was less cautious. Here the father becomes an incomprehensible and unjust figure—and he was distrusted all the more by a child who was unable to judge the various facets of his character. Pirandello described the relationship between his father and mother in his novel *The Outcast*, written in 1893.

He was taller than she . . . his build was enormous. . . . It was impossible to reason with him.

For many years she had learnt to judge every sorrow, every grief, not on its own terms but in terms of the rage it would arouse in her husband. . . . Sometimes all that was needed for the entire house to be plunged into mourning was that an object should be spoilt or broken— not even an object of any great value, but simply an object which could not be immediately replaced. . . . When the neighbours heard about it they used to laugh; and they were right. All that fuss about a little bottle, a little picture, any little trinket! But you had to see him, her husband, when the object was broken. He regarded it as a lack of respect not for the object, which was relatively valueless, but for himself. . . . Was he mean? Not at all! He was capable of breaking up half the house, and all for a trinket worth a few farthings!

In so many years of marriage she had managed to mollify him a little, by treating him gently, by forgiving him offences which were not always slight, but without infringing on her own dignity and without making her forgiveness weigh on him. But still he would sometimes fly into a rage over a mere trifle . . . and since nobody dared breathe a word he would sink into a black, silent fury for weeks on end. Of course, he was secretly irritated by the excessive care with which the members of his family avoided giving him the slightest pretext for grumbling. He suspected that many things were kept hidden from him —and if he ever found out that something *had* even if it were years later, he would give vent to his accumulated irritation without even thinking that he was being unjust and that everything had been done simply so as not to vex him.

He felt like an alien even in his own house; he thought his family regarded him as an alien and he consequently distrusted them.

And in view of the total lack of understanding between them his wife was occasionally forced to do behind his back things of which he would have disapproved. She was forced to deceive him.

Throughout adolescence Pirandello remained actively rebellious. The rebelliousness came out in acts of disobedience to his father, but later this spirit of rebelliousness was to be strictly repressed and to reappear in countless forms of disguise, in the shape of antitheses, outrages, or anarchy in his writing. Even Pirandello's belated commitment to fascism may originate from these unresolved conflicts and from a final acceptance of external authority.

The second crucial episode in Pirandello's childhood is described by Nardelli:[8]

In those days Luigi had never seen a corpse but, one day, he heard that there was one in the tower used as a morgue. . . . As he was walking along the Via delle Falde on his own he couldn't resist the desire to see it, so he jumped down the slope and pulled open the huge grey door. When he was inside the tower he made for the strip of blue sky behind the loophole and almost tripped over the coffin. Suddenly he saw the body! A pair of large shoes on its feet, it looked about forty years old. . . . But at the same time, in the silence of the hall, Luigi heard a soft noise, almost a rustle. . . . He held his breath. He heard the rustle again, not a rustle of wings, or of air, but a strange, continuous, live noise. . . . At that time and in that part of the country women wore a long petticoat under their skirts which ended in a stitched frill. . . . And sure enough, it was a woman. Luigi peered through the twilight and gradually perceived two bodies, a woman and a man, entwined together and performing a slow, strange, uninterrupted motion, as though they were rocking, impelled by a spasm or regulated by a spring. They held each other tightly and the woman's skirts were raised. The starched frill, rubbing between the two bodies, produced that unforgettable rustle. Luigi watched them. Her head was not bare, like that of a peasant. . . .

It is with reference to this episode that the critic and novelist Leonardo Sciascia wrote[9] that 'In Pirandello's work love always retains a smell of death—not the idea of death, but the physical, putrefying aspect of death. It is either tarnished by madness or poisoned by incomprehension and betrayal. Never do his characters abandon themselves to the emotions and the senses and there is not one woman, however beautiful, to whom the author does not give some more or less repulsive characteristic.' Yet we can hardly say that episode alone—the encounter of an adventurous and precocious child in a dark hall with a double spectacle of horror—determined the subsequent behaviour of the man and the writer. The boy's disappointment with his relationship with his father may have been more important. But what is certain is that Pirandello's life appears to be the consequence of a period of traumas, and the episode of the morgue assumes a symbolic value.

Pirandello was constantly struggling with death—with death transformed into a body or a person, an individual with physical or mental features. Death, for him, was to remain a figure which bounces back on its feet as soon as it has been knocked down, so that the game should continue. He shielded himself from it by caricaturing it and mocking it, but at the same time he formulated a theory in order to eliminate it from the intellect. He said that everything stiffens and that everything moves—an insoluble contradiction in his philosophy but at the same time a philosophical transposition of what he saw in the morgue. He turned the normal perspective upside down: he claimed that life was a trap, that birth was a beginning of death, that the living repeat the words of the dead, but also that death does not really exist because everything is constantly being set into motion again, that being is becoming and that man loses himself in his existence. This is more a form of mysticism than a philosophy. It comes from his struggle against death and is one of Pirandello's main themes with a biographical origin.

Death for Pirandello was primarily his own death. And it was his own death which had to be abolished. 'Do not dress my corpse,' he wrote in his will. 'Let me be wrapped naked in a winding sheet. And no flowers on the bed or lighted candles. . . . Burn me. And as soon as my body has been burnt the ashes must be thrown to the winds, for I want nothing, not even my ashes, to remain.' The scattering of his ashes to the winds was also a desire to return his corpse to the universe. Pirandello's final wish was not merely his last, it was his life-long wish. The old, yellow scrap of paper on which he wrote his testament proves it.

Pirandello was not even fortunate in the choice of his tutor. The tutor's name was Fasulo and, being vague and distant, he was never aware of the exceptional qualities of his pupil. Pirandello even wrote about him, in a short story entitled 'The Choice' ('La scelta'):

I can still see him, in his shabby grey suit and his faded old hat. . . . In Sicily All Souls' Day is a children's holiday . . . and my mother sent me with my tutor to the toy fair.

I remember the feverish desire with which I gazed at the toys. Deafened by the noise I turned this way and that. . . . Old Pinzone [Fasulo] pulled me along by my arm, wrenching me away from one toy seller after another . . . and when the toy sellers saw him tugging me along they cursed and insulted the poor man. But he simply sniggered and shook his head at the insults, talking to me the whole time, repeating:

'Take no notice of them: they want to cheat you. . . .'

Some of them were more aggressive; they jumped down from their stands holding a toy in their hand, they surrounded us. I looked Pinzone in the eye.

'Do you want it?' he would then ask me, and I would continue to look into his eye and say the no that I saw in his face and heard in the tone of his voice.

And so we went round the fair; and then, as I did almost every year, I returned to the store where they sold the marionettes which I adored. But even there, with the French Paladins and the Moorish knights, shining in their brass and copper armour, hanging in endless rows from pieces of wire, I had to make up my mind, while in fact I would have liked to take them all. Which one was I to choose?

'Take Orlando, sir!' the shop-keeper advised me. 'The champion of France: I'll sell him to you for ten and a half lire. . . .'

But Pinzone, who had been cautioned by my mother, burst out:

'Ten and a half lire? It's not worth three farthings. Look at him: he's got a squint! Besides, he may have been Champion of France, but he was also a raving lunatic!'

'Take Rinaldo di Montalbano. . . .'

'Worse still, you thief!' exclaimed Pinzone. And Astolfo was a braggart, Gano a traitor . . . in short Pinzone had something to say about every marionette I was shown. . . . Many years have passed: Pinzone is dead . . . but I confess that I still look enviously at a picture in which I am depicted in velvet knee breeches and with a trusted marionette in my hand. . . .

When Pirandello wept and stamped his feet because he was fed up with covering page after page of exercise book Fasulo told his mother that her son was 'backward' and that he had to go on doing his elementary exercises.

But as Pirandello grew older and learned to read and write his strongest natural tendencies came to light. He loved to read, and during all his school years until he went to university he read far more than the prescribed books; he loved the theatre, or rather a little theatre of his own where he could be both writer and producer. He displayed his passion for books almost immediately, although we know from his son Stefano[10] that all the household library contained was a four-volume edition of the Bible, certain novels by Walter Scott, and *La battaglia di Benevento*, an historical novel written by Francesco Domenico Guerrazzi in 1827.

In 1893 Pirandello dictated a 'fragment of autobiography'[11] about this period of his life.

My father is the proprietor of a large sulphur mine so he wanted me to study commerce. I was therefore sent to the technical school of Agrigento. But all those figures, all those rules, all that rigid mathematical order was repugnant to my impatient mind and my longing for complete liberty. Once I had been through the third form and had managed, God knows how, to pass the July exams, I told my father that I had failed in arithmetic and could not go to the country with my family since I would have to spend the holidays at Agrigento in order to study for and sit the exam again.

At this point Pirandello's mother intervened, together with his uncle Vincenzo who had since become a professor and who entrusted his nephew to a colleague, Professor Zagara.

My father didn't seem to mind and the money which should have been spent on hypothetical mathematics lessons was instead used for a real Latin lesson, because I so wanted to go to high school and to skip the first form. Everything went according to plan and in October I was admitted to the second form of the high school. My father didn't show too much interest in my studies: he was told that I had never lost a year and he was perfectly happy, far from guessing my prank.

I went to high school for the first two months with no worries whatsoever. But I was then betrayed by the pettiest of incidents. Even if my father did not look too closely into my studies he unfortunately had to sign my school report every two months. But I didn't have one because they didn't issue them at high school as they did at the technical schools ... so ... I managed to get away with it for the first term and invented some elaborate excuse which my father accepted.

But, wrote Pirandello's son Stefano,[12] Pirandello's father 'realized that he had been deceived when he had to sign the report at the end of the second term, and he made a terrible scene. ... For several months he neither looked at nor spoke to Luigi who studied as hard as he could, to prove that it wasn't a whim.' Yet Pirandello was a mediocre pupil during his first year at high school. A school friend of his, Antonio De Gubernatis, recalled[13] that he 'never gave any proof of possessing a superior intelligence' and that only once did the astonished schoolmaster ask Pirandello whether he had himself written an Italian essay which he had stood up to read. Nor had he done much better at the technical school where it appears from the school register that he rarely got as much as half marks for his essays. According to his son 'he was anything but serious and conscientious as a child. He was extremely vivacious; together with his younger brother and sister, Innocenzo and Anna, he was up to all sorts of tricks. One year, without ever having been to the theatre, they even organized a "performance".'

Pirandello had supplemented his father's library by buying serial novels and anything else he could lay his hands on at the local stationer's. It was then that he read Silvio Pellico's autobiographical *My Prisons* (*Le mie prigioni*) and his play *Eufemio di Messina* which inspired him to write tragedies. When he was twelve he wrote a five-act play entitled *Barbaro* which he produced with his brothers, sisters, and schoolmates, on the landing of a steep flight of steps in their garden— an event that ended in a riot when a boy he had excluded from the cast hid behind a pillar and urinated on to the stage. And, in his 'private theatre', he also staged works by other authors, including one by Goldoni.

The Pirandello family was comfortably off. Stefano was constantly going to the esplanade; he had a coach and horses at his disposal and a coachman of his own, and he was now rich enough to speculate on the sulphur market. He lent capital to the manufacturers and charged them interest; he bought up the supplies when the price dropped on the international market and sold them again when it rose, while correspondents informed him of the movements of the Stock Exchange.

But Stefano Pirandello was only relatively able as a speculator and he fell in with two mine owners who got him to lend them almost his entire capital, 600,000 lire. They went bankrupt; the Pirandello family was reduced to poverty; Stefano Pirandello had to ask his eldest brother, Felice, for help, and was put in charge of a sulphur deposit at Porto Empedocle. Since he had to go to Palermo every week to show his accounts he decided, after a while, to install his family there.

Luigi Pirandello may have felt a certain sadness at leaving Agrigento. He was later to recall with a trace of nostalgia in 'The Annuity' ('Il vitalizio') 'those steep lanes, cobbled like river beds, deep in shade, the walls of the houses rising oppressively on either side, with that little patch of sky which one could just see above them if one stretched one's neck right back, and yet could hardly see in the blinding light between the high gutters.' But, at the same time, like the correspondent of *La Gazzetta d'Italia* who visited Agrigento in 1874 and described it[14] as a 'mass of huts and hovels' whose 'hotels, full of insects and filth, send shudders down one's spine', Pirandello emphasized its more sordid aspects[15]—'the narrow, steep, ill-cobbled, dirty lanes, infected by the

evil smells coming out of the shops as dark as caves and the hovels of
those poor women who spent every day sitting on the door step, watching the same people at the same time, listening to the same quarrels...'.
It made too deep an impression on him for it ever to disappear. His
memories of it were to recur in his short stories, his novels, his plays—
even in his earliest poems written in Palermo, where he arrived in
1882[16] aged thirteen, and where he was to remain almost uninterruptedly until 1887.

He arrived in Palermo with the adventurous attitude of an adolescent
and with a sense of relief about the virtually permanent absence of his
father. This, he was sure, was to be a new era of his life. For Palermo
was *the capital*. Ever since his childhood he had been accustomed to the
idea of Palermo as a distant and marvellous place, fabulous, remote,
sumptuous, resplendent, beautiful, and so very different from the
squalor of Agrigento and the brutality of Porto Empedocle. This idea
of the city was to survive his experiences of living there and, even when
he was in his forties and fifties, Pirandello was still to see something
magical about it.

In Palermo the Pirandello family went to live in Via Porta di Castro,
now a workers' quarter, but then a semi-aristocratic district behind the
walls of the Royal Palace. They rented the first-floor flat of a two-floor
house and, on the second floor, there lived a well-to-do family with a
little girl who spent most of the year at the 'Maria Adelaide', the school
frequented by girls of the bourgeoisie and the local aristocracy. Her
name was Giovanna; she can hardly have been more than ten; and
Pirandello fell in love with her. One day, according to Nardelli, 'Luigi
Pirandello was on the balcony looking intently at the girl who was
standing on a higher terrace. They looked so fixedly into each other's
eyes that Luigi, who was sitting rashly on the parapet, his nose in the
air, forgot himself and almost fell over the edge. Just as he was about to
fall he seized hold of the parapet, while the little girl screamed, and, in
his effort to hold on, he hit his mouth against the bar and broke a tooth.'

Pirandello's family remained in Palermo from 1882 to 1885. From
Via Porta di Castro they moved to Via Borgo opposite the church of
Santa Lucia. 'Luigi,' his son Stefano tells us,[17] 'was engaged in translating the entire works of a Latin author only one of whose books he
was studying at school. Between the ages of thirteen and eighteen he
fulfilled his aim of obtaining a direct knowledge of Greek, Latin, and
Italian literature.' But Pirandello does not seem to have read with a
docile enjoyment. Not even when he was a boy did he belong to that

category of writers who are both omnivorous readers and immediately
capable of either a profound or a superficial assimilation of other
people's styles. Pirandello always had difficulty in assimilating things.
He had the characteristic self-sufficiency of the self-educated man as
well as a mental fixity of his own. Only when he was starting to write
did he perform certain experiments in imitation but they had no lasting
effect on him. He discovered that he had a literary vocation at an early
age, but only very rarely did he view it as a pleasurable career or as a
source of narcissistic satisfaction. Indeed, he devoted himself to it with
a precise ethical purpose, and as a means of release.

His education in these years and the way in which he studied remind
one of the poet who tied himself to his chair. According to more than
one account[18] he would remove the mattress from his bed at night, after
his mother, and later his aunt, with whom he stayed, had gone to sleep,
lie down on the wooden bedstead so as not to fall asleep, read until late
into the night by candlelight, wake up early and start reading again.
He often read reluctantly, only in order to cover as wide a field as
possible according to late-nineteenth-century standards of education
and also, perhaps, in order to assimilate the great writers and poets of
the past. A few years later in an article written in Bonn,[19] Pirandello
confessed how much patience he had needed to read Tasso's dialogues
(whereas he had less difficulty with other writers, like Benvenuto
Cellini and Giordano Bruno—and Goldoni, whom he adored). 'I
remember that when I was a boy my schoolmaster always told me to
read Tasso's dialogues and, however unwillingly, I obeyed him. But,
may Tasso's ghost forgive me. I used to fall asleep over them as if
mesmerized by some dark power...'. Yet one or two excessively
literary words were later to appear in his writing in the most unexpected places—a consequence, no doubt, of his reading the books borrowed from the Biblioteca Vittorio Emanuele.

What he most enjoyed reading in this period were the poets,
especially the romantic poets of the nineteenth century, from Carrer
and Prati to Carducci and, above all, his adored 'master', *his* Arturo
Graf. When he was fifteen Pirandello wanted to become a poet and he
practised conscientiously and untiringly. The poems written in 1883,
which are among the very few surviving documents in Pirandello's
own hand before 1886, are forty-two in number, and all but one were
written between January and May (twenty in May alone). Yet they can
hardly be more than a fraction of a far vaster production. They include
long poems of five verses of twenty lines each, a ballad of seventy lines,

and long stories in verse. The fifteen-year-old poet appears bravely to have attempted every medium (lyrics, lyrical epics, romances, idylls) with no thought of correct spelling, but with a concern for fine handwriting, friezes, designs, and every sort of decoration as well as an enthusiastic abundance of exclamation marks (as many as ten in fourteen lines) and an indiscriminate imitation of a variety of models—Carducci, Rapisardi, Stecchetti, Leopardi.

These poems are mainly interesting because of their autobiographical element. They show us how much attention the fifteen-year-old Pirandello paid to literature and the extent of his somewhat generalized interest in poetry. And, though there was a predominant tendency to look back to the romanticism of witchcraft, of mysterious and dramatic forests, he also displayed an understanding of some more modern representatives of realist, bourgeois poetry and even read and imitated the youthful d'Annunzio. Then there are some essentially autobiographical traits—patriotic references to his maternal grandfather's death in exile, references to his precocious interest in religion, and continually recurring images and personifications of madness and death.

This was the period of Pirandello's first literary triumphs. One of his poems, 'The Little Pilgrim's Dream' ('Il sogno del piccolo peregrino'), 'was read to the Giacomo Leopardi Club in Palermo', wrote the author proudly in a footnote; another one, the sonnet 'Dead Flowers' ('Fiori secchi'), 'was published in the fourth number of the paper *Sogni e fiori*'. And, when he was seventeen, Pirandello published his first short story, 'The Little Hut' ('La capannetta') in a Turin newspaper—*La Gazzetta del Popolo della Domenica* of 1 June 1884.

In these years Pirandello lived in Palermo with his family, while his father continued to commute between the capital and Porto Empedocle. At the same time, however, Stefano was having a love affair which his family, and above all Pirandello himself, found deeply offensive. Whenever he came to Palermo he had secret meetings with a woman. Pirandello, who was then about fourteen, was indignant, and the outrage done to his mother induced him to perform a dramatic gesture of protest. The episode has been recounted by Nardelli:

Stefano Pirandello had been engaged to a cousin of his [a niece, to be more exact]. And they had broken it off after a row. She married somebody else and, when her husband died, had fallen on evil days. So she wrote to Stefano [she was the daughter of one of his sisters] to ask for his help. Since an enormous quantity of letters, mainly business letters,

arrived in the Pirandello house every day and since they were invari-
ably opened and sorted by Caterina, it was Caterina who gave her
husband the letter and begged him to help the girl. He did so and his
old flame revived . . . .

To start with they met cautiously in the parlour of the Origlione, the
convent of which Stefano's sister Francesca was prioress. And it was
his sister who was (probably involuntarily) his accomplice in the
adultery. What followed has been told by Pirandello himself in his
short story 'Return' ('Ritorno'):

[He] knew that every Sunday morning the two met in the little parlour
reserved for the prioress of the San Vincenzo monastery, who was an
aunt of theirs. They pretended to go and visit her, and his aunt, who
probably attributed the affectionate intimacy of their meetings to the
fact that they were related, enjoyed seeing them sitting opposite each
other on either side of the little table beneath the double grating: he . . .
with his blue suit . . . she, pleasing in an essentially carnal way, but
placid because satisfied, dressed in black satin gleaming with gold
ornaments in the twilight of that parlour which had the austerity of a
church.
They gave each other, a mouthful each, the innocent little cakes of
the convent and, from the little glasses, they took turns sipping the pale
rosolio scented with essence of cinnamon. And they laughed. So did
their aunt, the prioress . . . she split her sides with laughter, behind the
grating.
He had gone there one Sunday in order to catch them out. His
father had just had time to slip behind a green curtain hanging in front
of a little door on the right; but the curtain was too short and beneath
the still swaying fringes he could see his two large shoes of smooth,
shining patent leather. She had remained seated at the table, the glass
still in her hand, drinking.
He had gone up to her and had pulled himself back a little so as to be
able to spit at her more violently. His father hadn't budged from behind
the curtain and, when he had gone home, he hadn't touched him. He
hadn't even mentioned it. [After all those years] that woman's face
suddenly appeared beautiful to him, with the indelible memory of how
she had looked at him, the spittle still hanging from her cheek, an
uncertain smile, of almost gay surprise, shining on her teeth, between
her red lips, and with such grief, so very much grief, in her eyes.

In the short story Pirandello relates that he never saw his father
again. And, sure enough, Pirandello hardly had anything more to do
with him, except for very brief meetings. But when his mother died in

1915 Pirandello invited his father, half blind and virtually helpless, to stay with him in Rome and took as much care of him as he could. According to Pirandello's great friend Arnaldo Frateili[20] Pirandello would ask a few close friends to 'play long games of cards with his father. The old man, though almost blind and deaf, remained overweening and authoritarian, holding his tall body completely straight, and insisted on that evening's entertainment to which even Pirandello himself contributed, submitting himself to the boredom of the card game and the obligation to lose continually so as not to displease him.' But Pirandello retained a feeling of guilt. He mentioned it in that same short story written in 1923, and he must have felt it every time he thought of the incident.

In Palermo, after that mortification inflicted on the forbidding figure of his father, family life cannot have remained particularly serene, especially since Pirandello's younger sister fell ill during her adolescence and appeared to go almost insane. This was the first time that Pirandello came into contact with madness. As for Stefano, he seems to have been overcome by the most appalling remorse, as though it were a providential punishment for the outrage he had committed against his family. Or so at least Pirandello told Nardelli. And such was his grief, and the silent sorrow of his wife, that Stefano decided that his family should leave Palermo and move to Porto Empedocle where he acquired a house in the country, Le Due Riviere, near Monte Rossello. At the same time he arranged for his niece to marry another man who, on the payment of a sum of money, was prepared to legitimize the child to whom she was about to give birth.

So Luigi remained alone in Palermo and went to live in Via Maestro d'Acqua in a furnished room together with his fellow student at Sant' Agata Militello, Carmelo Faraci.[21] It was his last year at the *liceo* but he did not go there very frequently: on the contrary. 'He hardly ever went to the lectures,' wrote his son Stefano,[22] 'so as not to lose time. At the end of the year the academic council had to decide whether or not he should sit the exams.' His friend Faraci sensed that his room-mate had some hidden talents which deserved respect and devotion and he started providing him with all his practical necessities. He did the shopping and the cooking while Pirandello dedicated himself to his studies, his poetry, and to the love which he had suddenly begun to feel for his cousin, Linuccia.

Pirandello was eighteen by now but he had started thinking about Linuccia when he was fifteen and he had even dedicated a short madrigal to her, 'Smile' ('Sorriso'). She was four years older than he and she had a quantity of admirers. Flirtatious as she was she and her relatives appear to have poked fun at Pirandello's infatuation and at his gratuitous jealousy which welled up whenever she showed a liking for anyone. Pirandello felt a little like David with nothing but a sling with which to defend himself. His weapon was his poetry and, as time went by, his love became increasingly obsessive.

Linuccia Pirandello came from a large family and Luigi had made friends with one of her brothers who was his own age. He could therefore visit her house but he did not dare declare his love, which appears to have been as agonizing as he was shy. 'Until, one day,' Pirandello recalled in 'Between Two Shadows' ('Fra due ombre') 'who knows why, maybe out of pique, or because of some unexpected disappointment, or in order to get her own back on somebody, she had approached him lovingly and had become engaged to him.' She consequently rejected her other suitors, friends of her older brother, sailors who frequented her parents' house, and there developed a tacit commitment to Pirandello who was too passionately in love to judge what was happening to him with any degree of objectivity.

In the meantime Faraci had left Palermo when a brother of his died and Pirandello had moved to Via Bontà to stay with a widowed and impoverished aunt who took him in as a paying guest. Matters with Linuccia grew complicated because she turned down a serious proposal (while another of her admirers had tried to kill himself for her). A rich widower from Palermo, an important trader in textiles, wanted to marry her and, in view of the advantageous match, her parents urged her to accept and put an end to Pirandello's visits.

Pirandello thought he would die of it, but this time Linuccia was faithful. When her family was certain of her refusal, they virtually forced Pirandello, who was now considered responsible for her future, to ask for her hand. Pirandello, Linuccia's mother insisted, should leave school at once and join his father in the sulphur trade since Linuccia could not possibly be expected to marry a pauper. At first Pirandello did not understand what was being asked of him, and impelled by a blind happiness about his dream which was at last about to come true and by the irrevocability of what was happening to him, he hurried to Porto Empedocle to obtain his father's consent.

All Stefano Pirandello could see in the whole business was a plot hatched against a couple of children at the expense of both father and son. Indeed, his fortune was again large enough to attract people. To

start with, therefore, he tried to obstruct his son's wishes 'wisely pointing out that a commitment of this description was far too sudden; that
his cousin was four years older than he was and that he would have to
wait at least six more years before making her his'.[23] Then, when confronted by the determination of his son who argued obstinately for a
whole month, ready to make any promises or to swear any oaths, and
by the solicitude of his wife who, however opposed to the match she
might be, did not want to displease Luigi, he gave in. But in the meantime he decided that Luigi should return to Palermo to end the academic
year. Stefano wanted to take his time.

Once he had finished his studies at the *liceo*, Pirandello found himself
back in Porto Empedocle, ready, he thought, to embark on a completely new life quite different from the one to which he had been
attached ever since childhood. With the exception of very brief visits
he had not been back to Agrigento or Porto Empedocle for seven years.
But now he was back, an involuntary fugitive from poetry and without
a single book—indeed, having lightly repudiated all books. He was
forced to stay there. In those summer holiday months, July, August,
and September of 1886, Porto Empedocle was a pit of sun and sulphur,
an inferno, oppressive and hostile. Pirandello retained old memories of
it, rough and violent ones. Even though he had only heard people tell
of it he could not forget that every morning, at a shout from the town-
crier, the convicts used to file out of the Torre Carlo Quinto, the
'square and murky' Bourbon prison on the sea, in order to lay the rocks
to form the harbour wall.

As a man of letters turned into a sulphur miner Pirandello found
himself surrounded by the shouts of 'bare-chested, bare-footed' men,
among piles of sulphur and metalwork. 'From dawn to dusk,' he
recalled in *The Old and the Young*,

all you hear is a constant grinding of carts loaded with sulphur being
driven from the railway station or from the nearby sulphur mines in an
endless turmoil of barefooted men and animals, bare feet tramping on
the wet ground, quarrels, oaths, and shouts amid the din and the
whistles of a train crossing the beach to one or other of the two reefs
which are always being repaired. . . . Crushed by the weight, water up
to their waists. Men? Animals! . . . the drains are still uncovered on the
beach and people die of the plague; with all that sea out there there is no
drinking water and people die of thirst! No one thinks about it, no one
complains about it. They all look like lunatics, maddened by the savage
war of profit.

For three months Pirandello, covered in sweat and yellow sulphur dust, weighed sulphur, constantly wary of being cheated. Whether he liked it or not, in those months he got an idea of the economic problems of the sulphur industry. This remained the only job he ever held outside the world of letters and one of his very few contacts with a life of trade and physical labour. In these three summer months of commercial apprenticeship Pirandello studied with curiosity the whole process of sulphur production, before and after the mineral arrived in his works in those romantic yellow trapezoidal shapes. Of course he was too much the writer not to confuse the hard facts of industry with his poetic and literary judgement of them and, above all, he was interested in the men who, like himself, felt the impact of brute economic needs in their own bodies and minds.

It must be admitted that Pirandello's temperament and education predisposed him towards a somewhat reactionary nostalgia for the rustic idyll of the nineteenth century and towards a still more distant, Rousseau-like myth of nature. In such a state of mind he approached the problem of the countryside burnt by the smoke of the sulphur smelting ovens, and described the peasants dazed by this new phenomenon of the green and peaceful fields suddenly abandoned to the painful and unromantic production of minerals. Even the miners were fascinated by the fields surrounding the arid areas in which they worked. 'No sooner,' wrote Pirandello in the short story entitled 'Fumes' ('Il fumo'), 'did the miners come up from the depths of the pit, short of breath and their bones aching with exhaustion than they looked for the green of that distant hill which closed the large valley to the west. . . . That distant hill was like a dreamland.'

The world of the sulphur mines came to assume an obsessively symbolic significance: 'oppression', 'the agony of asphyxiation', 'brutalization' are words which recur whenever he writes about men connected with the sulphur trade—and, beneath the ground, there is death; the miners are so many 'busy corpses'. Although he was on the side of the owners Pirandello also protested, in a realistic and philanthropic tone, about the lot of the little boys aged between eight and twelve who were set to work, the *carusi*, one of the most iniquitous phenomena in the Sicilian sulphur mines. 'After throwing down the load from their bruised and grazed shoulders,' Pirandello wrote in 'Fumes', 'the *carusi* would sit down on the sacks to breathe in the fresh air, covered as they were with the chalky liquid lining the galleries and the damp broken steps leading into the pit.'

The *carusi*, S. F. Romano tells us,[24] were used by the miners 'to carry on their shoulders up to twenty kilos of mineral up the shafts. . . . Not without reason was the lease of child labour accorded by the parents for a sum of money known as "renting human flesh". A slave-like dependency developed between the miner and the *caruso*. The *caruso* was required to work as hard as possible. At any sign of exhaustion the miners whipped him or hit him with the full consent of his parents . . . and the *caruso* might remain in that capacity until the age of thirty.' It was on this situation that Pirandello based one of his best short stories, 'Ciàula Discovers the Moon' ('Ciàula scopre la luna') —the story of a *caruso* in a sulphur mine near Agrigento who had to submit to the violence of a miner who, in his turn, was bullied by the overseer, a cowardly wretch who 'used to face the miners with a re-volver in his hand'.

Everything in Porto Empedocle appeared absurd and wrong to Pirandello—'the pressure exerted on the wretched man who hired the sulphur mine', the rents, the taxes, the obligations, the fact that the miners had no idea of what the sulphur would be used for apart from matches in those distant lands where it was immediately transported by 'English, American, German, French, even Greek ships' while 'our own riches, the riches which should be ours, leave the veins of our mountains, and we stay behind like blind men, like ninnies, our bones aching with exhaustion and our pockets empty.'[25]

Above all, however, his experience at the age of nineteen at Porto Empedocle enabled Pirandello to gauge how very alien all practical matters were to him. It was as though he tended to perceive a lack of substance in things, a purely abstract and symbolic quality in energy, and an absence of material values. He grew aware of his own incapacity to measure the things of this world in a manner which people regarded as normal. When he spoke of the activity of Porto Empedocle, which cannot really have been as violent and deafening as in his obsessive recollections, he could only do so with a fascinated disgust and, even if he could not help loving that land, so much a part of himself, he always tried to confine his love to those restful surroundings: the sea, 'between the flames of those magnificent Mediterranean sunsets which make the infinite expanse of the waters tremble and shimmer as if in a delirium of light and colour . . .',[26] the countryside, and the cemetery on the white marly heights that rose overhead.

During those three months Pirandello's father had had time to work out a way of upsetting his son's intended marriage with Linuccia. He was realistic enough to know that as time passed Pirandello would grow increasingly reluctant to commit himself to a marriage which would take him away from his favourite studies. Time, in other words, would quench Pirandello's ardour—and it was as well to help it to do so. At the end of the summer, when he could sense Luigi's desperation, Stefano Pirandello summoned him to his office and told him that, since he was sure how ill-equipped he was for such a job, he proposed to send him back to Palermo where he could go to university. He was well enough off to be able to afford it. Luigi would read law and, once he had a degree, would be in a position to provide for his family by working as a lawyer.

Thus Stefano won four years and so, for that matter, did Pirandello. He left at once for Palermo, to go to university and to join his fiancée. After the experience at Porto Empedocle, he knew within himself that the only career open to him was a literary one. He did not take any explicit decision or make any precise gesture which might clarify his future for him. Instead, and probably without even being aware of it, he began to hedge, to arrange things in such a way that, without forcing anything or anyone, only one course of action would be open to him. He started off by reading both law and literature. Then, for the whole of his last year in Palermo, he concentrated on trying to work out the problems facing a young man who was very much in love but who, at the same time, felt himself *called*, exclusively and disinterestedly, by an intellectual career, by art and poetry. The letters he wrote in this period to his favourite sister Rosalina were a continuous admission of an anguished state of mind.

The tinges of heroic romanticism, the enjoyment of secrecy which his love for Linuccia had offered him when it had still been a vague and mysterious source of poetry, had changed, suddenly and brutally, into the enforced observance of conventional forms. The official engagement, the fact that the couple were constantly chaperoned and pointed to as a sort of monster, 'the fiancés!', the obligatory visits to relations, the escorted trips by carriage to the Foro Italico past the sea and the flowers, exposure to the public in a box at performances at the Politeama Garibaldi, and then the difference of age which, for a temperament like Pirandello's, so sensitive to objective disharmonies, caused some embarrassment—all these things were no longer fully compensated for by his affection for Linuccia. 'When he was introduced to people,' he wrote in 'Between Two Shadows', 'still so young and with-

Pirandello as a child, with his mother and his sisters Lina and Anna

Pirandello at the age of fourteen

out any status, as Lilli's future husband, he felt ridiculous, especially in front of the other young men who had flirted with his fiancée.'

Linuccia, on the other hand, was fonder than ever of Pirandello. She appears to have been a beautiful girl, lively and sensual, but in Pirandello's eyes she began to assume the shape of an evil fairy, a bewitcher, both a friend and an enemy. He was incapable of enjoying so straightforward a form of happiness. Even if he did find pleasure in being together with her in spite of all the imperfect things and people surrounding them, in spite of all the compromises their engagement involved, he was incapable of suppressing one powerful urge within himself: his vocation as a writer. He required very different experiences and horizons from the ones provided by marriage with Linuccia. This, or so he thought, would necessarily have interrupted his life as a poet. It might even have constituted a complete repudiation of literature.

With Linuccia he had his first and probably his only complete love affair. Jenny Schulz-Lander was to be more a part of university life, and his wife would be a very different matter. He measured his strength with Linuccia and became aware of his own particular sentimental ineptitude. Between them, between his own sensuality—which must have been considerable—and hers, there intervened an all-absorbing Platonic screen in which his every word lost its value and his every gesture its force. His was a necessary advance towards the disappearance of every concrete experience, a step towards life that can be written but cannot be lived. In the poems he wrote at the time, 'Troubled Joy' ('Mal giocondo') and 'First Notes' ('Prime note'), Pirandello reveals his state of mind in continuously recurring images of constriction and of joy that has been lost and was doomed to be lost.

The faculty of law at Palermo University was a hotbed of ideological and political ferment, and Pirandello was in the midst of what his friend Francesco De Luca, one of the most influential leaders of the workers' movement known as the *Fasci Siciliani*, described as 'that enthusiastic atmosphere created primarily by university students'. 'Almost a mystical enthusiasm,' De Luca was to recall, 'with which intellects in search of something new welcomed a new theory of social reform'.

In his novel *The Old and the Young*, a book which evokes, in a somewhat distorted manner, the Sicily of Pirandello's youth, Pirandello was later to emphasize the enthusiasm and the devotion of the leaders of the *Fasci* even if he modified their historical value, and, when he was twenty, he may well have been seduced by them. Even in the novel he was uncertain whether to take sides with the noble-minded socialists or whether to hold aloof from them in an attitude of wisdom and irony.

Enrico La Loggia, who was also from Agrigento and almost certainly knew Pirandello since he too was reading law in Palermo, wrote, in March 1894 in the *Giornale degli Economisti*, that the leaders of the *Fasci* had been trained within 'a single generation of students at Palermo University. The faculties of law and medicine were citadels of radicalism, formed mainly by students from the provinces.' As we shall see, Pirandello, however distracted by his private preoccupations, definitely came under the influence of these young radicals.

But he did not remain in contact with the university of Palermo for long. The proximity of Linuccia prevented him from studying and, because the day of their marriage was approaching, he had to hurry to complete his studies. He therefore decided to leave Palermo and go to another university where, far from all distractions, he could concentrate exclusively on his work and return to Palermo with a degree and ready to marry.

We do not know how Linuccia reacted to this decision—she is unlikely to have felt enthusiastic about it. Pirandello's parents, on the other hand, were in full agreement. They would send him a monthly cheque in Rome where his mother's brother, Rocco Ricci Gramitto, was living. And so, in November 1887, Pirandello set sail from Palermo. As none of his letters to his fiancée survive, we have no information about their separation. It must have been difficult for Linuccia, and less difficult for Pirandello, as he was to imply in his poem 'Troubled Joy' in which he presented his arrival in Rome as a moment of melancholic liberation.

Pirandello left Sicily at the age of twenty. What effect had the island had on him? The Sicily in which he was brought up was a region where history moved very slowly, despite the unification of Italy. Social life was based then, far more than it is now, on landed property and feudal customs: even the sulphur industry had numerous aspects which can only be described as medieval. The caste system only *appeared* to be capable of change; in fact the structure remained virtually immobile and all that happened was the substitution of certain individuals by other individuals.

The rigidity of society corresponded to the Sicilian character. Particularly in the lower classes the violence suppressed in every individual sometimes burst out in one irremediable gesture or else never came to the surface at all. Repression and explosiveness were to remain a fundamental characteristic of Pirandello's Sicilian temperament.

At the age of twenty Pirandello already had an inflexible attitude towards the family and female behaviour. In Germany he was delighted to find a freer, simpler relationship between the sexes. 'The way in which one meets women,' he was to write to his sister from Bonn, 'is very simple. When a young lady goes out late in the evening and is afraid of coming across some drunkard she goes up to the first young man who looks like a gentleman and asks him to accompany her. . . . I am sure that if I told this to any friend of mine in Sicily he would wink, as if to say: "I know what you're getting at!" And I would call him a fool. But I also see that such a custom would never work in our own country, where hypocrisy is king and nearly all men lack good manners.' But he did not, for all that, shed the austere views he had developed in his youth and his adolescence. We shall see him declare his aversion for all the movements of female emancipation of the early twentieth century and only later, in a highly dramatic sphere, would he recognize the woman's right to an autonomous love life. On a social level, however, he remained caught in a network of conformity which was far closer to atavistic Muslim–Catholic Sicily than to the conventions of contemporary Italy.

Pirandello embraced, however unconsciously, the Catholic concept of the sins of the flesh, and any release of the senses represented something far more serious than a social failure or a betrayal of the loyalty and trust of other people. It represented a total moral lapse. At the same time he nurtured a prejudice about sexual morality which was still more extreme and radical. He regarded virginity as sacred. In the Sicily of the last part of the nineteenth century a woman's 'dishonour' was punished, far more promptly than it is today, by death. Thus any rebellious attitude towards chastity came as a traumatic shock which was even greater for Pirandello himself than for his characters: hence the dramatic effectiveness of the numerous conflicts concerning this theme in his plays.

But the element of his Sicilian upbringing which had the most powerful effect on Pirandello and his work was the formality of the Sicilians, the custom imposed by others, against which one can only rebel at one's own risk. 'No sooner do you arrive in Sicily than you feel yourself confronted from all sides by a verdict to which there is no reply. Everybody judges you. The Sicilian is exposed to many pressures including the constant domination of his compatriots.'[27] Hence a number of Pirandello's most excessive and most unconventional reactions. A violent need for independence which was constantly smothered in his youth by the heavy, pervasive, and oppressive climate of petty social rites was to be one explanation of his future attitude. Once Pirandello left Sicily he tried to adapt himself to everyday life and to the new social dimensions in which he found himself, but he was always prevented from doing so by a pre-existing instinct of rebellion, by a social trauma which had affected him deeply when he was a boy. Furthermore, for Pirandello, formality was always to be the net which excluded men from liberty. Yet he was born in a country, a world, and a century where formality was predominant. Pirandello's life and work, therefore, were composed of a mass of compromises and were torn between the acceptance of conventions and proprieties, and a still more fundamental rejection of them.

2

UNIVERSITY

Pirandello arrived in Rome in the middle of November 1887, eager for novelty, ingenuous, curious (even if he displayed a certain scepticism to the world) and at the same time, as his letters to his sister reveal, profoundly disheartened. Yet he had certain youthful advantages and a scholastic and literary competence which made him self-assured. He had read the Italian and Latin classics attentively and knew most contemporary Italian poetry. He had acquired a technical ability of his own and, before coming to Rome, he had had the satisfaction of writing over half his collection of poems *Troubled Joy*. In addition to this he had a further, though paradoxical advantage: his scepticism had given him something to fall back on. Shortly before he left for Rome he had written to his sister Rosalina:[1]

Meditation is a black abyss, peopled with dark ghosts, guarded by desperate discomfort. A ray of light never seeps through, and the desire to have light plunges you ever more deeply into the dark. . . . It is an unquenchable thirst, an obstinate fury, but the darkness fills you, the silent immensity freezes you. We are like the poor spider which, in order to live, has to weave its fine web in a corner; we are like the poor snail which is forced to bear its fragile shell on its back to survive; or like those poor molluscs in the depths of the ocean, each dependent on its own shell. We are spiders, snails, and molluscs of a nobler race, admittedly; admittedly we do not need a web or a shell; but we do need our little world, both to live in and to live from. An ideal, a feeling, a habit, an occupation—that is the little world, the shell of this snail or man, as they call him. Without it, life is impossible. When you manage to live without an ideal, because life, when observed, seems a great farce with no link or explanation; when you no longer have any feeling because you have managed to lose all respect or care for men and things —when, in a word, you live without life, you will think without a thought, you will feel without a heart—and you will no longer know what to do. You will be a wayfarer without a house, a bird without a nest. I am like that. Greatness, fame, glory no longer stimulate my soul. Is there any point in exhausting one's brain and one's spirit in order to be remembered and appreciated by men? Ridiculous! I write and study in order to forget myself—in order to save myself from despair. . . . But don't think that my lack of illusion and hope will destroy me. A positive and scientific concept of life makes me live like all the other worms.

Despite these words Pirandello retained, until his marriage, a capacity for illusion and trust. He was often on the verge of declaring himself a failure but was still more often on the verge of making a choice, of announcing to himself and others the direction his life would take. They may have been illusions, but he could tell himself: 'I shall be a poet', and later, 'I shall be a philologist and a poet', just as he could tell himself, when he was about to make a catastrophic marriage: 'I shall be happy.'

In Rome Pirandello went to stay at 456 Via del Corso, with his uncle Rocco Ricci Gramitto who, almost thirty years earlier, had been a hero of the anti-Bourbon resistance in Sicily (see above p. 3). Now he was well over fifty, a *consigliere di prefettura*,[2] and he had become so lazy that he did not even want a successful career in spite of his powerful political protectors. He turned down the appointment of *prefetto* in order not to have to leave Rome even for a few months.

In him Pirandello observed with amazement the metamorphosis of the hero who had deteriorated into a shadowy and dilapidated ruin. From this unexpected encounter with the 'dazed patriot' Pirandello developed a sense of humiliated history and consequently derived the theme of *The Old and the Young*. Uncle Rocco became the prototype of the old fighters of the Risorgimento who had been reduced to misery by the political events of United Italy. Besides, Rocco had taken to living what was then known as an 'irregular life'. He lived together with an erstwhile singer whom he later married and who filled his house with friends and relations as well as with every sort of animal— cats, dogs, parrots, and monkeys. So bad was her reputation that, a few years later, Pirandello was to refuse to let her have anything to do with his future wife who had been educated by the nuns of San Vincenzo in Agrigento. Just before their marriage he wrote to her that he had found a beautiful house in Prati di Castello but 'I dropped the idea of taking it, although I liked it enormously, since it is too close to where that terrible Nanna, Rocco's wife, lives.'³

Pirandello could not adapt himself to his uncle's house and, in the middle of December, he moved to a boarding-house at 9A Via delle Colonnette, behind the building on the Corso where his uncle lived. The street was so narrow that it was easy to communicate between his uncle's terrace and Pirandello's room and, twice a day, he was summoned to his uncle's house according to the irregular hours of lunch and dinner. The building, since destroyed, looked on to the Ripetta district and the bend of the Tiber between Ponte Margherita, Ponte Cavour, and Ponte Umberto. It is described in *The Late Mattia Pascal* (*Il fu Mattia Pascal*) written seventeen years later. Pirandello's room, according to his brother Innocenzo who lived in the same boarding-house, was that of Mattia Pascal. The windows 'overlooked the river. In the distance one could see Monte Mario, Ponte Margherita and the entire new district of Prati as far as Castel Sant'Angelo. The room dominated the old Ripetta bridge and the new one which was being built next to it. Further off there was the Ponte Umberto and all the old houses of Tordinona which followed the wide bend of the river. And in the background, on the other side, were the green heights of the Janiculum with the fountain of San Pietro in Montorio and the equestrian statue of Garibaldi.'

Pirandello arrived in Rome with a definite vocation as a playwright. He had already written to his sister Rosalina from Palermo in November 1886 to say that he had completed a play derived from classical Greek drama. It was a prelude to his later theatrical innovations, and was called *The Birds in the Sky* (*Gli uccelli dell'alto*). By means of a scenic inversion the auditorium turned into the stage and the spectators, having become actors, performed a function similar to that of the chorus in classical drama. The 'birds in the sky' are 'cranes'. 'Lina of my heart,' he wrote to his sister on 31 October 1886, 'have you ever seen cranes flying? Those poor birds are mad and hardly ever land. They are thrashed by the wind and the storms but they fly on and on, not knowing where they are going. All they know is that they are going forward. Cocks and hens, those middle-class birds, peck around in the mud and laugh at the birds in the sky which fly overhead screaming, as though they are praying for something. . . . What do you think

cocks and hens can understand about them?' On 25 March the following year he said he had burnt this play together with all his other
papers: 'The beaks and the feathers of my poor little birds in the sky
gave off the most terrible smell of burnt horn among so many ashes…'

Pirandello came to Rome with a five-act play, *The Happy People*
(*La gente allegra*), which he intended to have performed at the Teatro
Valle by Cesare Rossi in the season of 1887–8. ('Do not be deceived
by the title,' he wrote, 'it is one of the saddest plays you can imagine.')
He had also written *The Women of the People* (*Le popolane*) which he
gave to Cesare Rossi and to his leading actress Graziosa Glech. Another play written in these years (on his return from Bonn) and never
performed shows by its title the interest that Pirandello already had for
a 'play within a play'. It was called *Rehearsing the Play* (*Provando la
commedia*) and had as its subtitle 'Theatrical Scenes' (*Scene teatrali*).
In this first winter spent in Rome he was about to have a play (we do
not know the title) performed at the Teatro Manzoni by Enrico
Dominici. On 10 December he wrote to his sister: 'I still don't know
whether I can come to see you at Christmas. A play of mine is about to
be produced at the Teatro Manzoni and the manager of the company,
Enrico Dominici, told me today that it would be staged in ten or
twelve days' time.' He added that 'catcalls or applause' mattered little
to him, but the play never appears to have been performed.

The products of this particular theatre season have been swept away
by time. The texts have been destroyed and the difficulty or the im-
possibility of performing them induced the young playwright, after a
last futile effort, to give up the idea of the theatre for many years to
come and even to regard it as hostile. But the plays that seemed suddenly to come into being in miraculous abundance during the First
World War were really the result of a lengthy incubation period and of
a theatrical vocation which had long been repressed, but which finally
pushed its way to the surface.

Throughout his university years, in Palermo, Rome, and Bonn,
Pirandello wrote frequently to his sister Rosalina. She was two years
older than he and had been his playmate in his childhood and his confi-
dante in his adolescence. Pirandello remained deeply attached to her for
many years as we see from his countless letters and, when she married
Calogero De Castro in October 1887, one month before he left for
Rome, he wrote a poem for her in Sapphic metre. It was to his sister
that Pirandello disclosed his first impressions of Rome—an impression
of mournful gaiety joined (we find in his poem 'Troubled Joy') with a

literary contempt for 'the crowd'. Indeed, this sense of his own superiority, of a capacity for judging others, was to remain in all his work. It was not really Luciferian presumptuousness, since Pirandello was to feel himself obliged to share in other people's misery, to take pity on it; but, in the intervals of his compassion, there was derision, disillusion, contempt—even hatred, but a hatred directed just as much against himself as against others.

In 1889 while Pirandello was still in Rome, the collection of poems entitled *Troubled Joy* was published in Palermo, thanks, in part, to Enrico Sicardi, a young critic from Palermo, who was a friend of Pirandello and had been to university with him. The publisher was Carlo Clausen's Libreria Internazionale Pedone Lauriel, a firm which was connected with radical and socialist circles and which published the work of the more committed young Sicilians of the time, like De Luca.

The book had a certain success even outside Sicily. Arturo Graf, to whom Pirandello sent all his first collections of poetry as to a master, acknowledged that *Troubled Joy* contained 'much good together with the bad'. Giuseppe Gargano reviewed the book in *Vita Nuova*, a Florentine review which had published some of Pascoli's first poems, and described Pirandello as a 'new poet'.

In the meantime Pirandello felt ever less attached to his fiancée Linuccia, but he did not know how to get out of his commitment to her. He lacked the courage to do so. Linuccia fell ill and had attacks of hysteria. In the first months of 1889 the Pirandello family put her up at Porto Empedocle so that she should have some form of distraction. Pirandello went to visit her. He returned to Rome in despair. He wrote to his sister on 13 March 1889:

I would like to live in silence, like a stone, for the rest of my days. The great bitterness I have in my heart poisons my words as they are born, even before I write them. . . . Try and forget me. If I don't kill myself it is for your sake, but please don't force me to behave as if I were alive. I have death in my heart. My last remaining illusion has collapsed—love. . . . I cannot, I simply cannot manage, however hard I try, to love that poor sick girl any longer. As a sister, as a friend, yes—but as a future wife, no, never again. . . . Don't make me talk about it. . . . The scenes I witnessed, the words I heard (I burn with shame and sorrow merely to think of them), what gestures, what acts. . . . The fine net of illusions that is love which a breath of wind can undo . . . the beautiful, sweet net is all torn. . . . What remains? How much better it would have been if she had died! As far as I am concerned she has been struck

by the worst malady of all. How undiscerning of them to make me go
and see her in that state, hear her words. . . . I know I am no longer
myself. A cold, black night has fallen on me. What will happen? Don't
worry. I know my duty—it's bitter, but I will do it. I have a mother
and a father, I have you. I will be strong and do my duty but, please,
don't ask me to do more.

His duty was the duty of commitment, of the word given by his
parents, of the Sicilian custom which did not allow people to get out of
a marriage promise easily. But was Pirandello really set on keeping this
promise?

In Rome Pirandello gave up law since he no longer thought he
should sacrifice his literary vocation for a woman he did not love and,
with the minimum of enthusiasm, he studied literature. With very few
exceptions there were no brilliant professors at Rome University. The
vice-chancellor was the Venetian Onorato Occioni, almost sixty years
old, who taught Latin literature. Despite the veneration that Gabriele
d'Annunzio had had for Occioni, who used to ask him to come forward and recite Horace, Pirandello found that his course was too
elementary and one day the two had a quarrel which ended in Pirandello's having to leave the university.

Occioni was translating Plautus' *Miles gloriosus* during a lecture,
and made a mistake. He realized it slightly too late and made a clumsy
effort to correct himself. But the damage had been done. Pirandello was
seated in the first row next to a young priest who knew Latin well. The
two nudged each other at Occioni's slip, the priest could not suppress
a smile, and the professor lost his temper. He started shouting insults at
the priest but would not tell the other students why. Pirandello could
stand it no longer. He stood up, told the others why Occioni was so
angry, and walked out of the room haughtily. He was never allowed to
return. Using his authority as vice-chancellor Occioni summoned all
the professors of the faculty. Pirandello had to appear before a discipli-
nary council and was ordered to leave.

One, however, of the university professors had a high esteem for the
young Pirandello. This was Ernesto Monaci, one of the few professors
to keep academic studies alive and up to date. He was teaching a relatively new subject in Italy, Romance philology, and he was young
enough—forty-four—to have a close relationship with his students.
Indeed, in his letters, Pirandello addressed him in a studied but not
subservient tone. Ernesto Monaci had such an influence on him that,
for a few years, philology became Pirandello's speciality. Just as his

period at university was drawing to a close Pirandello decided to follow his professor's example and choose an academic career. When he went to ask Monaci's advice, Monaci suggested he should continue his studies abroad, in Germany and preferably in Bonn, where Monaci's friend and correspondent Wendelin Foerster had succeeded Diez, who had originally introduced the subject, as professor of Romance philology.

Pirandello accepted the idea of Germany but not, to begin with, the idea of Bonn. After obtaining an increased allowance from his father he was undecided whether to choose Berlin, a large capital city which seemed to him to have more to offer from every point of view than the provincial town to which his professor wanted to send him. But finally his sense of duty prevailed and he agreed to go to Bonn.

Before leaving for Germany Pirandello went back to Sicily to spend the summer with his family. From Palermo, in a letter dated 'the ides of September 1889'[4] he wrote Monaci an account of this last visit to Sicily. Within a few days of his arrival, he wrote, 'I succumbed to a violent attack of an illness which almost led me to death's door and from which I fear I shall never recover as long as I live'. 'Imagine,' he added, 'an endocarditis. This is the reason for my silence, and spare a word of pity for your poor Pirandello who constantly thought about you with affection and devotion and kept his promise to go, as soon as he could, to Agrigento to see whether there were any old manuscripts in the Lucchesi-Palli library. I found a great many and some, I think, are of value.'

Pirandello informed his professor that the library, run by 'an almost illiterate' priest called Schifano, 'is going to rack and ruin', that there were about a hundred 'ancient manuscripts' which 'are in such a poor state that some of them can hardly even be consulted', while the bishopric and the city council were quarrelling over who should own the building. He then gave a picturesque account of his first visit to the library:

... in the cool twilight of the large rectangular room, seated at a dusty table, I saw five priests from the nearby Cathedral and three *carabinieri* from the adjoining barracks in their shirt-sleeves intently devouring a cucumber and tomato salad. I stopped in amazement. The men looked up from their plates in surprise and stared at me. They obviously thought me a rare and inconvenient bird. I approached respectfully (why not?) and asked for the librarian. 'I'm the librarian', said one of the eight, his mouth full. 'I've come to ask your permission to see if there are any manuscripts in this ... (I did not say a tavern, but a library).' 'Over there, over there, in the far bookcase,' he interrupted me, his mouth full again, and the eight men resumed their meal.... The bookcase he had pointed to was open; anyone could have helped themselves; but no one had consulted those books except for rats and beetles....

After describing the manuscripts (which included some Arabic ones which had been 'an abundant source of study for the late senator Michele Amari who went to the library every day for three months') Pirandello said that, for reasons of health, he could not spend more than a week there. He concluded his letter with the words: 'I am now preparing to leave for Germany. On the 26th I shall undoubtedly be in Rome where I shall not be staying for more than three days, since I'm anxious to be in Bonn on time.'

But Pirandello could not go to Bonn at once. He fell ill again in Rome and had to spend twelve days in bed. Then he stopped in Como in order to recover before facing the Nordic winter and to have a few German lessons. He stayed with his brother-in-law at Cavallasca for a month in a villa which had belonged to the Imbonati family and had been used by Garibaldi as his headquarters just before the battle of San Fermo. Here in Como Pirandello fell in love—perhaps this was the first occasion on which he was unfaithful to his distant cousin—with a girl whom he would remember many years later when he looked back on the few loves of his life (in the poem entitled 'Meeting' ('Convegno') published in *La Rivista d'Italia* in October 1901). All we know about her is that she was dark and had unfortunately become 'a mistress of vices and an innkeeper of her body'. But she had loved him. He had seen her every evening, while she had talked to him of love and had sworn to be faithful to him. She had been 'sincere'.

In October he left Como for Bonn. His first reaction to the town was one of quiet surprise. He was almost totally incapable of communicating with the people. He could just understand some of the Germans who spoke a literary language but he could not understand a word of the dialect spoken by the townsfolk. His first letters are full of gaiety, and the eighteen months spent in Germany, despite his basic anxiety and ill-health, were probably the least unhappy of his life. He lived in a calm and isolated corner of the world, participating in the student life, and studying. His stay in Bonn was a period of trust and confidence.

He arrived with an adequate amount of money. His father wanted him to lead a comfortable life abroad and Pirandello was not cut out for a Bohemian existence. Dressed with dignified propriety he had easy access to certain middle-class families of bureaucrats and soldiers. Bonn was far from inhospitable and he immediately found himself surrounded by 'very pleasant people'. To his sister Rosalina, he said that life in the Hotel zum Münster where he was lodging was no more expensive than in Rome and that he had plenty to eat. 'Every morning a large quantity of milk and coffee with bread and butter. At half past nine . . . a thick sandwich; at twelve for lunch some broth or some very tasty soup, a fine piece of well-cooked meat, with plenty of vegetables, a further dish, fruit, pudding and coffee; at four, free, a beer, or a coffee, or a thick sandwich; at six for supper a plate of meat or fish, a salad, a little cheese or fruit.' The 300 marks his father sent him every month were more than enough. After less than a month he moved from the hotel opposite the Catholic cathedral and, together with an Irish student called William Henry Madden, he went to stay with a certain Herr Mohl who had a shop of textiles and let out rooms to students.

Here, at 1 Neuthorstrasse, Pirandello paid 'twenty-five marks for two rooms, nine marks for breakfast, four marks for the light, and three for the service—in all fifty-one marks a month.' The two rooms, 'elegantly, splendidly furnished', were 'each more beautiful than the other'. Pirandello, accustomed at best to the decorous style of bour-geois houses in Sicily, was very favourably impressed by the warm comfort of a Nordic household, and enthused about 'the carpets on the floor, the curtains and hangings on the windows and the doors, a very elegant sofa, two armchairs, a settee, fully padded chairs, cloths on both tables—all the same colour as the wallpaper, in other words very dark, as I like it—then bookshelves, cupboards, a wall cupboard, a little stand for portraits, stands in the corners with vases full of plumed reeds, all in black wood, a very beautiful large oval mirror hanging over the settee, etc.' In short the whole house was so magnificent that his sister 'would not even be able to imagine how beautiful it is'.

From the balcony 'there is a simply enchanting view: the Rhine, the mountains, the countryside, the town. . . . The window near my desk looks out on to Neuthorstrasse which runs down the Rhine, with woods of centenarian fir-trees on the left. The other two windows over-look the square of the magnificent Protestant Gothic church. (Fate has decreed that I should always be opposite a church in Bonn, but, fortu-nately, this one is Protestant.) . . . Bonn is a silent town *par excellence*, but this new house of mine is a symbol of silence.'

In his first days there, in order to escape from the countless difficulties of the new language, he used to spend his time with a Venetian who was restoring the mosaics in the dome of the Catholic cathedral. Then, in his new boarding house, he made friends both with the Irish polyglot, William Madden, and a young German called Karl Arxt, a master of arts who was 'very cultured and intelligent' and had been repudiated by his father because he had stopped studying theology, and expelled from the university because he was dangerously social-democratic. (Bonn was an excessively conservative town: even the emperor had gone to university there.)

Pirandello started giving Arxt Italian lessons in exchange for German ones. He did not feel he knew the language well enough to go to lectures and he waited for the end of the winter semester before signing on. At the University of Bonn there were some excellent professors of international renown like Franz Buecheler who taught Latin and Hermann Uesener who taught Greek, but the German they spoke was not for beginners. Finally, at the beginning of the summer semester, in other words after Easter, he was enrolled, and shocked the official who took down all personal particulars by candidly professing to be an atheist. 'No religion', he said, when he was asked to which faith he belonged. But then, in order not to complicate matters, he ended up by admitting that he had been baptized and was therefore a Catholic. 'Bonn,' he wrote to Rosalina, 'has almost 50,000 inhabitants: 51,000 are Catholic to the point of fanaticism.'

He had already called on Professor Foerster with a 'very flattering letter of introduction' from Monaci and had been 'welcomed affectionately' by him.[5] He mentioned the meeting in a letter of 14 November 1889 to his Roman professor, written in German: '. . . We spoke about you at length: and I then told him about my plans and also described in detail my earlier studies. He promised me his advice and assistance for the future; and, on his advice, I resumed my study of the "Dialect in the Province of Agrigento". I have with me a large collection of "fables and popular and improvised songs" which I collected myself and which will now serve as a basis for my studies. I shall then have it printed as an appendix to my work.' (But Pirandello never did this. He must have collected the documents on folklore during his stay in Agrigento before leaving for Germany.)

Foerster was most hospitable to Pirandello. He invited him to dinner from time to time and thereby enabled him to get some idea of family life in northern Europe, a mixture of formality, intimacy, dignified reserve, and rather unimaginative routine. The professor would sit at the head of the table opposite his wife with, on either side, the guest, and the professor's two children, a boy and a girl, dressed in traditional student clothes. While everyone drank beer at table the host and his guest treated themselves to a good Rhine wine. Conversation was both learned and familiar, and the jokes were far from lofty. Pirandello felt extremely awkward and was on tenterhooks the whole time. On one occasion he did not catch Professor Foerster's invitation to dinner— and Foerster took offence. Pirandello wrote to Monaci on 7 September 1890: 'I hope that Professor Foerster will regain his esteem for me since I lost it largely because of a . . . disagreeable misunderstanding. I can hardly think about it *without blushing to the roots of my hair.*'

Pirandello started to work on his own, to see people, even to have fun, although he wrote to his sister: 'I have several *friends* but I keep them all at arm's length since I love my solitude, my modest spouse, more than anything else.' In his notes on Pirandello's life Stefano Pirandello wrote[6] that his father 'enjoyed the novelty of student life and was amazed by the closeness between the students and the masters for whom the transfusion of knowledge was like nourishment . . .'. He joined his fellow students in 'excursions to the villages close to Bonn, Poppelsdorf and Godesburg, with the wysteria in flower in spring on the legendary river: they played bowls and studied Provençal texts all day long. The evenings were spent at the Verein where the songs of the Commersbuch and the rounds of beer were interrupted by learned lectures on some scientific subject. In the Neuphilologischer Verein of Bonn there were students of every nationality seated in a row before a long table with jugs full of beer, and they fraternized.' Pirandello was hardly inclined by nature 'to sit in a row' but he adapted himself.

He educated himself by reading German authors such as Heine, Tieck,[7] and Goethe, whose house he visited in Frankfurt on 13 June 1890.[8] But, above all, he spent his time studying philological texts and early Italian poetry. His academic conscientiousness in those days is proved by a scholarly article for the Florentine review *Vita Nuova* dated 'Bonn am Rhein, a.d. XI Kal. Dec. 1889'. After Gargano's favourable review of his first volume of poetry, *Vita Nuova* had welcomed him and was the first paper in which Pirandello became known in the Italian world of letters. His article was about a journey made by Petrarch to Cologne and Pirandello seized the opportunity to show off his familiarity with authors and learned quotations, and to lament the fact that 'in Italy criticism of texts and the scientific method of preparing an edition of the classics are still in their infancy'.[9]

But however hard he worked Pirandello continued to take part in the life of the town: he went to the theatre, saw various young women and went on excursions with the groups of girls who came from Cologne on the first day of every month to regale the students of Bonn as long as their money lasted. On 17 November 1889 he wrote to his sister that he had 'heard Wagner's *Tannhäuser* which left a profound sadness in my mind . . . the music is simply marvellous'. (In later life he was to turn against Wagner.) He had two girl friends, Mary and Anna Rismann, 'two little devils made of flames' who went to see him and 'messed up my aristocratic room'. When he wrote to Rosalina about them he implored her not to be shocked or to think anything improper. 'Would I mention any women who were not honest to you, sister of my heart? They are very well brought up young ladies, from one of the richest and most respectable families in Bonn. . . . I occasionally go to their house and they come and see me. We talk, we laugh about trivia in the most human and honest way possible, without there being any old fogey to turn up his nose, as there would be in Italy, Lina! . . . This is a very different form of upbringing and far more human, one must admit, than the form of upbringing in our part of the world. . . .'

In the meantime Pirandello's health did not improve. He wrote a little later to Monaci[10] that 'I shall soon have finished my study on the Dialect of Agrigento with the help and advice of the great Professor Foerster provided that I am not afflicted with another misfortune, provided, that is, that I do not again succumb to my heart disease which recurred more violently than ever,' and which stopped him 'working and living in peace for some time'. Foerster took a great interest in him and gave him 'an extremely courteous letter of introduction to the celebrated Dr Schultze' who also taught at the University of Bonn. That doctor, he wrote to his sister on 28 January 1890, 'having examined me attentively, came to the conclusion that my illness derived primarily from my digestion and my appalling way of life. So he told me to work as little as possible, to work standing up, to go for long walks, only to eat healthy and well-mashed food and not to smoke or drink coffee. Impracticable advice!' Nevertheless, encouraged by the doctor to do less work and to enjoy himself more, he took advantage of the fine weather to go for long, solitary walks in the neighbourhood, to Poppelsdorf, Küdinhoven, and Friesdorf, leaving at dawn and coming home late in the evening.

He gave an account of one of these walks in a page from a diary found in a large notebook which he used during this period for noting his impressions, for his poems, and even for his drawings.[11] In this particular account there are certain touches which remind us of Goethe's *Werther*, but, however elaborate, the whole page is concentrated on the impressions which the young man had in that Nordic atmosphere, so full of clear contours and silence and, for him, so new and different. The page is dated 17 January 1890 and it recounts a trip to Kessenich.

I can't say that I spent a good night but all today I have been in the best of health and I have lived as I have not lived for a long time. Yesterday at Plittersdorf, this morning at Kessenich, another village close to Bonn ... I walked fast, the pure air and the cold morning breeze revived my spirits and gave me an agility, a lightness which made me happy and serene. I despair at night, but every morning the illusion returns that the long walks will bring me closer to the Great Mother and might restore my health. ... We [by this time Pirandello had been joined by another traveller] went up a short and narrow path flanked by very tall cypresses which led to a small clearing covered with crosses beneath a little church. What a fine view from up there and what immense peace and pure silence. How sweet and religious death appears to be in a modest village cemetery. ... We went down to Kessenich which consists of a single long wide street with plain, low houses, nearly all of one floor, with a very ancient aspect. We looked for an inn. On the threshold of a little house on the right, painted blue, stood a girl of about twenty, laughing gently at us. ... Attracted by that mischievous smile I decided to go up to her and ask her. She said there was no point in going any further ... and without waiting for our reply she ran off laughing and, as she crossed the large courtyard, she sowed havoc amongst a gossipy crowd of geese which gathered and followed her, their necks craned forward, bouncing along on their short feet and shaking their wings. ...

As a means of recreation Pirandello went to a party in the Beethoven Hall in the Market Square of Bonn 'where the carnival was being opened with a large masked ball'. 'I too,' he wrote to his sister on 28 January 1890, 'wore a domino and—well may you shudder—I danced, or rather jumped, or rather trod on the toes of my partner.' Here Pirandello first met Jenny. 'I was literally *forced* to dance by a blue mask with an *extraordinary* straw hat who latched on to my arm and wouldn't leave me all evening. At midnight, when we removed our masks, I was amazed to see in the diabolical stranger one of the most radiant beauties I have ever come across. Today, according to the custom, I went to visit her at home to enquire how she felt after the whirlwind of yesterday evening. She is called Jenny Lander, and is twenty years old. . . . I can't tell you what a carnival ball in Germany is like and what women become on these occasions. They allow you to do everything, even kiss them, and with no commitment.' Pirandello promised that he would paint her portrait 'and I had to buy paints and brushes and I will begin tomorrow'. He also, as he recalled later in a short story, 'Sunrise' ('La levata del sole'), went to Cologne where the carnival was celebrated in style.

Some time earlier he had sent Monaci his translation into Italian of a book by Neumann—a student handbook on Romance philology. Monaci had appreciated it greatly and had had it published. With the fee of 200 lire from his publisher Pirandello invited his fellow lodgers to Cologne, leaving in his room, in a purse embroidered by his fiancée, the monthly allowance sent him from Sicily. For two days he and his two friends had enjoyed themselves in the Höllestrasse and the neighbourhood, spending Pirandello's hard-earned money until, suddenly, they had to return to Bonn, summoned by a telegram. A maid of Herr Mohl's had stolen all their clothes and belongings, including a gold watch which Pirandello had prudently left behind—and they ended the month in penury.

Pirandello's health now deteriorated to such an extent that he had to return to Sicily for four months. 'I was suffering too much,' he wrote to Monaci on 24 June 1890, 'and here I felt too lonely to suffer, so, remembering my past sufferings in Sicily, I decided, after a night I shall always recall with terror, to return to Italy. . . . I stayed with Romolo Murri in Bologna and he told me to leave books altogether for a while. Then I went to my house in the country where I felt so much better that I decided to leave again after about four months. I went back to Bonn where the semester was almost over and I barely had time to have my sheet signed; but I couldn't see Foerster. I didn't feel well enough to resume my studies calmly and actively, as I would have liked, and so I wandered about trying to recover again by means of recreation.'

Jenny's friendship was of some consolation to him. She soon managed to persuade her new friend to change his lodgings and to stay with her at 37 Breitestrasse, where her mother used to put up university students whenever the chance arose. Jenny was a pretty and intelligent girl: she played the piano and sang, and a vivacious, even if not immediately intimate friendship arose between the two. In the Schulz-

Lander household Pirandello again had two rooms: a study and a bedroom. But here too he was assailed by his 'wretched disease', which, he wrote to Monaci, 'will not leave me. And I cannot remain idle here for long. If I'm not killed by my disease I shall soon die of idleness which plagues me still more. . . .' And, once again, he returned to Sicily where he remained for nearly the whole summer.

He was back in Bonn at the end of August. Just before he left he had written to his professor in Rome: 'I want to start work again. To tell you the truth, *I never really stopped*, and I have almost finished the translation of Meyer's *Grammar of Romance Languages* which I suggested that the Bocca brothers should publish (a proposal I was unable to follow up). I have also worked on three *humorist* poets of the thirteenth century, Cecco Angiolieri, Folgore di San Gemignano, and Cene della Chitarra, of whose poetry *I would like to prepare a critical edition* and an interpretation.' Then, after giving some technical explanations and asking for advice about the manuscripts and texts to consult, he asked the professor's permission to dedicate to him this 'first work' of his 'as a sign of long-standing and genuine gratitude and affection'. He added: 'In a few days' time I shall call on Foerster again and resume my study of dialects for which I have now gathered all the material. I shall write it in German as my *doctoral thesis*. As you undoubtedly know, here in Germany, in order to obtain a doctor's degree in Romance philology, one also has to sit an exam in natural sciences and mathematics. Natural sciences are all right, but how am I to do mathematics, I who lose myself like a blind man in the squares of the Pythagorean table?'

As a university student Pirandello does not appear to have shown much persistence. And Foerster half-reproached him for the speed with which he learnt things, saying that he would forget them just as quickly while his German comrades, who took longer, would have them engraved in their memory. So Pirandello set to work, regardless of his health, and this last semester was the most intense and exhausting of his entire period at university.

Pirandello's friendship with Jenny had grown increasingly intimate and, on his return from Sicily in August 1890, it had turned into love—above all as far as Jenny was concerned—with all the consequences of love. Little is known about the episode. Though the allusions to it are veiled in his letters to his sister, Pirandello provides a more open confessions of his feelings in *Rhine Elegies* (*Elegie renane*) and *Easter in Gea* (*Pasqua di Gea*), the poems written at this time. Pirandello appears to have responded to Jenny's devotion with a vague feeling of guilt. He could not feel entirely guilty or entirely innocent and he kept on advancing excuses, as though he was performing a work of charity. Nor could he separate the concept of free love from the idea of sin. Accustomed to the rigorously chaste behaviour of his own sisters and 'well brought up' Sicilian girls in general, Pirandello appears to have been unable to feel much respect for Jenny. When he returned to Italy he left her brutally and ungratefully—ungratefully because Jenny really had constituted a haven of affection and consolation for him while he had lived away from home. And Pirandello, who continued to write to her for some time after he was back in Italy, did at least keep the promise he made in *Rhine Elegies*: he never forgot her. Indeed, forty years later, in America, when Jenny, who had also become a writer, was an elderly lady she tried to see her slim lover of the past who was now a world celebrity, but Pirandello made sure that the meeting never took place, so fond had he become of the transfigured memory of the spring on the Rhine.[12]

In September 1890 Pirandello finished his doctoral thesis under the supervision of Foerster who was of the greatest help to him when it came to spelling, to the diphthongization of the 'a' and the 'o' in the dialects of Agrigento and Casteltermini, and when Schneegans or Meyer-Lübke offered little assistance.[13] He prepared reluctantly for the 'two ineffable exams of physics and mathematics'[14] and he was at last ready to take his degree.

In the meantime he continued to publish literary articles in *Vita Nuova*. He took pleasure in showing off his knowledge of Provençal literature, announced that a volume of his own on the influence of Romance poetry 'together with certain other works of minor importance' were about to appear, and said that Romance philology was 'the science to which I have dedicated myself and which I studied with great love and assiduous care'.[15] He also brought to Bonn *Mastro Don Gesualdo*, Verga's recent novel, and with youthful arrogance (which he was later to regret and condemn) he criticized it severely. He accused Verga of philological ignorance: '. . . For some time many modern story-tellers and novelists (including Verga) who are in search of a live and spontaneous prose have done nothing but round off their dialects as well as they could. . . . And the attempt might even be praiseworthy, were it performed with more sense, with more awareness of the value which the work should possess, if, in a word, our writers were not too deficient, as they often are, in philological knowledge. . . . It is not enough to have talent and the possibility of opening one's mouth and expect to leave it at that.'[16]

Over the 'question of language' Pirandello started a Discussion with Pietro Mastri who finally lost his temper and, with Florentine incisiveness, ended the discussion by publishing the three words 'Enough is enough',[17] although Pirandello's arguments were not totally contemptible.

During this German period Pirandello read the philosophers (since one of his final exams was to be in philosophy), but he does not appear to have attached much importance to them. When he reached the peak of his success it was said, in France, that his favourite German poet was Heine. But he denied this, as Benjamin Crémieux witnessed,[18] and said that his favourite German poet was really Goethe—and this was true. He had in fact concentrated on the young Goethe, the Goethe of *Werther* and the *Roman Elegies*, as well as on Tieck and Heine. Only later, in his maturity, was his cultural background to become richer and more complex and only later did he get to know (whether directly or indirectly is not clear) Kant's *Critique of Practical Reason*, Hegel, and Schopenhauer.

Pirandello took his degree on 21 March 1891. It was not an easy exam. The *Doktor-Examen* was preceded by the *Magister-Examen* which consisted in a lengthy interrogation on three basic subjects, philosophy, history, and natural sciences. In all three Pirandello's performance was qualified *genügend*—satisfactory. He was asked every sort of question about philosophy and history, mathematics and zoology. At some of the questions on mathematics he became so confused that the professor played with him as with a child and proved to him that he had eleven, not ten fingers.

In his doctoral exam Pirandello also had to prove his knowledge of Latin and here Buecheler kept him for hours on end answering questions about grammar and the history of texts, and about Romance philology (specific aspects of Italian, Spanish, and Provençal). He was qualified as *im ganzen gut*, 'good in everything', in Romance philology, while his knowledge of Latin had no special qualification (or so it would seem from the surviving documents at the University of Bonn). The entire oral examination was qualified with the formula *rite superavit* while his thesis was judged as *observatione accurata et docta expositione probabilis*.

Finally, after answering all his opponents' questions (one was an older student, the other a graduate in Pirandello's own subject), Pirandello came down from the podium where his exam was held, a toga was laid on his shoulders and the large ritual hat was placed on his head. He took an oath on crossed silver rods held by the beadles, and could at last enjoy the painfully won *summos in philosophia honores*, *doctorisque nomen, iura et privilegia* (the highest honours in philosophy and the title, rights and privileges of doctor).[19]

No sooner was his thesis, entitled *Laute und Lautentwickelung der Mundart von Girgenti* ('The Phonetic Development of the Agrigento Dialect'),[20] published than it was reviewed by the great professor of Romance philology, Meyer-Lübke, in the *Literaturblatt für germanische und romanische Philologie*, on 11 November 1891. Then, after a brief stay in Wiesbaden and a promise from Professor Foerster that he would be given the post of assistant lecturer in Italian, Pirandello went back to Italy. He seems to have been pleased to do so. Before he left, when his sister asked him whether he proposed to remain in Germany to continue his academic career, he said that he not only did not intend to do any such thing, but he never wanted to set foot in Germany again. 'I propose to keep my room in Rome for ever. . . . I want the sun, I want light, and here you don't get either: here the days pass away like continuous sunsets.' In one of his *Rhine Elegies* he had said how alien Germany was to him.

Yet this declared dislike of Germany was true only up to a point. He was to retain a certain affection for the Germans (witness the portraits in some of his short stories, 'Sunrise' , 'The Pensioners of Memory' ('I pensionati della memoria'), 'Grandfather Bauer' ('Nonno Bauer'), 'Berecche and the War' ('Berecche e la guerra')) and, above all, he was to use his experience of the north, which was soon reduced to an idealized generalization, as a contrast with the image of the barbarous and uncultured Sicilian south. In the short story 'Far away' ('Lontano') he was to retain the sense of an antinomy between a metaphorically honest and clean north and a dirty, impure south, between the civilized countries of the north and the irremediably corrupt society around him.

Though he opposed the Triple Alliance Pirandello was never totally averse to Germany. After all, it was there that he spent some of his most receptive years as far as his cultural formation was concerned. Even if he could never really be fond of a country which he felt was so alien to his temperament he did become fond of the memory of that period of his youth and that stage of his intellectual development. Germany came to represent a period of fantasy and poetry, a period when he could love and express his ephemeral love. He had an ambivalent relationship with the country, in which an admiration for the seriousness of the German and Protestant culture prevailed, even if he occasionally yielded to his impatience with the inflexible and un-Mediterranean characteristics of the German people.

Now that his university studies were over, however, he wanted to *flee* from Germany for ever. But to return to Sicily entailed a return to the suffocating pressure of his long-standing and reluctant engagement. Linuccia welcomed him with terrible scenes of jealousy[21] because of the dedication of *Easter in Gea* in German to 'Jenny Schulz-Lander, meine liebe, süsse Freundin'.

Pirandello, who was still feeling ill, went back to the house where he was born in order to recover. Here, in the white light of spring, overcome by irritation, he wrote the misogynistic poem 'Belfagor' which he had started in 1886. But if he could give vent to his antifeminism in a poem, he had to be more cautious in practice. On 11 August 1891,[22] he wrote a long letter to his father in which he gave a detailed account of the reasons for which his marriage could not take place. His father, against the marriage from the start, had no difficulty in provoking Linuccia's family to the point of breaking the engagement. He brought up certain questions of interest, certain quarrels between the various branches of the family, and, with mutual contempt, the marriage was called off. Thus Pirandello was free. He left Il Caos, Agrigento, and Sicily. His new home was to be Rome, a town which he considered more suitable to his dream life as a writer and a poet.

Of the thoughts and feelings of Linuccia we know nothing.

3

ROME

Pirandello, now twenty-four, arrived in Rome, where he settled permanently, as a 'man of letters'. His father gave him a handsome allowance and he spent a number of years, before and after his marriage, working as a professional littérateur. He had cut all worldly bonds. His younger brother, Innocenzo, had agreed to do military service in his stead while he devoted himself to writing. It was only with many reservations that he had envisaged a philologist's career after his departure from Bonn. In a letter written in May 1891 he described his poem 'Belfagor' as a virile poetic testament dictated before his philological castration:[1] 'In this beautiful Italy of ours, the cradle of art, one cannot live by art alone, and whoever has the misfortune to be born for art is obliged to cut off his most precious possessions. Before I cut mine off I want to prove that I have them and I want to surpass those who are castrated—an idea like any other. Only then shall I dedicate myself to the closed 'e' and the open 'e' and the various consonant groups, and then who knows? They may make me a *cavaliere* and a *commendatore* . . .'

Barely a year earlier he had written to Pipitone, a friend of his from Palermo who edited a review entitled *Psiche*, that his only ideal was poetry: '. . . My nightmare is that I shall be dissatisfied for ever, in exchange for feeling, just for one moment in the whole of my life, the only satisfaction to which I can aspire—that of having realized my ideal.' '. . . I understand everything, but I confess that I do not understand a mediocre poet. If, by the time I am thirty, I have not produced a really fine and lasting work, I give you my word that I shall never write another line as long as I live.'[2]

He was searching for a unique moment of great poetry. He had returned from the north with a slightly Bohemian appearance and, many years later, his childhood friend Antonio De Gubernatis recalled his large hat, 'a sort of sombrero' which hid his face and made him unrecognizable.[3] Luigi Capuana described him as follows:[4] 'Fair haired, with a Nazarene beard, rather long hair brushed back under his wide-brimmed beaver hat—he had nothing in his slim, distinguished figure and in the gentle expression of his pallid face that suggested he was Sicilian. Many people took him for a German student on his indispensable journey to Italy after his degree.'

The Rome where Pirandello settled was characteristically *fin de siècle*. It was full of writers, journalists, and poets who either lived there or came to visit it. They came from every region of Italy, but above all from the south and the centre; they were poor, as disinterested as it was possible to be, and for the most part honest and generous. The decade before Pirandello's arrival had seen the birth of Italian journalism, the foundation of a quantity of newspapers and reviews, and Rome had been the meeting-place of the leading writers of the country. When Pirandello arrived the cafés, restaurants, and clubs still echoed with famous names, but most of the writers themselves had retired to the provinces, while those who remained had formed somewhat narrow sects and groups. There was the select provincialism of d'Annunzio's followers and there was the simpler and healthier provincialism of the realists and the neo-realists whose work never went beyond their own petty-bourgeois vision. It was this second group that Pirandello joined silently and unobtrusively, believing it to be closer to his own way of thinking. His having studied in a German university gave him some prestige and the philosopher and sculptor Millefiori introduced him to the writer Ugo Fleres who, in his turn, introduced him to the editor of the review *Capitan Fracassa*, Faelli. Since Pirandello had already translated Goethe's *Roman Elegies* Faelli and Fleres arranged for an interview with the translator to appear, bearing Faelli's signature, in another review, *Don Chisciotte*.

Pirandello's friendship with Ugo Fleres, a fellow Sicilian from Messina, quickly became warmer. The two went for long walks together in the sites which Goethe had visited, or they went beyond the walls with paints and brushes to paint the sunsets. They were frequently joined by Tomaso Gnoli and Ettore Romagnoli, a translator of Greek classics under whose influence Pirandello was later to write two of his best 'Greek' poems, 'Laomache' and 'Scamandro'.

Pirandello favoured the realistic style of painting and, though an amateur, painted reasonably well. When he was much older and painted on holiday for relaxation he always returned to the same quiet, undramatic forms and colours. A few years later, in 1895, on the occasion of the Fine Arts Exhibition in Rome, he even wrote seven articles of art criticism for the *Giornale di Sicilia*.[5]

It was to Ugo Fleres that Pirandello owed the friendship and protection of Luigi Capuana. Since Pirandello was still uncertain which literary medium to choose, Capuana advised him to concentrate on the novel and it was at Capuana's suggestion that Pirandello wrote his first novel, *The Outcast* (*L'esclusa*, then entitled *Marta Ajala*). He wrote it on holiday in an abandoned convent inhabited by an innkeeper and a meteorologist and his family on the Monte Cave where he stayed in a former cell and worked, while the weather was fine, in the countryside, on the lowest branch of an ancient oaktree, occasionally receiving visits from his new friends. One day Pirandello dressed up as a monk and went with his friends to Rocca di Papa where he glanced diabolically at the passers-by from under his cowl.[6]

The literary meetings were held occasionally in Capuana's house,[7] but mainly in Ugo Fleres's house in the Lungotevere Mellini, then in Via San Nicola da Tolentino, and finally in Via Nazionale. They also took place at Giuseppe Mantica's or in Pirandello's room above the Porto di Ripetta and, after his marriage, in his flat, first in Via Sistina and then in Via Vittoria Colonna, in Palazzo Odescalchi. When Capuana was away Fleres, who was seven or eight years older than Pirandello, acted as the guide of the group and the mentor of style, his aim being to restore the traditional limpidity of Italian literary prose within the realistic context of the period.

The meetings had four or five regular attendants—the Calabrian Giuseppe Mantica, writer, teacher, and politician, whom Pirandello succeeded as professor at the Magistero in 1897; the short-story writer Italo Palmarini; the composer Salvatore Saya, a musician from Messina who taught music at the Synagogue and who, though he was not a practising Jew, put a number of Hebrew chants to music. From time to time he would sit at the piano and play for his friends. Then there was Ugo Fleres whose versatility as a poet, novelist, short-story writer, librettist, journalist, literary and art critic, designer, and caricaturist was an example for Pirandello who, to begin with, also tried to be all these things at the same time. And finally there was a younger man, Tomaso Gnoli, who has left a description of these encounters.[8] The friends spent their time reading and discussing their articles, short stories, and poems. Pirandello read his works out loud, including his novel, *The Late Mattia Pascal*, which he read in instalments as he wrote it. 'They went in for competitions,' wrote Gnoli, 'choosing a headline in a newspaper and writing about it for the following Sunday.' Pirandello joined in eagerly and always remained attached to headlines —according to Gnoli the short story and later the play *The Doctor's Duty (Il dovere del medico)* was the result of one of these exercises. Then, after the readings, the friends would end the day with a game of cards.

By the beginning of the twentieth century the writers of Rome were meeting more and more frequently in the literary cafés. Pirandello and his friends would assemble between five and eight at the Caffè Bussi in Via Veneto opposite the Excelsior Hotel where numerous other writers might join them.[9] But Pirandello did not like literary cafés and was never influenced by the ideas that came into fashion. Indeed, he developed an aversion for Roman literary society which he satirized in his novel *Her Husband (Suo marito)*, published in 1911 and probably written earlier, which caused such offence to the novelist Grazia Deledda that she prevented it from being reprinted until 1941. In the novel 'militant literature in Italy' is represented as a 'petty, gossipy village pharmacy' swarming with envy and malice. 'Everyone ... so jealous, concerned only with his own affairs, and this concern stops him thinking.' Pirandello describes a banquet of these 'ephemeral men of letters': 'the secret envy which prompted false smiles and poisoned compliments, ... the ill-concealed jealousies and malicious whispers, ... the unsatisfied ambitions, illusions, and frustrated aspirations enslaved these restless beings.'

Pirandello preferred the quiet company of his own friends, Sicilians and southerners for the most part, and they generally met at home. As was almost inevitable the idea of a joint review arose in 1898. A Shakespearean title was chosen: 'Ariel'. The title page, in bright red, was designed by Fleres and represented a demon next to the title brandishing an object which looked like a cross between a pen and a rod. The decision to found a weekly paper was made in Giuseppe Mantica's house and about ten friends joined, at a fee of a hundred lire each. The editors were Pirandello, Ugo Fleres, Giuseppe Chiovenda, and Italo Carlo Falbo, editor-in-chief.

The paper did not last long: it survived only until the end of the spring. Pirandello, now thirty, dictated its manifesto, an article entitled 'Sincerity'. He had coined the term 'sincerism' as a new 'ism' to be added to those which Capuana had enumerated in his recent essay 'Contemporary isms'. It was a reaction against the 'latest priests of the Venuses of style' and was in favour of a sincere open-mindedness, 'sincere in essence, sincere in expression'. 'No formula, no system, no pretence and above all no pre-established method in art.' The editors of *Ariel* compared the conception of a work of art to conception in the maternal womb. There was no great philosophical ability in the members of the Fleres–Pirandello group but a great desire to be sincere. Nor was Pirandello to display much ability as a theoretician in his literary essays ten years later. The truth was that he was never able to express, either then or later, anything that went beyond his own instinctive and romantic poetics.

Around him he had no models of a more rigorous poetic discipline. His contemporaries were immensely prolific, covering thousands of pages without paying much attention to detail, confident in their instinct and genius, following the example of the French realists. And prolific, too, was Pirandello. In *Ariel* he published an autobiographical short story, 'The Choice' ('La scelta'), another short story, 'If . . .' ('Se . . .'), and *The Epilogue*, a one-act play (based on his short story 'Fear' ('La paura')) which was his first dramatic work to appear, although he had written it at least six years earlier.[10] *The Epilogue*, which changed its title and became *The Vice* (*La morsa*), was given to Zacconi in November 1892 to be produced at the Teatro Valle; then to Cesare Rossi who had promised to produce it.[11] Subsequently Capuana read it one evening to the Neapolitan critic Eduardo Boutet who recommended it to Flavio Andò, one of the most successful Sicilian actors of the late nineteenth century. But Andò forgot about it and then provided a series of excuses for not producing it. Pirandello, who saw his theatrical début thwarted once more, wrote the actor a letter violent enough to warrant the exchange of seconds. The duel was called off at the last moment thanks to Boutet, but after this episode Pirandello shunned the temptation of the theatre for many years.

In a letter of February 1893[12] Pirandello gave a list of twenty-one short stories, novels, plays, and collections of poems which he had written or was writing, and complained that they were still unpublished. But around 1900, thanks to his friends, to Capuana and above all to

Fleres, he had his works published in Rome, Florence, Milan, Naples, Genoa, and in Catania and Oneglia. His poems, articles, and stories appeared in countless papers—*Vita Nuova, Capitan Fracassa, Fanfulla della Domenica, Nuova Antologia,* and others. But his most important contributions were to the Florentine review *Marzocco,* edited by Giuseppe Gargano, Pietro Mastri, and Angiolo Orvieto. The magazine mainly upheld the ideas of Pascoli and d'Annunzio, symbolism, neo-spiritualism, and neo-idealism, but Pirandello was welcomed despite his hostility to d'Annunzio. He, as a 'sincerist', declared his satisfaction when Enrico Thovez showed up some of d'Annunzio's plagiarism in the *Gazzetta Letteraria* of Milan and he even joined in the attack himself in an article entitled 'The Idol' ('L'idolo'), which appeared in Monaldi's review *La Critica* on 31 January 1896. In the same review, on 8 November 1895, Pirandello had already accused d'Annunzio's characters of being 'extraordinarily ridiculous' and his criticism of d'Annunzio's *Virgin of the Rocks* ended with the prophetic words: 'How many people will agree with me today? Very few, or no one! And tomorrow? Who knows?'

His antipathy for d'Annunzio was mainly instinctive, but he later developed a conviction that the poet had usurped success and fame at his own expense. Indeed, the specious and clamorous glory of d'Annunzio's poetry overshadowed Pirandello's more modest style for a long time. But in this Roman period he was to recall a deliberately elegant d'Annunzio 'with an inch of starched cuff jutting out of his sleeve, a high collar, a top hat and daringly cut jackets'.[13]

In 1896–7 Pirandello hoped to become the proprietor of the *Nuova Antologia* together with Domenico Gnoli who ran it. But when the deal was ready to go through and his father was about to send him the required sum of money a group of politicians succeeded in buying the review. Gnoli, out of pique, founded *L'Italia* and, in the August 1897 number, published both Pirandello's story 'Vexilla Regis' and Carducci's 'Church of Polenta'.

Pirandello's first books began to appear without publicity and in modest editions. In 1894, almost simultaneously with the appearance of 'Pier Gudrò' (the poem which Capuana liked so much) and the *Rhine Elegies,* Pirandello's first collection of short stories, *Loves without Love (Amori senza amore)* was published. But despite the quantity of his published work, Pirandello's name was far from being well-known and as late as 1901 his talent had not been seriously recognized in the publishing world. Again it was Capuana who came to his friend's assistance with his full critical authority. In an article published in *Roma di Roma* on 16 September 1896 he presented Pirandello as a poet with a 'good-natured and subtle irony', and he devoted one of his most flattering 'Literary Profiles' to him in *L'Ora* of 4 August 1901. 'Luigi Pirandello,' he wrote, 'displays the same qualities of subtlety, irony, and observation in the short story as he does in the novel. But the public has not yet had the chance to notice it. The volume *Loves without Love* did not have the success it deserved. The short stories, liberally dispersed in reviews and papers, have not yet been assembled. Luigi Pirandello is now thirty-four. But I am sure that he will emerge from the shade the minute a publisher with flair becomes aware of his value and can present him successfully to the public. He can wait, of course, with the certainty that his hour of glory will come.'

Capuana's advice was taken. One after the other Pirandello's books appeared with their strange titles which, in subsequent editions published by Treves, Bemporad, and Mondadori, were unfortunately changed. Between 1902 and 1904, in Florence and Turin, the first and second volumes of *Jokes of Death and Life* (*Beffe della morte e della vita*) appeared together with *When I Was Mad* (*Quando ero matto*) and *White and Black* (*Bianche e nere*). The first two novels written some years earlier were also published: *The Outcast* from June to August 1901 as a supplement of *La Tribuna* directed by Onorato Roux; *The Shift* (*Il turno*) in 1902 by Giannotta, a publisher from Catania who was a friend of Martoglio and Capuana. Then, in 1904, came *The Late Mattia Pascal*.

Pirandello continued to attend the Sunday meetings at Fleres's house until 1910. But from the first he appeared remote and absorbed by other things. Tomaso Gnoli recalls him dressed elegantly in grey, with his bright eyes and blond beard, rather phlegmatic even when he was being vivacious, and always outside, if not above, life. 'He smiled', wrote Lucio D'Ambra[14] 'but he never laughed. I can't remember having seen him laugh in twenty-five years. . . .'

What was there behind the smile and the solitary irony which Gnoli noted in him? An article in the Florentine review *La Nazione Letteraria* of September 1893, written when he was just over twenty-five—that is when he was embarking on his career as a prose writer—gives us some idea of his attitude towards the modern world. It was entitled 'Art and Consciousness Today' ('Arte e coscienza d'oggi'). In it Pirandello endeavoured to evaluate contemporary civilization. He saw the old men 'resign themselves with compunction to rest in the hands of God' while he, Pirandello, was an atheist and proud of it. ('I remember that he used to boast about his atheism', Tomaso Gnoli recalled.) Leo Tolstoy, who had returned to the faith, wrote 'absurd and puerile comedies'; and Paul Verlaine (whom Pirandello may not have known but whom he regarded, in accordance with Max Nordau's opinion, as 'the lowest form of degenerate, a vagabond imprisoned for offending the morals of society'), Paul Bourget, and Antonio Fogazzaro, 'spiritually helpless', clung like shipwrecked sailors to their old faith. The knowledge of modern science provoked such shipwrecks. It is 'the desperately sick modern spirit that invokes God like a repentant man about to die . . . I am amazed that something which is in fact pitch dark should be called God.' 'Modern philosophy [i.e. positivism] has tried to explain in the universe as a living machine and has tried to specify our awareness of it. Then it went on to establish man's place in nature, to interpret life and deduce its aims. . . . But science has assigned man a pitiful place in nature compared to the place he once thought he occupied.' (Here we can see Pirandello trying to match the pessimism of his primitive romanticism with that of positivist times.) And what is the result of all this? 'This poor earth of ours! A tiny astral atom, a vulgar little top thrown from the sun and moving round it, through space, in immutable tracks. What has become of man? What has this microcosm, this king of the universe become? Alas poor king! Can you not see King Lear hopping before you, armed with a broom, in all his tragic comicality? What is he raving about?'

Here we have Pirandello's 'raving' man, the man he would provoke, wound, and torture all his life and in all his work, the man he would despise but also regard with compassion, as the true image of himself. But at the time of this article Pirandello had not yet reached the point of transposing himself into the creatures of his own invention. Here he used the first person plural. 'Who is not a degenerate?' he asked. 'Who can call himself sane? All of us are marked physically and intellectually to a lesser or greater degree, by degeneration!' The article continued:

As for the old, you have seen what they do . . . they return to God. . . . The young present a still sadder spectacle. Born in a feverish moment, when their fathers thought less of love than of war to reconstruct the country; born in the din of debates when people were trying to put in order what had been won, though what had been won did not satisfy the ideals of everybody, amid the swirl of opposed political and philosophical currents; educated without any definite criterion and lacking any inherent vital force, but obliged at too early a date to find an artificial force, destructive to the organism; they are nearly all affected by a neurosis and they are morally inane. . . . In the meantime we nearly all have contempt for traditional opinions, as though we wanted to conceal the deep discouragement in our hearts and the presentiment of obscure fears. With discreet arrogance we feign indifference towards all the things we know nothing about but which we would like to know about, and we feel dazed, lost in a huge, blind labyrinth, surrounded by an impenetrable mystery. . . . The old norms have vanished and new ones have not yet been established: so it is not surprising that the concept of the relativity of everything should have succeeded in making us lose our sense of judgement almost completely. The field is clear for any theory. The intellect has acquired an extraordinary mobility. Nobody manages to have a firm and unshakable viewpoint. . . . Never before has our life been more disjointed ethically and aesthetically. Disconnected, with no principle of doctrine or faith. . . .

Now consider for a moment those who, to find even a momentary way out of the complete moral shipwreck of the world, have shut themselves into themselves, have cut themselves off, have freed themselves as much as they can from every bond, and have consistently reduced their needs and aspirations. After some time, of course, they start to feel themselves alien to life, uninterested and without curiosity. They also feel an invincible disgust for daily vulgarity; and the cold, dispassionate observation of the sentiments and actions of others, more or less always the same, makes them feel a heavy tedium and boredom. . . .

From indecisiveness of thought results indecisiveness of action. No ideal assumes the concrete form of a really intense desire. Possession will never satisfy desire, man will never shake off his chains. . . . And there will always be something before us which we cannot attain. It is the eternal torture of Tantalus. . . . We are at the discretion of life.

To yield to the discretion of life became, for Pirandello, a line of conduct, both voluntary and involuntary. Were it not for this basic, but barely conscious passivity it would be impossible to explain Pirandello's reliance on his father's choice of a wife for him. It was certainly not out of conformity to the current Sicilian custom of prearranged marriages, for Pirandello was profoundly independent, especially where his father was concerned. That Pirandello married the first woman who was presented to him as a bride involved a far more radical renunciation. It looked like remoteness, lack of interest, or scepticism at the moment of greatest danger—and there may also have

Improvised theatricals with friends on the terrace of Pirandello's
lodgings in Rome. Pirandello is on the right

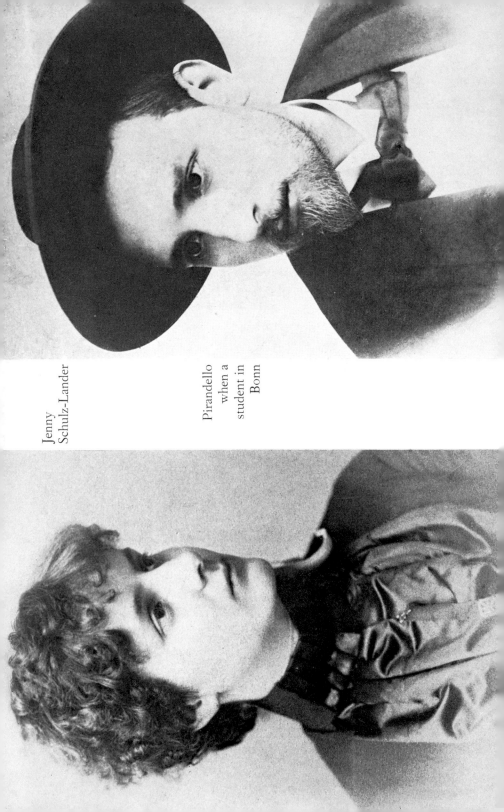

Jenny
Schulz-Lander

Pirandello
when a
student in
Bonn

been a touch of bourgeois cynicism which impelled him to make a marriage of convenience.

Hardly a year after he had broken off his engagement to Linuccia he received a letter from his father asking him whether he would agree to marry the daughter of Calogero Portulano, his business partner. Portulano had given him good advice in the past and appeared to have solicited the marriage himself, by leaving Agrigento for a while and entrusting to the care of Stefano two envelopes, on one of which was written: 'The dowry of my daughter Antonietta.'[15] It contained 70,000 lire, and between two Sicilians an allusion of this kind was fully understood and appreciated. The fathers agreed. All that remained was for the children to agree too.

Pirandello left for Agrigento where he waited till a meeting with the girl was arranged. His childhood friend Antonio De Gubernatis related:[16]

As we were walking along I asked him whether he really was in love with the girl living opposite his house, as people were saying. He said that he was not, but that he wouldn't appear on his balcony again as long as he stayed in Agrigento. Then, putting his hand on my shoulder, he told me he was getting married. I thought he was joking. . . . He said that his father, Don Stefano, a sullen but good man, had written to him suggesting a girl who was beautiful, good natured, and of excellent family: Antonietta Portulano. Luigi had agreed and was already contemplating marriage.

'Do you know her?' he asked me candidly.

'No. Do you?'

'No. I'm going to Porto Empedocle to meet her.'

The meeting took place more or less as described in *The Old and the Young*. The two families worked out how long it would take and two carriages set out from Agrigento and Porto Empedocle, one containing the Pirandellos, the other the Portulanos. They crossed, as had been arranged, on a level with Il Caos. Greetings were exchanged and the Pirandellos invited the Portulanos to their farmhouse. Here Pirandello and Antonietta could see each other and all precautions had been taken not to compromise the girl if Pirandello did not like her.

'When he returned that afternoon,' De Gubernatis went on, 'Luigi told me that he had seen her and had thought her "suitable to be a wife". That was all. After a long pause, during which he seemed to be thinking his own thoughts, he added that he wanted to make a real woman of her.'

There were further complications. Antonietta's father, together with her entire family, was terribly jealous. When she had gone to school with the nuns of San Vincenzo her father used to supervise her behaviour when she was taken out for walks with the other girls and, if she looked to the right or to the left, he made the most appalling scenes. Indeed, Calogero Portulano, who had fought with Garibaldi in the Trentino in 1866, had taken part in the anarchist revolts in Romagna, and had finally settled in Agrigento as a businessman and a money lender at an exorbitant rate of interest, was so jealous that he developed an ineradicable aversion for his future son-in-law, the man who was to hold his daughter in his arms, and the aversion became mutual. Portulano's first instinct was to call off the marriage which had been so laboriously prepared. He said that Antonietta was too young and insisted that Pirandello settle in Agrigento at the very time when he had found and decorated his house in Via delle Finanze in Rome. When Luigi refused to accept this condition Portulano denounced the agreement and looked for another husband for his daughter in Agrigento. He found a young lawyer, but Antonietta had obviously been attracted by Pirandello who was, by all accounts, an elegant, handsome young man with a romantic appearance, and she was not prepared to give him up. Finding her so stubborn her father yielded and the marriage was arranged all over again.

Pirandello, who was at Monte Cave writing the last pages of *The Outcast*, was recalled to Agrigento. This time Portulano was in a hurry. Pirandello was allowed to see his fiancée for just over a month and to meet her and talk to her only if in the presence of three or four other people. His daily visits lasted for two hours and took place in the presence of his mother and sister, and Antonietta's father and two brothers. The women sat on their own talking to each other. Antonietta was forbidden to look her future husband in the face and the men sat opposite them in silence.

Calogero looked at Pirandello out of the corner of his eye. Their mutual antipathy was never to diminish, even if their formal dealings were correct. Indeed, once he was married Pirandello often used to spend the summer in his father-in-law's beautiful house in the almond and olive groves of Bonamorone. Yet he enjoyed teasing him, and when Calogero died he yielded to his wife's relatives' insistence that he should write his epitaph and started with the words: 'Here at last lies Calogero Portulano.'

Once he was back in Rome Pirandello had to look for another flat for the new furniture. He at last found one on the corner of Via Sistina and Via del Tritone and the furniture, which had been sent back to Sicily when the engagement was broken off, was again dispatched to Rome. In a letter to Antonietta of 29 December[17] Pirandello protested in a sudden burst of rage: 'The forwarding agent should be flogged. I don't know who he is, whether Vajana or De Luca. All forwarding agents should be flogged! . . . All the glasses are broken, the roof of the shelves is broken; the clothes' stand has been ruined, split in the middle and without the plank for the umbrellas; that lovely writing desk has had its corners knocked off, and the friezes broken and lost! . . . I almost wept with anger!'

Pirandello arrived in Rome on 14 December and began corresponding with Antonietta at once. His first letters, both affectionate and pedagogical, show his intention to 'make a real woman of her'. They contain the hope of happiness, but his optimism cannot have been deeply felt for it was shattered as soon as he came up against the reality of Antonietta Portulano. Pirandello, who was essentially monogamous, was later to fall in love with Antonietta physically—she was a beautiful woman with long dark hair and a sad charm—but the radical intellectual and psychological differences between the two bode no good. Pirandello approached Antonietta very romantically. In his very first letter he told her what he had not said to her face: that she would be his salvation:

I cannot explain what I feel as I write to you. Nor could you understand it, since you are unaware of the condition of my mind before I met you in Sicily. I imagined life to be an immense labyrinth surrounded by an impenetrable mystery. Nothing made me want to go in one direction rather than another: all paths seemed to me ugly and inhospitable. Why should I go? and where? The fault is in ourselves, in our minds, and the evil is in life, a senseless evil—or so I said to myself.

We will never know anything, we will never have a precise notion about life, only a feeling, mutable and varied, sad or gay according to the circumstances. So nothing absolute. What is justice? What is injustice? I never found a way out of this labyrinth. . . . I felt neither desire nor affection: everything was indifferent to me, everything seemed vain and useless—I was like a bored and restless spectator who did not want to stay but could not make up his mind to leave; it was as though I had been pushed out of the river and was standing on the bank looking at the stream with no wish to be carried any further by it. My passionate love for art was the only rock to which I could cling in my

desolation, but modern life . . . has almost submerged this last rock, so
that to cling to it was tantamount to drowning. . . .

I have been foundering in a terrible night, Antonietta! My dreams of
glory were flashes immediately absorbed by the darkness. . . .

But now my sun is born! You are my sun, my peace, my purpose:
I have now emerged from the labyrinth and I see life differently. . . . I
have your image present and living before my eyes. On the journey
back I gazed for hours at the star you liked. I am awaiting your portrait
impatiently. . . . When will it come? As soon as possible, I beg you. . . .
Think of me, love me. . . . You will love me, you must love me because
I. . . .

The next day he wrote to her again:

If anyone had told me before I left for Sicily: 'You, my dear, will come
back cured', I would simply have answered: 'You don't know what's
the matter with me.' And this illness of mine really seemed to me incurable. I had freed myself from every bond; I watched others live, I
looked into life as into a complex of vain absurdities and of contradictions between people's acts and words, which were more or less always
the same. I had derived an oppressive sense of tedium and restless boredom.—And then? And then? I asked myself. Is this all? And will
it always be like this? So life is my illness and death alone will cure
me.

It seemed impossible that I could act, think, live like other men
whose actions, thoughts, and lives I had for so long followed without
interest or curiosity. It seemed impossible for me to fall in love, to feel
the joy of offering myself entirely to another person and to live almost
the same life as someone else.

Yet this is what happened and I feel I am dreaming, and I can hardly
believe myself, my heart. I think of you, of all the things that could
give you pleasure, of the best ways to embellish the life we will lead
together. I think of our nest, of the house which will welcome us; I am
building up a whole world of fine plans for the future . . . myself, this
black self of mine which I saw looming up before me; myself, who up
till a month ago poked fun at the stupidity—or so I said—of people
who were in love. Well, yes, life is made of these stupidities, and woe to
him who takes no notice of them! The dawn of my new life has put to
flight for ever the mists that were clouding my mind. Now the future
appears clearly before my eyes. I have at last been able to unite the two
supreme ideals: Love and Art.

And what do you think of me, Antonietta? What do your dreams of
me tell you? Don't let them lie to you or diminish the love and tenderness I feel! . . .

In his elaborate and passionate love letters Pirandello seems to have
lost his sense of proportion, to have lost sight of the object on which
his happiness depended. He forgot that Antonietta, brought up by
nuns, could only feel bewildered and still more distant from him after
the confessions of his intellectual crisis, she who knew nothing about
literature or philosophy. Both he and Antonietta were soon to pay
dearly for this miscalculation. But even in his third letter his expectation of absolute bliss and his more turgid feelings seem to have been
dampened by a somewhat unexalted reply. He no longer addressed her
as the woman of his salvation but as a little girl, in an affectionately
playful but not totally sincere tone. 'You do not want me close to you,'
he wrote, 'but it is no good! Resign yourself to having me always before your eyes. I am undergoing the trial of fire and it seems to me
centuries before I can see you again, never to leave you. Poor Antonietta! Breathe in these last few days of liberty which remain while I am
far away. . . .' But at the same time he appears to be answering a confession of her own intellectual ineptitude before so much intellectual
provocation.

You must understand me, Antonietta, and follow me along the noble
path allotted me by fate: the path of Art. You will warm yourself with
me before the purest of fires and your heart will open at the vision of
my high ideal. Your love will make up for the sadness which Art often
gives, and you will be the fount from which I will draw energy and
vivacity in moments of anguish. I too have my religion, as you see,
and no devotee has been or ever will be more faithful or pure than
myself.

Pirandello was not going to throw away this last chance of finding
an emotional refuge, and the next day he again wrote of his 'soul full of
an unusual tenderness', of a 'vast sense of expansion of the entire being
and sympathy for all things'. 'Have you communicated it to me with
your youth, with the promise of your hand, with the gentle and closed
simplicity of your ways?' But she answered that he should not invoke
her heart since *her* heart was 'behind her ribs'. 'Yes, I know,' he replied.
'As you say: your heart is behind your ribs. . . .' Her father and the
nuns of San Vincenzo must have told her to make that reply to whom-
ever spoke to her about love.
As a result of her prosaic replies, and despite spurts of renewed
tenderness, the tone of the letters gradually became less passionate; the
declarations of love became more artificial and insincere. Pirandello

wrote more about practical matters, such as the decoration of the house. By the beginning of the new year he appeared to have lost patience with the workmen and removals men who had turned the house upside down. He was on his own; his father was characteristically uncomprehending and did not send him the money he needed. Nobody wrote to him from home with advice, his Uncle Rocco had left for Monreale with Nanna and he had 'to run all over the place from dawn to dusk to prepare the house as quickly as possible'. He now called Antonietta his 'little wife'. 'I realize that I have given vent to my feelings for too long instead of talking of things which are more immediate. Forgive me, Antonietta, but you are already my little wife and I can talk of my troubles to you.'

In a letter of 3 January he asked: 'Are you as impatient as I am that we should see each other again? Don't let the delay weary you, Antonietta! Weariness breeds boredom and boredom prompts cold consideration of our own and other people's feelings.' And he added, to allay any suspicions that these may be *his* feelings: 'In any case impatience does not give way to exhaustion and still less to boredom. What should I do? I love you more and more!'

The last letter, posted on 7 January, two or three days before he left Rome, proves that there was no dialogue between Pirandello and Antonietta and made it clear that there would never be. If they had been unable to speak to each other during the engagement visits in Agrigento, the only one who now spoke was he. She remained enclosed within herself, intimidated, probably incapable of saying anything—

Don't you really know what to say to me? Do you really have to force yourself to write to me? I don't believe it! It's not at all true that you don't know how to write. Why haven't you got anything to say to me? Who knows how many thoughts our promises of love have inspired in you—and the approach of the day when our two lives will be united! Who knows how many feelings have been aroused in your heart! And you do not want to tell me? And if you don't tell me about that, what will you tell me about? For me your heart is still a closed book. Imagine how thrilled I would be if, at least once, something of your inner being was revealed to me: some secret thought or feeling. I haven't yet heard an intimate note in your words. You talk to me of external things, but you never talk about yourself, about what you think and feel. Am I really so alien to you? You hide behind the statement: 'I don't know how to express myself'. And I tell you: 'Try! You will be able to if you want to. If the feelings dictate, the hand writes. There is no need for teachers.' But it's too late now ... I am often sad and don't know why.

Is my sadness from the earth, from life, from heaven, or is it caused by my invariable ideals, by my goal which moves further away at every step, by my dreams, by time, by my problems? I do not know. Maybe by all these things together and by many other things too. . . . It's almost as if there are two people in me. You know one of them, but even I hardly know the other. I mean that I consist of a big self and a little self: these two gentlemen are constantly fighting each other; one of them is often extremely uncongenial to the other. The first is taciturn and continually absorbed in thought, the second talks with facility, jokes, and even laughs and makes people laugh. When the latter says something rather stupid the former goes to the mirror and kisses him. I am constantly divided between these two people. Sometimes one of them predominates, sometimes the other. I naturally prefer the first, I mean my big self. I adapt myself to and pity the second, who is basically a being like all others, with their virtues and their defects. Which will you love more, Antonietta? Here lies the secret of our happiness.

Pirandello returned to Agrigento and married Antonietta in the Town Hall and the church of Madonna d'Itria on 27 January 1894. He was twenty-six and she twenty-two. After the ceremony the guests and relations accompanied them to Il Caos and, after the wedding feast, they were left to spend the night on their own.

Calogero Portulano's descendants, whom I questioned, claim that Pirandello, 'with an exquisitely gentlemanly spirit', did not want to consummate the marriage that night, or for some time after, with a woman who was almost unknown to him and to whom he was completely unknown. In his letters all his approaches had been limited to 'handshakes', 'a *very strong* handshake', a handshake 'still stronger than yesterday' and, with a daily crescendo, '*two* very strong handshakes', then 'three, four, a hundred, a thousand very strong handshakes', and so on. It is impossible to tell whether such Nordic behaviour as the unconsummated honeymoon decided on by the bridegroom was well received by the Sicilian Antonietta. It may even have had a traumatic effect on a woman who expected a more violent assault on her virtue.

After a week Pirandello and Antonietta left Il Caos and went to Rome. Here they moved into the house which had been fully furnished with the help of Pirandello's cousins. He had described the rooms to his fiancée: 'The drawing-room is all Louis XVI, delicious!' and there were plenty of carpets, 'indispensable in Rome'. To begin with their married life was probably affectionate and serene. Pirandello worked; they were well enough off economically; and they shared the household tasks. But less than two years after their marriage, the poem 'Landing place' ('Approdo'), which appeared on 29 October 1895 in Monaldi's *Critica*, suggests nostalgia for Linuccia and his broken engagement.

Eighteen months after their marriage, in June 1895, their first child, Stefano, was born. In June 1897 (when the Pirandellos had moved to Palazzo Odescalchi in Via Vittoria Colonna), Lietta was born, and two years later, again in June, Fausto. With Fausto's birth Antonietta had her first nervous breakdown, but it was not too serious and their married life continued quite calmly. Pirandello, who had given up his own share of the profits of his father's firm, received a monthly cheque from his father which, together with the income from Antonietta's dowry, enabled them to live comfortably. Thus Pirandello could concentrate on literature without financial cares or distractions. He could write short stories, novels, poems, continue to see his literary friends, invite them home, and attend the Sunday meetings in Fleres's house. In 1897 he obtained a teaching post at the Magistero, a training college for future teachers. For the first six years of their marriage Antonietta's time was taken up by nursing her three children, but she had a latent psychic instability which turned into a chronic and incurable disease.

The fatal year was 1903. Antonietta felt that she had a right to some partial authority over her husband through her dowry and her active contribution to the family finances. The possession of property in Sicily, especially in those days, was more than a mere cause of prosperity. It could easily become a fundamental part of one's existence and she was the daughter of a man who had started off poor, had made a fortune on his own, and continued avidly to accumulate money and turn it into land and houses.

The dowry had been entrusted to the by no means able hands of Stefano Pirandello who had started exploiting a large mine near Aragona, spending on the equipment not only his own money but also the 70,000 lire belonging to Antonietta. The mine, a 'huge sulphur mine' as Pirandello described it in a letter to Angiolo Orvieto,[18] which would ensure the well-being of his father and all his children, was suddenly flooded, causing a loss of 400,000 lire which corresponded to Stefano Pirandello's entire capital in addition to Antonietta's dowry. When he returned from an afternoon walk Pirandello found his wife lying in bed, semi-paralysed. The letter from Agrigento which she had read and which she handed to him, explained everything. Her paralysis was the first serious attack of the illness.

In addition to the problem of his wife's health there was also the question of supporting his family. His children were aged eight, six, and four, and Pirandello had to find an immediate solution. An old woman working as a governess for him was ordered to take Antonietta's jewellery to the pawnshop and returned with 600 lire. Pirandello himself seriously contemplated suicide[19]—not a cowardly suicide but a suicide which would solve the situation for everybody. For Antonietta, on her own, together with her children, would certainly have been welcomed by her father who, after repeatedly advising his son-in-law not to trust Stefano Pirandello's speculations, now seemed ready to say: 'It serves you right'. But the idea of suicide was soon dropped.

On 15 January 1904 he wrote to Angiolo Orvieto,[20] the editor and owner (together with his brother Adolfo) of the review *Marzocco* to which Pirandello had hitherto contributed articles and short stories without payment, and told him that he had interrupted his collaboration owing to the need for immediate financial profit. He now had to support his wife and three children with his teacher's salary which was hardly enough to pay the rent. He offered to continue to write for *Marzocco* and to produce one short story a month if he was paid twenty-five lire for it. Angiolo Orvieto, who was appalled by 'the terrible ordeal' which his friend was undergoing, paid for all his past work (about 3,000 lire) and gave him thirty lire for each new story.

Even the short stories which had already been published proved profitable. Besides, he had now been contributing for some months, ever since Giovanni Cena had become its editor, to the *Nuova Antologia*. And the *Nuova Antologia* paid its collaborators slightly better than other reviews. Then there was his teacher's salary, low as it was. But all this hardly sufficed.

Finding himself forced to earn more money, Pirandello started giving German lessons and Italian lessons to foreigners (at five lire an hour), and increased his literary output. One of his notebooks of that period survives and in it we find a 'list of earnings' from 1904 (we do not know whether it is complete) from which we see that his life must have been exhausting. Much of his earnings came from his job as a professor and he was also nominated exam commissioner outside Rome, which entitled him to a travel allowance. Some of the short stories set in the Central Italian provinces were the result of this experience. He went to Alatri and Montepulciano and here we find him recording

Tuscan idioms—he listed at least eighty of them in his notebook. From
the short stories published in *Marzocco* and the *Riviera Ligure* respectively he received thirty and twenty-five lire each. For one short story,
'A Voice' ('Una voce') published in *Regina* he earned fifty lire. He got
over a hundred lire from the German translations of 'Sunrise' and 'The
Annuity', and he also managed to sell a copy of *Bagpipes* (*Zampogna*),
his collection of poems published in 1901. His salary came to 2,592 lire
and, in the whole year, he earned 6,203.61 lire.

It was to this pressing need for money that we owe *The Late Mattia
Pascal*, the first of Pirandello's novels to have an immediate success in
Italy and, soon after, abroad. Giovanni Cena asked him for a novel to
be published in instalments in the *Nuova Antologia*. He would give
him an immediate advance of 1,000 lire and Pirandello accepted, though
he had not written a single word of it and did not even have an idea in
mind. *The Late Mattia Pascal* was written at night while Pirandello
watched over his wife who lay in bed unable to move her legs. It tells
the story of a man who pretends to have committed suicide in order to
live a life of complete freedom and, in its introspection and its subtle
humour, it constitutes a turning-point in Pirandello's career. 1903 was
a decisive year in his life. His smile became sadder and more ambiguous,
his attempts to find satisfaction ever more repressed.

The Late Mattia Pascal's publication as a volume by the *Nuova
Antologia* is connected with Pirandello's encounter with Giovanni
Verga. Twenty years later Pirandello himself recounted the incident:[21]

I was at the newspaper's offices with Giovanni Cena when Verga came
in, just back from Milan where he had witnessed the failure of his play
From Yours to Mine (*Dal tuo al mio*). He had lost his self-confidence.
He thought of returning to Sicily and never writing again—and this
was what he did. From that day on the great novelist remained silent.
But he had undertaken to give the *Nuova Antologia* his work *La
Duchessa di Leyra*. He cancelled everything and wanted to give back
the money. But Cena insisted. After various alternatives it was finally
agreed that the *Duchessa di Leyra* be replaced by *From Yours to Mine*
in novel form. During the conversation the printer of the *Nuova Antologia* brought in the first six printed copies of *The Late Mattia Pascal*.
Verga picked up one of them, looked at it, and was about to put it
down again when Cena introduced me to him. So I gave it to him. He
was very grateful and said he would read it and write to me and, sure
enough, I received a letter from him six days later. He said some very
kind and very sad things. He felt that time had overtaken him and he
saw his own lantern go out next to the little light of my own art. I will

never forgive myself for losing the letter. Perhaps my poor wife destroyed it during one of her attacks.

The Late Mattia Pascal was translated into French by Henry Bigot as it appeared in the Nuova Antologia and, in 1905, it was translated for the Viennese Fremdenblatt by Ludmilla Friedmann. In Paris Bigot's translation almost appeared in the Revue de Paris edited by Ganderax, but Matilde Serao, who was then far more famous than Pirandello, had managed to persuade the review to publish her own novel, After the Divorce (Dopo il divorzio)—which was also appearing in the Nuova Antologia—instead of Pirandello's. Consequently The Late Mattia Pascal appeared in France a few years later. But the success of the book earned Pirandello the interest of the publishing firm Treves, which was then the ambition of every Italian writer. In 1906 Treves published Two-faced Erma (Erma bifronte) and, in 1908, a volume edition of The Outcast. In 1920 Pirandello left Treves for Bemporad and, in 1929, Bemporad for Mondadori.

Despite the martyrdom and the dramas of his family life Pirandello could be sincerely affectionate, patient and obstinately docile. He was prepared to meet people and would often participate in vacuous and pointless discussions in a friendly and jocular manner. At the same time, however, he felt an irresistible urge to protest and an anarchistic desire to break with everything, as if out of malice. All these contradictory elements come out in his work. In his dealings with his family, his friends, and others, the contradictions were more or less resolved. Pirandello was endowed with considerable perseverance. He was self-disciplined but behind the silence and solitude which anyone who saw Pirandello had occasion to observe and which gave all his words a quality of detachment and alienation, there could occasionally be glimpsed his most vindictive side.

Once, when his wife reproached him for keeping a large portrait of her when she was young and serene, he pointed at the portrait and replied: 'I keep it because it is her, and not you, who made me happy.' Equally, he occasionally took pleasure in making one or other of his pupils at the Magistero cry. On one occasion he bitterly reproached one of the girls for having 'copied' her essay from a short story by Edgar Allan Poe. The girl's excuses were to no avail. It was in vain that she said that she had never even heard of Poe, and she wept desperately, without being able to move him. Then there were his outbursts against his father, his violent letters (written to other people) about him. But these episodes are few and far between. Those who knew him generally retained a memory of his humanity and goodness, even of moral superiority towards others. For Pirandello spilt his venom more into his written work than into his daily life, and he managed to achieve a certain equilibrium thanks to his incessant activity as a writer.

4

POLITICS AND WAR

In 1908 Pirandello published his third novel, *The Old and the Young*, which appeared as a supplement to *L'Italia Contemporanea* between January and November. It is not a great novel, but it is indicative of Pirandello's obsessions and anguish. He started writing it when he was almost forty and felt the need to concentrate his opinion of contemporary society in a single book.

Based as it is on the *Fasci Siciliani* and the events accompanying the scandal of the Banca Romana *The Old and the Young* contains Pirandello's political ideas. These ideas appear to be pronounced heatedly and passionately, but in fact Pirandello was more absorbed in an introspective examination. Both at the beginning and at the end of his career Pirandello insisted on the distinction between the artist's work and his political views.[1] Moreover, although he lived in isolation and managed to see deep into the motives of others he had no insight into the political society which surrounded him. Because of the superficiality of his political reactions Pirandello lacks any real autonomy as a public figure and simply merges into his social class. Whatever he says can always be traced back to a current opinion among his contemporaries.

Pirandello felt an immediate and instinctive impulse to protest, even if the object of his protest was ultimately indifferent to him. As a young man he had been with the Radicals, the direct heirs of Mazzini's 'Party of Action'. As an old man he was a fascist. In the intervening period he managed to be at the same time an extremist, a violent opponent of the Prime Minister Giovanni Giolitti, a supporter of Garibaldi, 'an individualist anarchist', and a supporter of Giolitti's reformism. He could share the moderate opinions of Albertini's *Corriere della Sera*, participate in Benedetto Croce's type of liberalism, and in the interventionism of the First World War which reconciled all contrasts. Where he was more consistent, beneath the occasional outbursts of rebellion, whether anarchist or fascist, was in his participation in the lot of his class. As a social being he was no different to the other members of the Southern Italian petty bourgeosie who were moderate first and fascist later.

This side of Pirandello's personality might appear to contradict some of the better known aspects of his work and indeed, in a sense, it does. But, point by point, it is possible to document my conclusions. To do so we should glance at Pirandello's reactions to the various periods of Italian policy. He left for Bonn, from Rome and Palermo, with some rather confused ideas ranging from humanistic and bourgeois patriotism to a radical socialism which he had picked up at the University of Palermo when he came into contact with De Luca. And however much his commitments changed he retained one constant idea, imbibed, so to speak, with his mother's milk: the patriotism of the Risorgimento.

In Bonn Pirandello seemed to forget every political ideology, for the quiet little town on the edge of an empire which was constitutional only in name and where the Kaiser was Kriegsherr and king by divine right, provided few occasions for political distraction. The Germany of 1890 was tidy and reactionary. Bismarck had abandoned his Kulturkampf over ten years earlier to side with the conservatives and the Catholic Centre, and had outlawed the socialist party. The struggle of the workers' party, led by Bernstein and Kautsky, took place far from the little university town, and the Neue Kurs had no more effect on Bonn than the Second International of 1889. Socialist students were expelled from the university named after Friedrich Wilhelm.

When Pirandello crossed the Italian border on his return from Germany it was as though he were returning from limbo. In Italy and Sicily he found a heated political climate. For the first time, on 1 May 1891, the Italian workers celebrated May Day. In the same year Filippo Turati founded *La Critica Sociale* and when the prime minister, Crispi, fell he was succeeded, after Di Rudinì's brief ministry in May 1892, by a group of men of the left led by Giovanni Giolitti. It was therefore possible to found the Socialist Party of Italian Workers legally.

It was at this moment that Pirandello resumed his friendship with his former radical acquaintances, part of whom had gone over to the socialists, and, when he settled in Rome, he remained in touch with them. When the new elections were announced in October 1892 he supported the candidate of the *Fasci*, Giuseppe Salvioli, professor of legal history at the University of Palermo, who was running in Agrigento, and he even sat on an electoral committee. In the electoral supplement of *La Riforma Sociale* in November 1892, the review edited in Agrigento by Francesco De Luca, Pirandello's signature appeared together with that of other sympathizers. He had also wired from Rome on 25 November 1892: 'If sincerity counted, my vote alone would ensure Professor Salvioli's triumph.' But Salvioli was not elected.

In September 1893, the year in which the organization of the *Fasci* spread to almost all the Sicilian provinces, Pirandello mentioned the socialist movement in Sicily in an article in *La Nazione Letteraria* published in Florence. But he did so in an ambiguous and hesitant manner, and, rather than set forth the facts in Italy and discuss the difficulties which faced the few volunteers who were endeavouring to arouse the Sicilian masses, he simply referred to the matter on a literary level.

Pirandello's article ended in the expectation of a vague catastrophe: 'Everything seems to be so shaky and unstable. I do not share the confidence and calm that some people feel . . . We are on the brink of a great event. . .'.

The end of 1893 was marked by the scandal of the Banca Romana in which men of the older generation like Crispi as well as younger men like Giolitti were involved. Pirandello appeared to favour the anti-Giolitti campaign and, after the massacre at Aigues Mortes in August, when thirty Italian immigrant labourers were killed by French workmen, he was won over by nationalist and anti-parliamentary propaganda. It was on this occasion, perhaps, that he developed his historical-political view that there were two generations in Italy, the generation of the Old who had thrown in their hand after the unification of the country and that of the Young who seemed totally incapable of seizing the reins of power. This may have been a superficial view, but it appealed to Pirandello and survived *The Old and the Young* until the First World War.

In the meantime the venture of the *Fasci* had miscarried. Crispi had returned to power, had proclaimed a state of emergency in Sicily, and had brutally repressed the rebellions of the peasants and the workers. The leaders were court-martialled and given excessively heavy sentences; even Francesco De Luca was sentenced to many years in prison. The socialist party was banned.

Pirandello hated the government's repressive 'anti-Sicilian' policy but, curiously enough, when he wrote *The Old and the Young* some years after the event, he absolved Crispi of responsibility for the massacres and the violence. In the novel, written in about 1908, he seemed to share the renewed nationalist sympathies for Crispi and praised him unconditionally, referring to him as 'the great old statesman', 'that venerable old man with child-like illusions about the country's future.'

After the repression in Sicily Pirandello appeared to share the anti-socialism of Crispi's followers. He refrained from joining the new 'League for the Defence of Liberty' in which the socialists were backed by all radical and republican groups. His anti-socialist attitude came out in some of his writings in 1895 and 1896. At Christmas in 1895, when his former travelling companions were serving their second year in prison he, together with a number of other writers, suddenly turned towards Christ. On 23 January 1896 he published in Monaldi's *Critica* a review of *Storms* (*Tempeste*), a collection of 'socialist' poems by Ada Negri. When he read these poems Pirandello's irritation knew no bounds: 'I deny,' he wrote, 'that Karl Marx's algebraic books can really inspire a poet!' The socialists fighting in the streets who addressed their followers with 'ready-made phrases, empty commonplaces' and who inspired the 'rebel poetess', were nothing but 'so many outsiders, professional charlatans who, today, have of course become socialists'. The socialist party had now become 'a party in fashion'.

In 1896 Crispi resigned again, this time for good, and the last years of the century in Italy were marked by a succession of attempts to restore authority. The heroes of the moment were King Uumberto I, Rudinì (under whose government the massacres of Milan in 1896 took place), and General Luigi Pelloux, Rudinì's Minister for War. The desire to discredit Parliament and curtail its power was now prevalent among the ruling class. Pirandello's position was uncertain. He was in personal touch not with the socialists but with the republicans and radicals. In July 1897 he wrote to Napoleone Colajanni[2] offering to collaborate on a forthcoming radical newspaper. Though he did not express any particular political allegiance in his letter his attitude was implicit in his offer to write a column in an opposition paper: '... I really do need to earn more than my wretched salary as a teacher ... and the small sums from my writing, so badly paid in our country. I would therefore willingly join the editorial board of the newspaper which the radical party plans to launch in Rome next October and write some literary articles, on the theatre or anything like that. Could you recommend my name to one of the more influential members of the radical party? I would be very grateful to you.'

A few years later, in 1901, Pirandello wrote a brief poem entitled 'Good old fellows' ('Bravi vecchietti')[3] which was a synthesis of the potentially chauvinistic and anti-parliamentarian attitudes of Italian nationalism, but which retained an anticlerical and masonic note. His Francophobia which had something of Crispi's post-Risorgimento ideology is constantly in evidence in his work. Usually it appears in the shape of a literary nationalism intended to defend the originality or the superiority of Italian works of art against foreign works, and to combat the imitation of things French (above all, of course, to combat d'Annunzio). In a letter in verse published in Monaldi's *Critica* on 28 March 1896 he asked France ironically what books ought to be read that year and whether d'Annunzio should be considered a great writer simply because he had been translated into French, and he ended with a curious epigramme against the French symbolist poets (with whose work he does not seem to have been well acquainted).

Again, in his essay 'Humour' ('Umorismo') in 1908 Pirandello warmly defended the independence and even the superiority of Italian humorist writers compared with foreigners and, in 1936, in a state of euphoria after winning the Nobel Prize and being hailed as foremost European dramatist, in a preface to a *History of the Italian Theatre*, he sustained the theory that Italian theatre was then, and always had been, superior to that of any other nation. However, Pirandello's chauvinism was only incidental to his activity as a writer. He occasionally conformed to contemporary journalistic propaganda but without trying to fit into the culture of his time. He was far from the moralism and post-Hegelian idealism of a man like Oriani and from the expansionist and imperialistic concepts expressed in Corradini's nationalist paper *Il Regno*.[4] He was far, too, from the obstinate rhetoric of d'Annunzio and Pascoli, from the irrationalist ideas of Maurice Barrès, and from the pseudo-rationalist views of Maurras and the 'Action Française.'

When Giolitti was in power Pirandello opposed the government because of his allegiance to Sicily and because Giolitti's economic policy favoured the north at the expense of Sicily and the south. Pirandello's scepticism towards social struggles found continual confirmation in the disorder and corruption in which negotiations between classes now took place. Basically, however, he agreed with the new policy of moderation and, in *The Old and the Young*, he even suggested a plan for social reform. He considered illusory the socialists' confidence that 'with their sermons . . . they can penetrate the hard secular shell of stupidity mixed with diffidence and animal cunning which encrusted the mind of the Sicilian peasant and sulphur worker. How could they believe in a class struggle where there was no strength of principle, where there was not even the most rudimentary culture or consciousness?' But he added: 'A class struggle is impossible in these conditions; instead, class cooperation should be attempted, since in every social category in Sicily there is deep resentment against the Italian government owing to its indifference towards the island ever since 1860.'

Pirandello's attitude was cautious; he advocated a *slight* reform of labour agreements, a *slight* increase in wages, all to be obtained with time, *little by little*. But this appears as an afterthought: we have no idea what was Pirandello's immediate reaction to the revolutionary explosion of the *Fasci Siciliani* and the repression which followed it. We must keep in mind that when *The Old and the Young* was being written labour organizations were again permitted to help workers improve their standard of living. The government made a point of not intervening in economic disputes. Mythological and apocalyptic socialism was extenuated as its minimum programme was fulfilled; and industrialists and land-owners were being encouraged to take a more active part in solving the social crisis. It was a period of creative reformism and Pirandello shared the political moderation of the time even if he retained his paternalistic tone.

Yet there is one passage in *The Old and the Young* which might lead us to draw a different conclusion. It is the only passage in which Pirandello's theory of the perennial destruction of form under pressure from the vital flux is adapted to the idea of a social revolution which would 'destroy the basis of an order of things convenient for the few but iniquitous for the majority of men, and awaken in this majority a desire and a feeling that would bring about the destruction and dispersal of all these century-old forms.' These lines are reminiscent of certain revolutionary theories of maximalist socialism or of certain concepts dear to Gramsci, but there is no element of Marxism in Pirandello and it is most unlikely that he knew the work of the socialist ideologist Antonio Labriola or the anarchist Carlo Cafiero. Pirandello's propositions have a highly personal origin, and are related to the subjective problem of the author as the character—to the individual yearning for an anarchistic destruction of reality.

Indeed, Pirandello liked to call himself an anarchist. One of his more vivacious pupils at the Magistero asked him one day what his political ideas were, and the following dialogue ensued:[5] 'Monarchist?' 'No.' 'Republican?' 'No.' 'Socialist?' 'No.' 'Anarchist, then!' 'That's right, anarchist individualist.' 'Well then, why are you in the government's pay?' 'Because I give the government what it asks me for conscientiously and it pays me for what I give it.'

After writing *The Old and the Young*, however, Pirandello's social and political ideas became more and more like those of the ruling class. In 1909 we find him contributing to a 'three-weekly political-military review' allusively called *La Preparazione*. Here, in an article which appeared on 11 February, we even find a prelude to Pirandello's future admiration for the Duce of fascism. 'We need some great captain,' he wrote, 'some great statesman for the war of tomorrow who will allow us to live in peace today; for the peace of today we need someone who will lead us to war tomorrow. But one does not come across a great captain and a great statesman at every turn . . .'.

In *La Preparazione* Pirandello had the opportunity to expound other reactionary myths. His attitude towards women's emancipation, for instance, was one of irritated irony. He wrote an entire article on the subject, 'Feminism' ('Feminismo') on 27 February 1909. The woman he examines as a model of 'feminism' is supplied with 'spectacles which enlarge her eyes enormously and confusedly' and she speaks with a 'guttural, masculine voice' which sounds 'as though it comes from the depths of the earth'. 'Feminism' is a bladder full of air, and 'history is full of such burst balloons.' 'To assume that the woman who is constantly dealing with men will become too masculine; to foresee that a home, without the assiduous, intelligent and loving care of a woman will lose some of the intimate and precious poetry which is the greatest attraction of marriage for a man; to suppose that a woman, contributing with her own earnings to the upkeep of the house, will no longer feel that devotion and respect which gives men such pleasure: these are not prejudices. . . .' For Pirandello, women had no brains. 'A curious destiny,' he told his pupils, 'has ordained that I should teach women to write',[6] or, as he wrote epigrammatically in a poem, 'a woman seldom thinks about what she feels.'

He was also misogynistic on a conventional, petty-bourgeois level: marriage was ruinous, celibacy an ideal state, he believed, even before his painful experience of marriage. These notions are similar to those of the clubs Pirandello used to frequent in the south of Italy, to which women were not admitted. Women were confined to adulterous love affairs, to a bourgeois marriage, or to romantic love; otherwise they were spoken about spitefully or jokingly. As late as 1924 Pirandello still considered women to be creatures of pure instinct, and he added:[7] 'I don't think much of the woman of letters. Of course, she must not be regarded as a woman. The woman is passive and art is active. This does not mean that an active female mind cannot exist. It simply means that it isn't a woman's.' The female characters in his work, even when they are surrounded by a respectful halo of idealization (as happened above all after he had fallen in love with Marta Abba), are represented as instinctive animals. He preferred an immobile and mythical, or simply a neo-romantic, image of the woman which oscillated between raw nature and an animal-like, inscrutable 'eternal feminine'. At the end of *The New Colony* (*La nuova colonia*), for instance, the woman becomes the mother and saviour of the human race. At other times the woman, incapable of thought and inexhaustibly mobile, is a symbol of Form's resistance to death. Elsewhere the woman appears, according to a Biblical and Christian pessimism, as a vessel of vice, a temptress, a bearer of sin.

In 1909 Pirandello started publishing his short stories in *Il Corriere della Sera*. After his failure to find an outlet on a radical paper, he wrote for moderate, liberal, and conservative newspapers. He got on well with Albertini, the owner of *Il Corriere della Sera*, for several reasons. Albertini was far from being opposed to anti-parliamentary campaigns. He favoured patriotic and nationalistic propaganda. He was anti-socialist and he was constantly insisting on the importance of gradual reforms—views fully shared by Pirandello and declared in *The Old and the Young*.

In 1908 Pirandello had published two collections of essays, *Humour* and *Art and Science* (*Arte e scienza*). The first was published by Carabba at Lanciano and the second by a Roman bookseller and publisher called Modes. They were aesthetic and literary essays which helped Pirandello compete for the chair of 'Italian language, style and grammatical rules and the study of classics, including the best translations of the Greeks and Latins' in the Magistero in Rome. He was nominated on 28 November 1908.

The appearance of the two books marked the beginning of a curious battle, consisting mainly of punches below the belt, between Pirandello and the philosopher Benedetto Croce, and it even continued long after Pirandello's death. In the five years between 1863 and 1867 three men were born who were to occupy the three corners of a triangle of Italian culture and poetry: d'Annunzio, Croce, and Pirandello. All three of them were from the provinces and none of them ever really freed himself from his provincial and southern background. When one examines the biographical details of their relationship—a relationship of mutual incomprehension—one reaches the conclusion that each man's temperament rendered it impossible for him to communicate with the other two. Pirandello had no respect for d'Annunzio. He attacked him with a sense of superiority but the same cannot be said of his attitude to Benedetto Croce. To all appearances Croce emerged victorious, yet Pirandello can hardly be considered a loser. He appeared to succumb because he felt a definite sense of inferiority towards the philosopher after opening an attack on the most unfavourable terrain (from his own point of view)—that of philosophy. And on this terrain Croce had no difficulty whatsoever in disposing of his adversaries.

Pirandello, with his back to the wall, insulted his opponent impetuously, both in private and in public, while the philosopher had the appearance of sublimating no less authentic a hatred in a relaxed and ironic superiority. Pirandello's insults mask considerable respect for the opinions of Croce, and Croce's feigned moderation hides a note of pique.

Pirandello opened the attack in *Art and Science* saying that Croce's *Aesthetics* was 'abstract, incomplete and rudimentary', that it was 'an intellectual aesthetic system without intellect', and that Croce 'insulted logic' with false premises, sophisms, and contradictions, which resulted in 'confusion'. In *Humour* he dismissed Croce's opinion that humour was an indefinable psychological state, a pseudo-concept, and not an aesthetic category, and defended the aesthetic autonomy of humour.

Croce replied almost immediately with a review of *Humour* which appeared in *La Critica* (VII, 1909). He showed that he was unaware of the attack in *Art and Science*, and he treated Pirandello condescendingly. He started off by asserting that Pirandello was unacquainted with the authors he cited in his essay: '. . . and though he is unacquainted with the works of Baldensperger, of Cazamian, of Spingarn, and probably has no direct knowledge of my own essay, he has heard about my negative theory and objects to it. But there is not much point in discussing it since Pirandello is far from strong in the field of methodology and scientific logic.' Then he added: 'I do not want to take advantage of his doctrinal inexperience . . . since the author's difficulties are quite evident. Whenever he picks up an idea it loses its shape in his hands. . . .

If he thinks he can define things with precision I do not know what is meant by precision.'

Despite his public declarations to the contrary Pirandello was convinced he was an expert in philosophy but, when confronted with Croce's self-confidence, he began to doubt his abilities. Consequently, he nursed his vindictiveness in a typically Sicilian manner and finally gave vent to it eleven years later, in 1920, when *Humour* was reprinted. He then changed a few pages and added a few notes in an attack on Croce. He accused him of bad faith. 'It is not true that Croce does not understand. He does not want to understand. . . . All this is really pathetic.' And he added in a note: 'Excessive philosophical education (my own, as everyone knows, is minimal) has led Croce to this edifying conclusion. We can refer to this or that humorist. He has nothing against that, on a philosophical level. But we cannot talk of humour! Croce's philosophy immediately becomes an iron gate which will not budge. We cannot get through! But what is behind the gate? Nothing. Merely this single equation: *intuition equals expression*, and the affirmation that it is impossible to distinguish art from non-art, artistic intuition from common intuition. Very well! But surely we can by-pass this closed gate without paying any attention to it?'

Then, in 1921, Pirandello's chance came. When Croce's famous essay on the poetry of Dante appeared Pirandello demolished it in *L'Idea Nazionale* of 14 September 1921. This time he had the upper hand. He was not arrogant in the way that Croce could be: he was bitter, sarcastic, relentless. With a scandalized air he stressed Croce's famous distinction between poetry and non-poetry, between poetry and structure in the *Divine Comedy*, and pointed out all the contradictions in Croce's essay. 'But taken as a whole,' he wrote, 'Dante has committed the grave offence of not fitting into Benedetto Croce's aesthetic theory—and we all know what that is and what fruits it has borne.'

This time Croce thought it better not to reply and he seemed to forget about Pirandello, preferring to ignore his worldly success. Yet it is worth noting that the Biblioteca Nazionale of Naples, largely influenced in its choice of books by Croce, never purchased Pirandello's works systematically. Even today it does not have a complete edition of the *Short Stories for a Year* (*Novelle per un anno*) and if it contains his complete theatrical works it is due solely to a private legacy. Croce managed to spread his dislike at least in Neapolitan cultural circles, and his oldest and closest friends still talk of Pirandello as 'a disagreeable man'.

When Pirandello won the Nobel Prize at the end of 1934 Croce, who had not suspected that he would win it, could not contain himself and, on the spur of the moment, wrote, and printed in *La Critica* of the following January, a hurried, misleading, and prejudiced essay on Pirandello's work. He commented that Pirandello had a certain artistic potential but it was 'suffocated and disfigured by a convulsive and inconclusive philosophy. So it is neither art nor philosophy'. As a result he found Pirandello's work pretentiously empty.

Pirandello was furious. In a letter which appeared as a preface to an essay by Domenico Vittorini published in Philadelphia in 1935, he said that of the many critical interpretations of his work 'the most idiotic' was 'that of Benedetto Croce'. Shortly before he died, in *L'Illustrazione Italiana* of 23 June 1935, he defended himself again against Croce's unjust attacks: 'Nothing was more bitter and suffocating than the vulgar opinion that I was an expert littérateur who had had the fortune to hit on a catchy and captious technique like a juggler of ideas. I, who have spent my entire life, a life rich perhaps in nothing if not in energy and feeling, attempting to find a few words to say, as a man, to other men.' After Pirandello's death, Giovanni Gentile took up his defence against Croce's statements.[8]

Croce did not change his attitude, even after Pirandello had been dead for some time. In *La Critica* of 1938 he again emphasized his failure to understand philosophy, and commented: 'He was undoubtedly a tormented man and not just a theatrical manipulator working on the matter of an imaginary torment; but he had no real appreciation of beauty; and I do not think that anyone, after a story or a play by Pirandello, has sincerely exclaimed: "How beautiful!" ' These last words suggest the basic reason for the two men's aversion to one another (and explain the rival camps of Italian critics, for and against Pirandello).

Pirandello taught at the Magistero from 1897 to 1922, the year of *Henry IV* (*Enrico IV*). He had no vocation as a teacher: indeed, he was fundamentally anti-pedagogic. But a no less imperious sense of self-discipline forced him to do various things—to be a faithful patriot, a loving husband, and a competent, even if an unenthusiastic, teacher. That he was so, for a considerable number of years at least, is confirmed by his former pupils. But in 1907, as he was inclined to cancel his classes at the slightest excuse, his students' infuriated parents complained to the Ministry of Education. Pirandello defended himself, emphasizing the amount and the importance of his creative work, in a letter to Giuseppe Aurelio Costanzo,[9] the head of the Institute and a friend of his.[10] In the last years of his teaching career, with the beginning of his success and his ever more feverish activity as a playwright, he became increasingly vague and inattentive. One of his pupils recalled that in 1921 'when word got round that *Six Characters in Search of an Author* (*Sei personaggi in cerca d'autore*) was being rehearsed at the Teatro Argentina, the pupils organized delightful excursions to the Villa Borghese'.[11] He did not even like the subject he taught. The teachers at the Magistero, he wrote to Massimo Bontempelli in 1908,[12] 'are subjected to the full rigour of the laws and rules of the university, but without the [university teachers'] grade, the privileges, the authority, or the salary.' There were other injustices at the Magistero: after eleven years' teaching as an assistant 'without a single penny's increase in my salary,' he was still not on the regular staff. And, he wrote to Bontempelli, owing to a bureaucratic paradox 'in order not to have his career irremediably ended', he would have to enter a competitive examination as an assistant teacher competing for the post of assistant teacher.

Ultimately he could enter another examination, based on degrees, but he had wasted too much time and energy in preparing the essays on aesthetics. 'I shall send you my volume of essays entitled *Art and Science*,' he wrote to Bontempelli, 'written especially for the competitive examination. Another essay is going to press in May, on Humour. Thank God for the latter! But what misery, my dear Bontempelli! I have hardly been able to breathe for over a year, and I have had to put aside a novel I was writing and take no notice of all the requests for short stories coming in from all sides. . . .' As for the subject Pirandello was teaching, the exam commissioners, 'five university professors, professors of Italian literary history, naturally have no idea of what "style" actually is. And who *does* know? I have been teaching it for eleven years. I teach style? I teach aesthetics, or rather that part of aesthetics which refers to the art of the word. . . .' Pirandello regretted having chosen the teaching profession—or at least he regretted being at the Magistero. 'These two institutes of Rome and Florence,' he wrote, 'are frowned upon, and probably rightly so, by university professors. If only you knew how much I regret having wasted so many years of my life on it, without any reward.'

Accounts of Pirandello as a teacher are few and largely anecdotal, mainly because former pupils wrote much later and were unable to separate their genuine recollections of their teacher from a romantic ideal of him. The most convincing account is by Professor Maria Alaimo of Agrigento who later wrote the first introduction to Pirandello's work. She said:[13]

He liked Leopardi and especially the *Zibaldone*. When he spoke of Leopardi both his attitude and his tone of voice assumed a certain resonance. He did not refer to his own work. . . . Only occasionally, when he was criticizing one of our essays, did he make a passing allusion to some short story—as if to compare his manner of expression with our poor efforts. He liked pages where his pupils went in for reminiscences or where they created a world of their own. . . . Sometimes he was distant, aloof, and seemed to lack human understanding, as a man, as a professor, as an examiner, as man to man, as person to person. It was as though he stood on the podium more out of dire necessity than out of inclination.

He did not display much friendship for the other professors, his colleagues. He always kept to himself. Not that he put on a pose, no, but his whole attitude was strange. Even the way he dressed, even the way he spoke. . . . He used to talk to the beadles in the corridors and he talked to them humbly.

He nearly always dressed in grey. He was very distinguished . . . His hat with its broad brim, a cigar nearly always in his mouth, his eyes half-closed and remote.

He liked to gesticulate with his hands: he used his thumbs a great deal, almost like a sculptor. . . .

The authors Pirandello selected for his lectures were the doyens of Italian literature: Dante, Ariosto, Tasso, Manzoni, Leopardi. He chose particular aspects of them: for example, he gave a course on 'comic irony in epic poetry', and one on the 'resuscitated dead in Ariosto'; a series of lectures on 'devils and tragedy in Dante', on which he later based his 'Lectura Dantis' which he held in Orsanmichele in Florence in February 1916. And he spoke at length about the unhappiness of Tasso. His essay on humour, too, was largely based on a lecture course held at the Magistero.

He concentrated, furthermore, on his pupils' composition and spelling. He was not generous with his praise:[14] 'He nearly always demolished our creative efforts with a few ironic sentences. We stood up, trembling with emotion, to read the essays we'd written with such care, in the vain hope of hearing a word of encouragement from his lips, half-hidden between the moustache and the grey goatee. But

Pirandello sat in his customary position, his elbow on the desk and his forehead in his hand, as though he were so tired, so terribly tired. . . .'

Another student, Paola Boni-Fellini, recalled the time when Pirandello's beard was still ash blond and his brown hair was only beginning to thin. She remembers him as an unfeeling breaker of hearts who 'conquered all the girls'. The day-pupils at the Institute went to meet him when he arrived on foot from Piazza Indipendenza, and another, more emotional group of girls—boarders on the floor above the Institute—made a god of him.

Since he held his classes in the early afternoon the girls had time to make themselves beautiful for him in the lunch-break. According to Paola Boni-Fellini[15] 'it took all his reserve, his seriousness, his sense of responsibility to stop his lessons turning into a court of love.' So the girls had to content themselves with decorating their essays with multi-coloured ribbons. That was all the professor allowed. Once a student wrote to him that she would kill herself because of his indifference, and Pirandello had to go to the director in order to liberate himself from the responsibility. Another girl took to hiding love letters in the pocket of his overcoat. When he received the third Pirandello complained about the incident in class, tearing the letter as he did so into tiny pieces (which were then patiently reconstructed by the girls).

Pirandello might have enjoyed such flirtatious advances (although according to his son he was annoyed by them). At all events he did nothing to provoke them and the enamoured pupils of every new lecture course believed him to be hard-hearted. At the beginning of his scholastic career Pirandello's only concession to vanity was to dress with painstaking elegance. According to an involuntarily pejorative description by Lucio D'Ambra:[16] 'He was careful about the cut of his tight-fitting clothes, the crease of his trousers and the immaculate dove- or slate-grey colour of his wide-skirted overcoats, so wide that Pirandello could have fitted into them four times over. His silk bow ties, his bright patent leather bootees with tender-coloured gaiters! There was only one bold note in this fashionable elegance—a grey hat with such a broad brim that it looked like an umbrella. . . .' Then, gradually, Pirandello dispensed with this somewhat provincial modishness and, in later years, his clothes assumed an ever more functional simplicity.

His wife was jealous of the students, of the ribbons on their essays, of the court they paid him. She sometimes went to fetch him at the doors of the Institute and she spied on him from behind the trees in

Piazza delle Terme. She had recovered from the paralysis incurred by the news of her father-in-law's bankruptcy but she was now overcome by the Portulanos' maniacal jealousy, and she took every opportunity of starting a quarrel with her husband. Antonietta's jealousy was irremediable. Pirandello soon started writing about it and he continued to write about it for many years. It appears that Antonietta decided never to read another page of her husband's work after she had read one of the stories inspired by herself.[17] The absurd, obsessive climate of domestic jealousy between a bourgeois couple tied by the bonds of a poisoned, twisted love (and he was the one who was in love, not she, for she took an attitude of sullen irresponsibility) is that of such short stories as 'The Widower's Outing', ('L'uscita del vedovo'), 'You laugh' ('Tu ridi'), many pages of *Her Husband*, and *Shoot (Si gira . . .)*. In 'The Reality of the Dream' ('La realtà del sogno') we have a portrait of Antonietta at the beginning of the marriage. He, the husband, 'maintained that the awkwardness, the embarrassment she felt in front of all men was a fixation. In the four months before the wedding he had not been allowed either to touch her hand or to whisper a word to her. With the jealousy of a tiger, her father had inculcated into her a veritable terror of men ever since her infancy. They said that he had never allowed one into the house. All the windows were shuttered and the few times he had taken her out she had had to bow her head, like a nun, looking at the ground. . . .'

In 'The Widower's Outing' we have Piovanelli who was the victim of a jealous wife: 'That was really bad luck! Jealous of him! A man of dog-like devotion by nature; one woman was enough for him even when he had been a bachelor. His friends had teased him about it in his youth. But what could he do about it?[18] He didn't like to change. Perhaps . . . yes, maybe he didn't know how.' 'That woman,' Pirandello continued, 'hated the human race, both men and women, because of her terrible illness. . . . Now he, who had always behaved with the greatest respect and reserve before women, he who had never dared perform an act or utter a word which might seem at all risqué, he who had always believed every sentimental conquest to be terribly difficult, he felt ambushed on all sides and walked down the street with his eyes on the ground. And if a woman looked up at him, he immediately looked away; if a woman squeezed his hand he turned a thousand colours. Every woman on earth had become a nightmare for him, an enemy of his peace.' Paola Boni-Fellini noted Pirandello's sudden blushes before his eighteen-year-old students and a neighbour of his had confirmed the fact that women were a source of dread for him and that he would suddenly walk off in the middle of a conversation out of fear of Antonietta.[19] In order to avoid her scenes he announced the exact time of his departures and arrivals. He had entrusted her with the household money and every day, before he left the house, he made her give him the money for the tram, the newspapers, his cigar. But she would never stop worrying, would never leave him in peace. In *Her Husband* he wrote:

He felt his bowels tighten and his heart turn sick at the constant mockery and fierce denigration. For he felt the atrocious absurdity of his tragedy: to be the target of madness, to suffer martyrdom for imaginary faults, for faults that were not faults and which he had never even dreamt of committing, even at the risk of seeming ill-mannered, arrogant, and peevish, so as not to give her the slightest excuse. But he seemed to commit them unconsciously, who knows how and when. He was obviously two people: one for himself, another for her. And this other person she saw in him, this sad phantom whose every look, smile, gesture, the very sound of whose voice, the sense of whose words were transformed in her own mind—this other man came to life and lived for her while he himself no longer existed . . . except in the debasing, inhuman torture of seeing himself live in that phantom, and in that alone. In vain did he try to destroy it. She no longer believed in him. In him she only saw the other man and, as was perfectly right, she treated this other man with hatred and contempt. . . . Who knows how and who knows when this other man would succeed in escaping from his prison, with his phantom-like inconsistency created by a veritable attack of lunacy, and would run through the world perpetrating every sort of misdemeanour. . . .

Such was Antonietta's hatred of 'the other man' that she no longer wanted to live with him. Time and time again she begged to be separated from Pirandello, to go and live on her own. But Pirandello would not let her go. He kept her at home by force, because he would have been unable to live without her, and he wrote to his father-in-law in Agrigento imploring him to hold her back, for Antonietta obeyed her father and, even at a distance, he retained his former authority over her.

Pirandello continued to suffer Antonietta's jealousy which grew all the worse the more she felt herself to be imprisoned. Pirandello continued in *Her Husband*:

She knew nothing of his ideal life, of his superior talents. She saw in him nothing but a man, a man who had been violated, excluded from any other life, deprived of any other satisfaction, and who, because of these renunciations, sacrifices, and privations, was obliged to seek from her the only recompense she could give him, the only outlet he could allow himself with her. Hence the bad idea she had of him, hence the phantom she had made of him which she watched without even understanding that he was only like that for her, because he couldn't be any different with her. But he couldn't prove this to her for fear of offending her virtue. Assailed as she was by continuous suspicions, she often indignantly refused him that one recompense, and then he would be still more indignant over the slavery to which she had reduced him. But when she was more inclined to yield and he took advantage of her ... he would shudder with indignation at the dark oppression of his sated and exhausted desire. He saw the price of sensual satisfaction obtained from a woman bereft of sensuality herself but who made him into an animal ... sentencing him to the perversity of that necessarily lustful union. And if at that moment she was so unguarded as to resume her mockery his rebellion burst out again, stronger than ever.

When Antonietta's father died in 1909 she felt herself freed from the chains of obedience and for Pirandello and his children a new period of torture began. There were continual scenes and separations. Pirandello would have to leave the house himself or she would go off, either on her own or with her daughter Lietta. Sometimes the children would have to seek refuge with one of their relations. Whenever Pirandello had to leave the house (on one occasion he lived for two months in Via Balbo):

He felt lost in a world from which he had excluded himself for so long; he realized at once that he had no roots in it and could no longer throw any, not only because of his age, but because the idea that other people had formed of him after so many years of austere cloistering weighed on him like a cape, dogged his steps, imposed with malevolent vigilance a reserve which had by now become customary and which condemned him to be as others believed and wanted him to be. The surprise which he read in so many faces as soon as he appeared in an unusual place, the sight of people accustomed to living freely, and the secret realization of his awkwardness and unease before the insolence of those fortunate enough never to have had to answer to anyone for their time or their acts, troubled him, humiliated him, irritated him. . . . Everything inspired such a sense of disgust in him, such a dreadful sense of humiliation, such a bitter and black sadness that he withdrew at once from contact with others and, on his own again, empty and horribly lonely, he would contemplate his misery, tragic, ridiculous, and irremediable. He couldn't even detach himself enough to return to work, the only thing that could save him. And then all those excuses began to loom up ('his duty towards that woman . . . the pity which he, sane of mind, knew he should feel for her, who was insane'), excuses which he pretended to believe were the reasons for his slavery. They loomed up, instigated primarily by the instinctive and ever more urgent needs of his virility, by the enchanting memory of her embraces. And he returned to his chain. . . .

'On the very rare occasions,' his son recalled,[20] 'often after a reconciliation, when one or other of my parents returned from exile to family life, in other words when those separations which constellated Pirandello's married life tragically and continually were patched up for a moment and Antonietta was serene for a day or two and welcoming towards him, we children were appalled by the total nullities we became for those two passionate lovers, those two fugitives in a heaven of their own where the poet could not find means enough to glorify his Goddess; and the disproportionately extravagant gifts he showered on her. . . .'

Once, in 1913, Antonietta went back to Agrigento, taking with her Lietta and Fausto, while Pirandello, together with Stefano, went to live at 15 Via Antonio Bosio, the house to which he returned shortly before his death. In September 1914 he went to fetch the children so that they should go back to school in Rome and Antonietta refused to go with them. A few months later, when she was alone in Agrigento (she lived in a flat in Villa Catalisano beneath the Passeggiata) she had an attack of madness. She barricaded herself in and started screaming that people wanted to hurt her. The neighbours rushed to her assistance, her brothers were called, and the magistrate said that she should be interned in a lunatic asylum. Pirandello and the children arrived at once, and, as soon as she saw him, Antonietta fell into his arms and begged him to help and protect her. The family was reunited under the sign of Antonietta's madness. Her health deteriorated still more and, in her exasperating presence, Pirandello wrote the novel, *Shoot*, in which he described her at length with a sense of renewed despair. Nene, the character who corresponds to Antonietta, is a woman affected by a 'typical form of paranoia, with a wild persecution complex. . . . Typical, typical! Poor Nene even went as far as to believe that he and her daughter wanted to kill her in order to get hold of her money. . . .'

And then there is poor Luisetta [Lietta], left all alone in that inferno, all alone with her mother who has lost her reason. . . . Ah, it takes real heroism, believe me, it takes great heroism to put up with her, and I

probably wouldn't put up with it were it not for my little girl. . . . I
know it's a disease. . . . If I didn't know that she was mad I'd throw her
out, I'd leave her, I'd defend my dignity at any price. But . . . I know
that she's mad! And I also know that I have to reason for two people,
for myself and for her. . . . But to reason for a mad woman, when madness is so supremely ridiculous, means to cover oneself with ridicule!
It means putting up with having my dignity massacred, in front of my
daughter, in front of the maid, in front of everybody, in public. It
means the failure of all my efforts to hide my misery.

In September 1914, just over a month after the outbreak of the First
World War and about nine months before Italy's intervention, Pirandello published a short story entitled 'Another Life' ('Un'altra vita') in
the *Rassegna Italiana*. It remains an interesting document revealing
both the interest and the lack of interest he showed in that first phase of
Italian neutrality. The current opinions of the moment reappear as the
views and feelings of the various characters in the story. We find the
concept of *useful neutrality*, dear to Giolitti and Croce, which was
shared by the majority of the public; the passionate tone of the irredentists; and the idea of public and private renewal which was supposed to result from the war. But what strikes us more than the list of
contemporary opinions in the story is Pirandello's particular interest in
some of these opinions—as, for example, when a character says:

On the whole, however terrible the events and the consequences may
be, we can at least be pleased about one thing: that we will be allowed
to witness the dawn of another life. For forty, fifty, sixty years we have
thought that things could not go on, that the tension was becoming so
strained that it would have to snap; that the explosion would at last
take place. And now it has taken place. Terrible. But at least we will
have watched it. The anxieties, the unease, the anguish, the agitation of
such a long and unbearable wait will have an end and a resolution. We
shall see what becomes of it. Because everything will necessarily change
and we shall all certainly come out of this ghastly mess with a new
spirit.

Pirandello had voiced a similar attitude in *Shoot* when he wondered
'whether this noisy, whirling mechanism of life which grows more
complicated and accelerates day by day has not reduced humanity to
such a state of madness that it will soon burst out frantically and upset
and destroy everything. That might even be all to the better.' But in
'Another Life' he was more pessimistic. Though the rhetoric of the

Futurists rang in his ears, with their idea of 'war as the sole hygiene of the world' and their frenzied appeals to 'a hot bath of blood', he approached the war in a highly subjective spirit and his apocalyptic visions were followed by sadly humdrum ideas resulting from his wretched day-to-day routine.

The sole character in the story (who has dozens of traits in common with Pirandello) remains on his own, beset by fears for the future:

The nightmare of general destruction, which would put out the light of science and civilization in the old Europe, weighed more and more heavily on his mind. . . . How would it end? What new birth would there be once the terrible conflict had died down on the ruins? . . . At heart he was tired and sad, with a sadness that events could hardly change. Whether the French, Russians, and English won or the Germans and Austrians, whether or not Italy was dragged into the war and assailed by the misery and squalor of defeat or by the frantic jubilance of victory . . . whether or not the map of Europe changed, one thing would never change, that was for sure: his wife's sullen spite and the regrets brought on by a life which was fading away without any real memory of joy.

Indeed, for some time Pirandello had been in a hopeless rut: the future did not seem to hold anything in store. When Italy declared war on Austria on 24 May 1915 he had no reason to expect the critics to alter their opinion of his work. He was almost fifty and was content with his relatively modest reputation and the appreciation of his friends. He continued to write with the same disciplined passion for the written word, fulfilling his obligations to the newspapers. In the previous three years he had written over fifty stories, many of which were not short; a novel, *Shoot*, had appeared in 1915 in the *Nuova Antologia*; and he had rewritten most of *The Old and the Young*. In all these works there was no indication of any innovation, merely a little external polishing. Pirandello wrote almost the same things, with almost the same spirit as ten years earlier. His most original features continued to be submerged in a mass of undigested inventions. The critics were hardly to blame if they associated Pirandello with writers who were in fact infinitely inferior to him.

He could see no likelihood of change in his career as a writer and there were no prospects of improvement in his private life either. His children, Stefano, Lietta, and Fausto, were twenty, eighteen, and sixteen years old. He loved them deeply, with no reservations. He does not seem to have let any of his forebodings of crisis affect his feelings

Antonietta Portulano, Pirandello's wife

A family group: Pirandello is standing behind his parents, with his wife
on his father's right and his sister seated on the ground

for them—indeed, even in his works we nearly always see ties of blood taking priority over any movement of reason. And, in his loneliness, Pirandello's love for his children appears as a necessary outlet for his emotions; a means of filling the desert of his emotional life.

The war years clearly illustrate this aspect of Pirandello's character for, in that period each of his children was to undergo an ordeal and to risk their lives. Stefano was studying literature at university. His father had looked after him with the care which one lavishes on a rare plant. He saw that he had inherited his own literary inclinations—a love of poetry and a talent as a writer which made his education all the more rewarding. From Stefano's earliest infancy Pirandello had used him as his confidant in his moments of greatest despair. On the other hand, Lietta, who was eighteen, constituted a considerable source of anxiety since her mother tyrannized her and cast a blight over her entire youth with her continual scenes of jealousy. Fausto was at secondary school and already showed signs of talent as a painter.

What with his children, whom he loved as a last resort, a wife who was only capable of rancour and hatred, a thankless job as a teacher, and a form of literary confession which, all too rarely, turned into the consolation of art, it was difficult for Pirandello to retain any stability in his mind. His own life and the world around him appeared to be cruel deformities. But he had not experienced anxiety and persecution to the full. Paradoxically enough, it was the blow of Stefano's departure for the front, the sudden awareness that his own distress coincided with the laceration of the world outside, the correspondence of the absurd public agony with his own private pain, the confirmation that every-thing was vain and iniquitous, and the renewed taunts of his wife, that freed Pirandello from despair and showed him the liberating path of true art.

At the outbreak of war Pirandello was caught up in the wave of patriotic infatuation, and he took his stand in favour of intervention. The newspapers, the rabble-rousers, and the government succeeded in instilling patriotic enthusiasm into a large section of the public. In the first days of May even the policy of the parliamentary majority was reversed. After having favoured Giolitti's neutral policy parliament became interventionist almost overnight and voted full powers to Salandra who was responsible for the Treaty of London, by which Italy entered the war on the side of the Allies.

Despite his disappointments, Pirandello retained an obstinate faith in heroism. He retained a belief in the myths of the Risorgimento and in heroic idealism. However well he interpreted the crisis of the twentieth century Pirandello retained a decisive nineteenth-century component which accounts for this sudden surge of patriotism. For, in both the Ricci Gramitto household and in that of his parents, the value of the *country*, *la patria*, had never been doubted. It was a romantic and idealistic term, an absolute which one could curse or sin against, but which one could not criticize.

On 5 May d'Annunzio delivered a speech at Quarto near Genoa. The immense crowd had clamoured for war. From Genoa d'Annunzio was called to Rome. On his arrival he was met by over 50,000 people and, from the balcony of the Hotel Regina, he delivered a further speech. He said, amongst other things, that Italy was no longer 'an inn', or 'a museum', or a 'garden for courting couples'. 'Around us,' he said, 'there is a smell of treachery and this treachery is taking place in Rome. We are about to be sold like a cheap flock of sheep. Our human dignity, the dignity of each one of us, is threatened. . . .' We know from his son that Pirandello 'was greatly distressed by the fact that the contemptible d'Annunzio (he always regarded him as contemptible) had been taken on as the spokesman of feelings which would inevitably be contaminated by his participation (or intrusion).' Pirandello was not at the Piazza della Stazione to welcome d'Annunzio, nor did he listen to his other speeches at the Campidoglio and the Costanzi. But in spite of everything Pirandello must have been impressed by d'Annunzio's eloquence which, even if he did not hear, he probably read about in the papers. For, in 'Berecche and the War', a short story written in the first year of the fighting as a sequel to 'Another Life', we find the same images and expressions which d'Annunzio had used in his address to the Romans.

In fact Pirandello had very little in common with d'Annunzio's brand of enthusiasm. His own interventionism was far more simple and resulted largely from his view of the Risorgimento. For the moment all he wanted was a fourth war of independence. His sympathies were for the 'irredentists' of the Trentino and Venezia Giulia, and, by August 1915, his statements in favour of intervention had become far more definite than they had been in September of the previous year. But, in August 1915, Italy had already entered the war and his son Stefano was fighting on the Austrian front.

Stefano had been following an officer's training course since January 1915 and, as soon as war was declared, he volunteered, like so many other university students stimulated by the propaganda of nationalist

interventionism. He left Rome in July. Pirandello, like his character
Marco Leccio, 'could not say no. He could not oppose his favourite
son's desire to enlist . . . he could not do so because of the education he
had given him. But to part from his son . . . for whom he would perform any act of cowardice at the mere thought of the risks he would
run; no, he could not part from his son. . . . At the station, just before
the train left . . . he was tempted to jump on to the train, hide among
the soldiers, leave as well.' Such was Pirandello's state of mind, both
because of his overpowering paternal love and because he felt partially
responsible for Italy's entry in the war. He would have liked to have
participated in the war actively, as a soldier on the battlefield. According to Nardelli he was about to 'apply for admission into the voluntary
mounted guides'. For a moment he thought it essential to continue the
Risorgimento heritage of his family in his own person.

As always Pirandello could write about life but not live it. And so he
dramatized and parodied in his writings all his thoughts of volunteering.
Two of Pirandello's characters, Berecche in 'Berecche and the War'
and Marco Leccio in 'An Episode in the Life of Marco Leccio and his
War on Paper', are old and deeply grieved about not being able to leave
for the war with their sons. They watch their sons leave for the front
and decide to enlist. In both cases the result is comically heroic and
pathetic. Berecche, a schoolmaster married to a mad woman, lives in the
same street as Pirandello and wants to join the voluntary mounted
guides. But he has no idea what to do, knows nothing about horses,
and therefore gets one of the Hoepli handbooks on riding. After studying the theory of riding for a whole night he goes to a riding school in
Via Po. He gets on to a horse and, after various mishaps, 'he closed his
eyes and started whipping his horse along the track, imagining himself
in a charge led by Garibaldi. . . . And the faster the stable-lad ran in
front of him with his red shirt and his fixed bayonet, the harder he
whipped his horse: Onwards! Onwards! Viva l'Italia! . . .' Berecche
falls off his horse, cuts open his forehead and returns home defeated,
his head in a turban of bandages.

In 'An Episode in the Life of Marco Leccio' Pirandello gives a still
more satirical image of himself facing medical visits and the officers at
the recruiting office. Marco Leccio is old and ill. He arrives at the
'Board'. When he sees the colonel he delivers a brief speech:

We are old, we're almost through, and yet we have to send our sons to
the front, our sons who probably do not feel nearly so much disgust

and hatred as we do! But we should go before them, sir, old as we are!
. . . Our sons should see us fall so that they should feel as vindictive as
we do and fight with a strength which we lack. . . . I would like to
enlist as a trooper, sir.

'The Board,' Pirandello continued, 'was quite ready to take him on
because of a general tendency to welcome veterans in view of the prestige of their appearance and of their past. He would have been given a
uniform, but the Board really couldn't send him to the front. He could
be of great use working in administration. But more than that, he
could not be expected to do.'

'I can't dress up simply for appearances, sir,' Marco Leccio tells the
colonel. 'Administration—that means working as a clerk? Sitting here
and writing on paper? If it's paper work I have to do, I have all the
paper I need at home . . . I'll fight this war at home, on paper.' And
so Marco Leccio returns home and simply follows the war on the map.
Pirandello attacked his autobiographical hero bitterly:

Aren't you ashamed of yourself when you read every evening of all the
twenty-year-olds who died that day, of all the old men, of sixty, seventy
even seventy-six who go off to the front and fight as troopers? Don't
you blush with shame? Did you see that old man on the train yesterday? He must have been at least seventy, and off he went! Think of
how he will die and of how you will die!

But Pirandello could not abandon his younger children to the mercy
of his wife, with no means of subsistence. Besides, Stefano's departure
coincided with a worsening of Antonietta's malady. She isolated herself more and more in a savage world of her own where everyone
appeared to be persecuting her—and there were also outbursts of
maternal fury against her husband whom she considered responsible
for her son's departure. Periods of crisis followed periods of serenity
and lucidity. But there were indications that there was no hope of her
health improving and that she would have to leave the house. She had
been making appallingly violent scenes for years. Pirandello had sometimes woken up with a start in the middle of the night to find her lean-
ing over him, looking at him fixedly with a thoughtful expression on
her face. She had once even tried to strike him with the scissors and a
hatpin.

Stefano had not been gone long when Pirandello's mother died. It
was a terrible blow. Pirandello was in great need of comfort and since

nobody around him could give him any real support he yielded to his loneliness, shutting himself into it as if into a secret cell, resorting to the hermetic chamber of visions and the consoling evocation of his dead mother. Thus, Pirandello's mother turned into one of the vivid characters with whom he discussed his most intimate problems. This—and it was an extremely important moment in Pirandello's life—was the time when he yielded most to his strange dealings with the creatures of his imagination. He entitled his stories of 1915, in which he reported these episodes, *Conversations with Characters* (*Colloqui coi personaggi*).

Pirandello's mourning for his mother's death, therefore, is connected biographically with his anxiety about his son. Stefano had left in July and had been sent to the front. It was from that moment that 'the constant anxiety about my son', as Pirandello put it in *Conversations with Characters*, began. 'While I tortured myself helplessly and was obliged to wait and to satisfy all the little material needs of life, he was risking his life up there; and every moment that elapsed could be his last, and I would have had to go on living this terrible life.'

Pirandello's agonizing wait for his son's letters began. He counted the days to the next one; he would start counting all over again, and would then decide that every calculation was pointless because by the time Stefano's letter arrived the worst might have happened. To Stefano he wrote on 24 October 1915: 'If your postcard of the 19th had arrived we might have known whether you were going to fight in the front lines or the rear. . . . I realize that my anxiety is useless since the really important news, the news after the 21st, will not arrive until the 26th or the 27th —if then. I understand, I understand; but it isn't I . . . Reason tries to moderate the anxiety and trepidation of the heart: the heart doesn't, cannot listen to reason, and it frets itself to death. . . . But the best part of it is this: I act and talk: *I'm giving exams at the moment, you understand?* I'm giving exams. I go out every morning at eight, come home at twelve, go out again at two thirty, come home at six. Me! . . .'

Stefano was fighting in that unfortunate initial period of the war during which Cadorna, who had been entrusted with the supreme command of the Italian army, appeared unconcerned both about the bloodshed and about the morale of the troops. The soldiers were exhausted, humiliated, and sent to the slaughter with an indifference that eventually led to a rebellion of public opinion. Pirandello, who was experiencing all this through his son, was consumed with worry.

Soon, in November 1915, there occurred what Pirandello had

foreseen and feared. While he was engaged in one of those anonymous occupations of which he felt so ashamed, his son Stefano was impelled to perform an act of heroism. He was on Monte Calvario and, on the morning of 2 November, he was ordered to attack. As his men advanced he was wounded in the chest by a shell. His wound was dressed, he refused to remain at the first-aid station and returned to the attack. He and his men resisted the Austrian counter-attack while the rest of the line fell back until he was surrounded and forced to surrender. He was taken prisoner and transported, finally, to the camp of Mauthausen where he remained until the battle of Caporetto in 1917.

Once Stefano had been taken prisoner Pirandello was sure, at least, that his life was safe and he could stop worrying. His own life continued as before. The only event was his journey to Florence where, on 2 February 1916, he read the twenty-first canto of Dante's *Inferno* at Orsanmichele. His average day, as he described it in his letters to his son, consisted exclusively of work. He worked all morning and a good part of the afternoon. He wrote critical essays, newspaper articles, short stories. At the beginning of 1916 he started writing plays. On Tuesdays, Thursdays, and Fridays, from one to three o'clock, he gave his lectures on Italian literature at the Magistero. Every evening he went for a walk from his house in Via Antonio Bosio near Villa Torlonia (whose pines and cypresses he liked to gaze at out of his study window) to Porta Pia where he bought some newspapers. He would then return home and dine. After dinner he read the newspapers attentively. He continued to take a keen interest in the war because the destiny of his son and his return to Italy were closely connected with it, and he followed on a map the retreats and the advances of the Allied armies.

He wrote to Stefano every other day at least and sent him parcels which Antonietta herself would prepare and which he delivered every other evening at six o'clock at the Red Cross in Piazza Montecitorio. Then every evening, towards half-past nine, Rosso di San Secondo came to visit him, occasionally accompanied by Borgese. Martoglio and Frateili, too, were assiduous frequenters of his house and, talking about the war or about their profession, they would stay until midnight.

Pirandello could think of nothing but his son. He was deeply moved when his sword and ordinance box were brought back. 'We have left the sword as it was,' he wrote, 'wrapped in sack cloth.' In the box were two letters which Pirandello 'preserved religiously', 'because they both contain traces of my saintly mother: noble words, the last thoughts of her noble mind. Found there, in your box, they seemed to me like words from beyond the grave, and I couldn't read them without tears coming to my eyes.' When the sun was shining and Pirandello did not have to go to the Institute, 'after lunch' he and his family went down to the garden for half an hour and there, 'in the sun, we talk about you'.

In these letters to his son Pirandello wanted to seem serene, although there were moments when his secret bitterness about life and humanity as a whole suddenly came to the surface in an expression of contempt. But these were isolated moments, and he never ceased to encourage his son who might be driven to despair by his solitude and by that monotonously inactive prison life. It was as though, when writing to his son, he summoned up all the strength he had acquired through resignation to a life of continuous mortification. 'You know,' he told him, 'that these exhortations to patience come from a stout heart which has patiently proved its strength against so many unwarranted passions.'

But he wanted to do more. He wanted to prevent Stefano from losing touch with him. He wanted to share his pain and his resistance to pain: 'Take heart, Stefano. Do not yield to too much meditation, and work, work as hard as you can: there is no better remedy to this evil which is life. Nobody knows that better than I do.' 'Your last letter was unhappy. You too complained of being unable to work. Well, that's how it is. . . . But you know, these tantalizing interruptions are good for one. . . . We look round suspiciously, there seems to be no hope of gain, it seems as though the path is not leading to our true goal. But then confidence returns with the certainty that there has been some advantage . . . that the goal is always a trap and that what matters is to walk, to move forward. Everything helps!'

He also tried to 're-live' what his son had experienced: 'Yesterday, on 2 November, the anniversary of your capture . . . I woke up at six and my thoughts flew to where you were a year ago and I tried, in my imagination, to live through the terrible hours of that morning. You can imagine how much I suffered!'

But Stefano's capture was soon followed by other ordeals. First there was the departure of Fausto, who was called up as soon as he was old enough. Convalescing as he was from an operation for a serious intestinal disease, he was sent first to Florence and then to Castelfranco di Sotto for his military training. The army doctors, who had no consideration for anyone, not even for young soldiers who were ill, did not allow him a moment's rest. So Fausto, together with the others, found himself forced to take part in exhausting military exercises which

were almost unbearable even for those who were healthy. Unable to
stand it he asked his father for help. Pirandello arrived at once. He
turned up at the barracks while the soldiers were on parade and awaited
his son's return. As soon as he got back Fausto fainted in his arms.
Pirandello reacted violently, and though the objects of his wrath were
no less than the officers of the Italian army he had his way. He was
taken to see the general who settled the matter, partly because Pirandello had become a well-known writer by that time. Fausto was sent to
Florence to convalesce. But his health deteriorated and he was discovered to have tuberculosis. He recovered at home later.

In the meantime Stefano's situation was not improving. After
Caporetto an enormous quantity of prisoners came to Mauthausen.
Indeed, in the disorder of the retreat the Austrians had taken more
prisoners than they wanted. Conditions deteriorated. Austria was in
the fourth year of war and there had been a food shortage for some
time. The prisoners now went hungry. From Mauthausen Stefano was
transferred to Plan in Bohemia where he stayed until the end of the war
and where he was treated worse than before. The parcels his father sent
him as frequently as possible either through the Red Cross or through
Swiss and Dutch friends rarely reached him. They went through
famished territory—and no less famished than the prisoners were the
guards. The rain dripped through the roof of the wooden sheds where
the prisoners were confined and the benches were rotten with fungus.
In the damp and the cold even Stefano, although he had a tough constitution, contracted a lung infection. So both Pirandello's sons contracted
tuberculosis, and both were far from home.

Pirandello then decided to move heaven and earth in order to rescue
Stefano. Fausto was already obtaining medical assistance and was later
allowed home. But as far as Stefano was concerned the only possibility
was to try, with the support of the Italian government, to obtain his
return, via Switzerland, for reasons of health. An Austrian prisoner
would be given in exchange. But in these cases dealings were extremely
slow and difficult. It was not possible to go through normal diplomatic
channels: the Secretariat of the Vatican City alone was in a position to
act and Pirandello was hardly a writer who enjoyed much popularity at
the Vatican. It was not that he had not been objective whenever he had
stopped to consider the problems of the Roman Catholic Church—
indeed, he had expressed his deep regret at the death of Pius X in
August 1914. But the new Pope was Benedict XV who was reputed to
be a Germanophile. And Pirandello's particular anti-clericalism was

constantly appearing in the pages of his work—in *Better Think Twice About It* (*Pensaci, Giacomino!*) which had been staged less than a year earlier, and in *Liolà* which had to be withdrawn from the repertory after the riots caused at the Teatro Alfieri in Turin by young Catholics at the instigation of *Il Momento* and its mediocre dramatic critic Saverio Fino. [21] Pirandello had therefore to persuade someone to help him and he at last found the right person in Matteo Gentili, the editor of *Il Corriere d'Italia*.

Gentili managed to get into contact indirectly with Cardinal Gasparri, the Papal Secretary of State. This was fortunate for Pirandello because the Cardinal was a broad-minded man, sufficiently diplomatic and mundane not to take exception to Pirandello's plays. And besides, on this occasion Christian charity prevailed. The Cardinal saw to it that Benedict XV personally signed a letter to the Austrian government in which, through the ecclesiastical hierarchy in Vienna, he requested the release of Stefano Pirandello in exchange for an Austrian prisoner in Italy.

Once the letter had been posted the reply took a long time. In the Pirandello household, the anxiety became appalling. Moreover, Pirandello, his wife, and Fausto were all stricken with Spanish 'flu—but they soon recovered and when the reply from Vienna arrived Pirandello was summoned by Cardinal Gasparri who treated him with the utmost courtesy and told him that since Stefano Pirandello was the son of an important figure in Italian culture the Austrian government was not prepared to release him other than in exchange for three Austrian prisoners whose names were given. In other words the Austrian government had sensed a profitable bargain and wanted to make the most of it.

At this point the consent of the Italian government had to be obtained and Pirandello had to call on Vittorio Emanuele Orlando who had become Prime Minister after Caporetto. Orlando was Sicilian and had a high opinion of Pirandello. Common friendships made conversation between them easy and Orlando asked the playwright to give him time to gather information about the three prisoners whom the Austrians wanted back. As soon as he had received it he told Pirandello without adding any comment of his own, that they were three naval officers who had hitherto behaved in such a way as to suggest that they would not remain idle if they were released. So Orlando placed Pirandello in a dilemma. He did not want to appear to influence Pirandello's decision and simply said: 'It's up to you.' In the third year of the war

Pirandello felt his patriotism waning and in 'War' ('Quando si comprende'), written in 1918, he wrote 'there is one's country, yes, but inside us there is something much stronger—our love for our children.' Yet this dilemma with which the Head of State faced him could only have one answer. *La patria* must have priority and Pirandello could not commit an act of civic cowardice. So he lowered his head and said no, giving up all hope of his son's release.

Antonietta's madness is an essential part of Pirandello's vision of the absurdity of the world. In the last years of the war her moments of sanity grew less frequent. Not only did Antonietta feel an aversion for her husband: she was in the grip of a persecution complex which involved everyone around her. Under her very eyes, she believed, an alliance had been formed between her husband and her daughter to ensure her destruction. She convinced herself that Lietta wanted to replace her in everything, even in her physical person. Antonietta had gone out regularly with Lietta for walks in the afternoon or to do some shopping and had been letting her help with domestic chores but she now cut herself off and was constantly telling her daughter that *she knew*, and that she would defend herself. It was not easy to get the better of her and so, since she was sure father and daughter wanted to poison her, Lietta had to taste all the food first.

Lietta, obliged to endure ordeals which her father did not have the courage to prevent, felt she could no longer live at home. Her father, forced back into his solitude, sought consolation in his study, and as a result this was an extremely fruitful period as far as his dramatic output was concerned. But Lietta could no longer remain alone with her mother. One day Antonietta was explicit: she accused her daughter of committing incest with her father, and Lietta was so appalled that she tried to kill herself. She used a little old revolver which she found lying about the house but fortunately the barrel had been blocked by rust, and the bullet stuck. Lietta then ran out of the house and rushed through the streets of Rome in search of the Tiber. But her jealous mother had kept her at home nearly all her life, except for taking her for walks in the neighbourhood. Consequently she did not know her way about Rome and lost herself in a labyrinth of streets until she grew calm enough to ask some acquaintances who lived near Porta Pia to take her in. They informed her father who immediately found Lietta a place in a boarding school run by nuns, and then, a little later, took her to Florence to stay with her aunt Rosalina. Here Lietta remained until

Stefano's return from prison camp. Pirandello was now alone with his wife and if, to test her, he occasionally suggested that his daughter should return home, Antonietta would reply: 'Either she goes or I go.'

Pirandello was at a turning-point. 'He was confronted,' wrote his son, 'by the necessity of choosing between his needs as a man who could not do without his wife, however mad she was, and the responsibility of having sent away from home a daughter who had received little from him and who was now old enough to think for herself.'[22]

He did not find sufficient compensation in writing plays—an occupation which he often had to abandon for months on end on account of his work as a teacher. In his letters to Stefano he often complained about these obligations which interrupted his concentration during a period which he felt was essential to his art. 'I would like to remain at my desk,' he wrote. 'My mind is always fresh, agile and ready.' Instead, he wrote in another letter in the autumn of 1916, 'tomorrow the entrance exams begin: there are no less than 174 candidates which means that I shall have to correct 174 essays. And I am in the same situation as I was in July, involved in exams to the point of suffocation. . . .' And, in a letter of 29 June 1917, that is in the following year: 'I am writing to you from the Magistero in the middle of exams. They started on the 7th and will last till 20 July. I'm exhausted!' Then again in the autumn: 'I haven't done anything since 7 June: imagine! first the exams, then [a phrase has been censored by Stefano] . . . and I am still frittering away my time running this way and that!'

Pirandello's life, up to the beginning of 1918, had not undergone any change. 'Our life,' he wrote to his son, 'is the same as ever. You can envisage it perfectly well without straining your imagination. Just the same as it ever was and nothing new.' At times Pirandello reached a point of exasperation, as on the occasion when nobody had prepared his lunch and he had had to go to a restaurant. He thought that two young men were looking at him and laughing at him. So, in a fit of rage, he seized a bottle and threatened to break it over their heads. It was all his fault, his misunderstanding, and he apologized. But the episode reveals his state of tension. He could not leave his house for long for fear of his wife's attacks, nor could he attend all the rehearsals he would have liked to attend. And so the actors misrepresented his plays and this irritated him.

By the end of the year the war had ended and there was still nothing new in his life except for the rehearsals of *The Rules of the Game* (*Il giuoco delle parti*) at the Teatro Quirino and the presence of his sick son

Fausto at home. 'I didn't write to you,' he wrote to Stefano on 29 November, 'because I had a terrible cold for the last two days, as usual, and I still haven't quite recovered, and because exams have started again as well as the rehearsals of *The Rules of the Game* at the Quirino. The morning at the Institute; then I dash off to lunch; then, with my mouth still full, I go home to get a meal for Fausto; then from two to half-past six at the Quirino; then, dead tired, I rush to Salvaggi to get some food for Fausto, then I go out to dine at seven. So, after a day like that, one hardly has time to write a letter. . . .'

But in the last months of 1918 Pirandello's worst problems were almost at an end. 'Lietta,' he wrote to Stefano, 'has written a very affectionate letter from Florence for your return home. She is longing to see you and to embrace you again.'[23] Pirandello had taken a decisive step as far as his wife was concerned. He would await Stefano's return so that he too should be aware of his mother's condition and then, in agreement with his children, he would have her interned in a neurological clinic in Viale Nomentano, not far from his house.

When Stefano came back Antonietta had to be tricked into going to the clinic. Since she had been saying for years that she wanted to be separated from her husband she was now told that her wish would be granted but, for the separation to be approved by law, she would have to be proved sane of mind and would therefore have to go to a psychiatric clinic for observation. Antonietta became very docile and let herself be taken off. 'We awaited the day,'[24] recalls Stefano Pirandello, 'as a condemned man awaits the day of his execution and, after the "treachery" used to get her into that prison, we were like a family devastated by mourning and guilt. And Father's frenzied eagerness to have her back began at once.'

From then on Antonietta lived in her little room with the nuns looking after her. Pirandello wanted to see her but she frequently refused to admit him or received him like an enemy. But, said Stefano Pirandello:[25]

he had a single thought in his head, that of getting his wife back home, for she was as necessary to him as the air he breathed and he insisted on his children going to see her every day and telling him word for word what she said, if and how she had spoken about him. . . . This went on for years, not just for a few days or a few weeks, until five years later, in 1924, it seemed (although we children retained some doubts) that the time had come for Mother to return home, and we rented an isolated house at Monteluco above Spoleto for the summer. It was all ready for the guest, elaborate preparations were made for the journey, and then at the last moment she decided not to come. When the time came to leave her 'prison', from which, with a tortured voice, she begged us to liberate her, she suddenly clung to it as to a refuge which she was afraid to leave, and all her old aversion against her eternal enemy returned. . . . It was only then that Pirandello gave up the hope of ever taking her back. . . .

Antonietta lived in her clinic for a long time to come. She survived her husband and only died after the Second World War.

The house which Antonietta had previously filled with her terrifying presence suddenly appeared to Pirandello to be agonizingly deserted. ('Once she had left, my house suddenly seemed empty to me,' said one of the Six Characters. 'She was my nightmare, but she filled the house for me! When I was alone I felt like a headless fly in those rooms.') His children were back but that was not enough to remove his feeling of emptiness. Antonietta had represented something very different for him. For sixteen years Pirandello's life had been balanced precariously: his work as a writer had been conditioned in thousands of ways, every hour and every minute, by Antonietta's presence. Antonietta had inspired him: she had forced him, by continual onslaughts, to enclose himself still more within himself. He had understood a great deal by observing her: he had witnessed at first hand the deformations imposed by her psychological disease.

Now it was all over. All that Pirandello retained, once his daughter had also left him, was the physical silence of those rooms. He soon moved to another house. Antonietta had been a wall round Pirandello's art, the obsessive stimulation of his creativity. It was she who had insisted on the reality of countless things that did not exist. And Pirandello had given her credit for it. He was writing plays and preparing a novel to prove her right. *One, None and a Hundred Thousand* (*Uno, nessuno e centomila*) was inspired by this wife who helped him to see himself, Pirandello, as another very different person, but as the only person who really existed as far as she was concerned.

Once Antonietta had left and the strange, sometimes even monstrous fetters chaining him to that house had been broken, Pirandello felt himself terrifyingly free. It was an unbearable blow. He had always had a house, first that 'hermitage in the middle of the countryside' where he was born, then his mother's houses in Agrigento and Porto Empedocle, then the houses in Palermo and Bonn, and finally in Rome. Every domicile, however brief, had been a refuge for him. But soon home, every home, was to lose its value for him. He built himself a house but sold it almost immediately without any sense of sacrifice. His life as a nomad had begun. He was to choose as his residence hotels and the theatre—the most fictitious and equivocal of abodes. Only towards the end of his life did he return, significantly, to the house in Via Bosio.

5

THE THEATRE

There is nothing to mark the start of Pirandello's career as a playwright. Without pausing for breath, without a break in time, the prose writer simply started writing for the theatre. And he did so effortlessly, with amazing technical precision, with absolute mastery of the medium, as if, in the past, he had done nothing but practise and had only now decided to publish the results of his long apprenticeship. In fact he had had little practice—only a long-repressed dramatic vocation which he had unconsciously developed in his narrative prose.

After his youthful efforts, which lasted until about 1893, he had written a play in three acts, *The Hawk* (*Il nibbio*) in 1896, and some one-act plays, three in fifteen years, *Sicilian Limes* (*Lumie di Sicilia*), *The Doctor's Duty* (*Il dovere del medico*), and *Chee-Chee* (*Cecè*) which were no more than stage adaptations of short stories. From 1916 to 1924, however, he wrote twenty-eight works for the theatre: three in 1916, seven in 1917, five in 1918, and so on, two or three a year uninterruptedly, often taking no more than a week or two to write them.

Pirandello seemed suddenly to awaken to the fact that he was a great master of the theatre and was not excessively surprised about it: it came to him too easily. He hardly took what he was doing seriously, and, during the whole of this period, until after *Six Characters in Search of an Author*, he was constantly threatening to leave the theatre which, he said, did not interest him. Once he had fulfilled his obligations to this or that theatrical manager he would continue to write stories or novels, since that was what he principally wanted to do.

There are numerous indications of this surprising attitude towards
the theatre. Some of the men who were closest to him at the turn of the
century, Lucio D'Ambra, Ugo Fleres, Mario Corsi, and others,[1] refer,
in their recollections, to a reserve towards the theatre so artificial as to
resemble a pose. It was as though Pirandello wanted to flaunt his indifference to the theatre out of personal pique.

His friends, Giustino Ferri, Fleres, D'Ambra, and above all Boutet
and Martoglio, were either militant dramatic critics or playwrights and
producers and, in the cafés and at their meetings at home, they would
always go in for polemical discussions about theatrical works and
authors. Whenever this happened, Lucio D'Ambra recalled,[2] 'Pirandello would gather all his playing cards before him and, completely
aloof from our conversation and our excitement, would calmly start
playing patience. And those were the great days of contemporary
theatre. The first productions of Ibsen in Italy, the great controversial
and revolutionary premières of Becque's *La Parisienne*, Donnay's
Amants, Porto-Riche's *Amoureuse*, F. de Curel's *Nouvelle Idole*, the
tempestuous evenings of d'Annunzio's first dramatic works. . . . Pirandello was deaf to everything and refused to raise his grey eyes and
blond beard from the cards. The success of a game of patience interested him far more than thousands of contemporary plays.' 'The theatre
doesn't interest me,' he would repeat, and he would say that he had
stopped at the Greeks, at some Spaniard, at Shakespeare, that the
furthest he had ever got was Molière and Goldoni. 'After Goldoni,'
Lucio D'Ambra continued, 'there was nothing but darkness for him....
And he spoke of the theatre as of something that had nothing to do
with him, as if it were unworthy of serious people.'

From 1893, when Pirandello had been deeply offended by Flavio
Andò's attitude of indifference towards his play *The Vice* Pirandello
showed no desire to approach the theatre, and in his newspaper articles
and essays written up to 1915, he quoted no modern playwrights
except for Ibsen and him unfavourably. 'Have you ever been to a play
by Ibsen?' he wrote in 1893.[3] 'What does this Norwegian want? Nobody can really understand him, but it is enough for someone to seem
incomprehensible for him to be surrounded by a swarm of undecided
individuals as insistent, as oppressive as, if I may use so vulgar an
expression, flies surrounding a spittle.' To Rosso di San Secondo he
once compared the theatre to a rough form of painting with coarse
brush strokes.[4] Narrative prose, on the other hand, offered him the
possibility of a more precise penetration of truth and of restoring a

multiple complexity. 'If God will help me,' he wrote to Munzone in December 1909, 'I will never write plays. The theatre—not the work of art, of course—the theatre, for me, is the same as the vignette to the book it illustrates, or like a translation compared with the original: a reproduction which either spoils or diminishes the original.'[5]

In 1914 it was again Lucio D'Ambra who intervened in Pirandello's theatrical destiny. They had just come back from a holiday (Pirandello had been staying near Viterbo), and while D'Ambra was helping his friend to rearrange his books he came across a dusty old manuscript of *The Hawk* written in 1896. He asked for it and gave it to Marco Praga, the manager of the Repertory Company of the Teatro Manzoni in Milan, who was then staying in Rome. Praga, who was later to become a great friend of Pirandello, was amazed by the play—so much so that he wrote to Lucio D'Ambra from Milan saying that 'Pirandello is a master with his first step. I shall produce the play in Milan.' Pirandello was thus performed by a major company, directed by Marco Praga, in which Irma Gramatica was the leading actress and Talli, Ruggeri, Betrone, and Melato other members of the cast.

The play, whose title was changed to the more fashionable *If Not Like That* (*Se non così*), was performed on 19 April 1915. But things did not go as the author would have liked. The play tells the story of a middle-class wife who manages, with the weapon of moral blackmail and in the name of an ambiguous and abstract duty, to tear the illegitimate daughter of her husband from her mother 'like a hawk'. According to the author the play was to pivot on the thankless character of the sterile wife. Instead Irma Gramatica, in agreement with Praga whom Pirandello was unable to persuade otherwise when he went to Milan, preferred to act the part of the mistress whose part was more emotional. And so, thanks to Irma Gramatica's overweening dramatic personality, the focus of the play was shifted to a character who was not the one on whom the author's inventiveness had been concentrated, and, despite the applause of the audience, the critics received the play coldly.

Pirandello came back to Rome in the worst of humours, confirmed his rejection of the theatre, and returned to writing short stories. Then, when *If Not Like That* was published by Treves, also in 1915, he wanted to get his own back on Irma Gramatica and wrote a letter to precede the play full of annoyance about the leading actress who had ruined his work (even if he did not actually mention her by name). The letter was addressed to the real protagonist of the play. 'Dear lady,' it ran, 'I am sorry to have to say so, but you do not come out of this play too well. And maybe no self-respecting leading actress will ever want to act your part. . . . So stay here in the book. In our theatres, as they are and as you are, you have no hope of making your way, I can assure you. As you are, dear lady, you lack appeal. . . .'

The friendship between Martoglio and Pirandello, both Sicilians and of almost the same age, had become very close of late and the two fifty-year-old writers had been joined by Rosso di San Secondo, who was twenty years younger and who soon aroused Pirandello's esteem and affection. They were always together. Pirandello formed greater friendships with southern Italians than with northern Italians (his only close friend who was not from the south was probably Massimo Bontempelli), and he followed, with an air of benevolent superiority, Nino Martoglio's efforts to implement the programme inherited from Capuana and Alessio Di Giovanni to raise Sicilian dialectal theatre to a level of national culture. In the summer of 1915 Angelo Musco, one of the most famous and talented Sicilian actors, as eager as Martoglio to promote a Sicilian theatre, went to see Pirandello and asked him to write a play for him to be performed in Milan in the next season.

He found that Pirandello was anything but prepared to satisfy him. Stefano had only just left for the front and Pirandello was beside himself with anxiety. He felt completely alien to the man who had invaded his study and who, gesticulating and insisting, tried to win him over to the world of the theatre and wanted a play from him at any price. The actor even suggested an idea. He reminded him that some years earlier he had given the title of an unwritten play to Martoglio's company, *The Man from the Continent* (*Il continentale*). Pirandello hedged but Martoglio liked the idea and, in the days that followed, he and Pirandello decided on the general plot. At a certain point, however, Pirandello felt he could not go on—and *The Air of the Continent* (*L'aria del continente*) as the play was finally called, was almost entirely by Martoglio. Nevertheless it had an enormous success and remained Musco's war-horse for ever. It also earned Martoglio a large sum of money which he wanted to share with Pirandello, but which Pirandello refused, even if he later regretted the decision. 'In Milan,' he wrote to Stefano on 19 February 1916, '*The Air of the Continent* is being performed very successfully. To tell you the truth I made a considerable contribution to it: it was I who provided the subject matter and the structure of the work. We were supposed to do the whole thing together but at that very moment you were taken prisoner and I left the plot to Nino, telling him that it was all his. I thus lost at least 10,000 lire because the play had a huge success in Milan, Turin, Florence, Genoa, and Rome, and was performed hundreds of times. Well! . . .' He would in fact have earned a great deal more than 10,000 lire if it is true that Martoglio made almost 500,000.

Pirandello was in great need of money just then. 'The many expenses and this last, rather big operation of Fausto's,' he wrote to Stefano, 'made me stop work on another novel (*One, None and a Hundred Thousand*). I write short stories, one after the other. . . .' And a few days later he wrote that he would have liked to take his wife and daughter to see *Sicilian Limes* which Musco was giving at the Teatro Morgana, produced by Martoglio, but added: 'I might go . . . but I'm uncertain because Mother and Lietta are still in mourning [for Pirandello's mother] and have nothing to wear and I don't want to go alone.'

So, when Musco came back to Rome from Milan in triumph and asked the 'Professor' for another 'play' Pirandello overcame his prejudices against theatre of dialect and promised to adapt a short story. He could work with greater peace of mind now that Stefano had written to him from prisoner-of-war camp in Mauthausen. Besides, he had admired Musco's talent in *Sicilian Limes* and the character of the old Professor Toti, in his next play, *Better Think Twice About It*, was written for Musco. The play, which Pirandello translated into Sicilian for Musco's benefit, was performed at the Teatro Nazionale on 10 July 1916. On 11 July, in a letter to his son, Pirandello gave a description of the evening: 'I must give you a piece of news which will undoubtedly give you a great deal of pleasure: Yesterday evening (10th) Musco performed my play . . . with triumphant success: at the end of the third act the audience leapt to their feet and called me three times on to the stage. But I did not appear. The first act had four curtain calls, the second two. Twelve in all. But the whole thing is satisfactory because the work is very daring and the spectators had not been predisposed to applaud. The whole play was followed so attentively that it was quite awe-inspiring. Musco was great.—Are you pleased about it, Stefano? I thought about you several times during the performance and I would have liked to have had you close to me together with Fausto who kept me company in a third-rate box hidden away. Like him you too might have suffered and worried a little too much, but then you too would have had a very pleasant surprise. . . .'

This letter reveals an anxious Pirandello, sensitive about the success of his plays, counting the curtain calls and probably no less worried than his son 'hidden away' in his 'third-rate box'—in other words very different to the Pirandello described as being unconcerned about the success or failure of his works. It was only before others that he tried to appear so.

On 14 July he again mentioned *Better Think Twice About It*. 'The play has had a run of very successful performances and will undoubtedly be performed triumphantly throughout Italy. . . . I have undertaken to write another play for Musco to be performed next October and I hope to keep my word, although, as you know, the theatre does not really attract me. . . .' On 20 July, less than a week later, the new play had already formed in Pirandello's mind. 'I already have the plot, the script and the title, *Liolà*. It will be about a peasant poet, drunk with sun, of whom there are so many in Sicily. And it will turn out well, you'll see. . . .'

Liolà was to be the best play Pirandello ever wrote in the traditional medium and it was to be a landmark in the history of the Italian theatre. But on 18 August he had got another two-act play ready for Musco, *Cap and Bells (Il berretto a sonagli)*. 'Now I am writing *Liolà*,' he wrote to Stefano, 'a play in three acts. I shall then write *The Favourite ('U cuccu)*, if I can retain my interest in the theatre and I shall then close this theatrical parenthesis to return to my more natural work as story-teller.' By 25 August he had written the first act of *Liolà* and by 10 September, the whole play. *Liolà* was the only work of that period in which Pirandello tried to escape from his despair. Unlike *Better Think Twice About It*, which Pirandello translated into dialect, *Liolà* was actually written in Sicilian. Composed during his son's imprisonment, his wife's madness, and the abyss in which he said he conceived *Right You Are (If You Think So) (Così è (se vi pare))* it shows more than any other work Pirandello's capacity to shut himself hermetically into a private world of fantasy.

Early in October, in another letter to Stefano, Pirandello was worried about not being able to attend the rehearsals of *Liolà* at the Teatro Argentina since he had to supervise exams at the Magistero. But he finally managed to attend. Musco, who liked to improvise when he acted, remembered him as 'a difficult author'.[6] 'He was difficult,' he said, 'in the sense of being impossible to please. The rehearsals rarely satisfied him. He sat on the stage, his face in his hands, or resting on one hand, while with the other he fiddled nervously with his grey beard. . . . Even if he didn't say anything we could tell that he wasn't satisfied. And I said nothing because I thought: we'll see what happens on the first night.'

Indeed, the playwright still tended to look down on Sicilian actors[7] and he did not trust Musco who was undisciplined, refused to learn his part, and could not resist improvising. Pirandello wrote to his son that *Liolà* 'aroused great expectations', that he hoped it would turn out well, that it was the work he cared most about after *The Late Mattia Pascal*, and that he was terribly jealous of it. On 4 November, the day of the first performance, during the dress rehearsal, Pirandello realized that none of the actors knew their parts. He could contain himself no longer and wrenched the script from Musco's hands. 'Pirandello took the script away and forbade me to perform the play that night,' wrote Musco: '"Professor," I shouted, running after him, "it's no good your taking the script away. We're going to improvise tonight. You don't realize that we're like racehorses who don't start unless they hear the starting pistol. If we don't see the footlights and the audience we don't act."' Pirandello grew still angrier at such a display of irresponsibility and rushed out of the theatre. Only later could Martoglio calm him down and prevail upon him to return the script. 'And that night,' Musco went on, 'when *Liolà* was a tremendous success, Pirandello came on to the stage and kissed and embraced me enthusiastically, with the affectionate and sincere emotion of a gentleman and a Sicilian.' '*Liolà*,' Pirandello wrote to his son, 'went very well on the first and on subsequent nights' but, he added, he could feel no real joy because of the painful conditions in which he lived.

In the meantime Pirandello continued to produce other narrative works. In 1915 *Shoot* had appeared and was followed by two collections of short stories, *The Trap* (*La trappola*) and *The Grass of Our Garden* (*Erba del nostro orto*). In 1916 there appeared in *Nuova Antologia* the 'profane mystery' *At the Gate* (*All'Uscita*), and in 1917 Treves published a further collection of stories, *Tomorrow, Monday* (*E domani, lunedì*), while *La Rivista Italiana* published *By Judgement of the Court* (*La patente*), a one-act play based on the homonymous short story written in 1911.

The year 1917 marked a new phase in Pirandello's dramatic work. His Sicilian plays had served as a springboard for his great prose works. Two plays in dialect, *Cap and Bells* and *The Jar* (*La giara*) were still being performed at the Teatro Nazionale in Rome on 27 June and 27 July but they were already a year old and had only been performed at the insistence of Musco. At the same time Pirandello collaborated with Martoglio on two plays in dialect, *Cowardice* (*'A vilanza*) (which was performed on 8 September by Giovanni Grasso Junior at the Teatro

Argentina) and *Capiddazzu Pays for Everything* (*Capiddazzu paga tuttu*) which was never performed. But Pirandello's mind was on something very different. *Liolà* and *The Jar* had been his farewell to the Sicilian theatre which was too close to a narrow tradition of realism for him to be able to give a more universal expression to his ideas. Ever since the beginning of the war he had been living in a daze. Even if he appeared to be an active patriot, poring over maps of the war, he was in fact prey to a dark state of mind from which he could not and would not free himself. To his son he had written on 24 October 1915: 'I feel that my whole life is devoid of meaning, and I no longer see any reason in the acts I perform or in the words I say, and it astonishes me that other people can move about outside this nightmare of mine, that they can act and speak. . . .'

There was no reason to do one thing rather than another. The world was bereft of value. Every good intention had failed and the prevalent current of feeling in the world seemed to be hatred. Pirandello's problem of the knowledge and identity of reality, the problem that had always induced him to ask himself *philosophical* questions, was now resolved in the most negative of ways. While the father wrote to his son on 23 December 1916: 'I have read all the books of philosophy for you and when you return I shall tell you what they told me: very, very little. . .', the dramatist was preparing the most sceptical of his parables, *Right You Are (If You Think So)*. Pirandello used the theatrical technique of continuous *coups de scène* each of which destroys a hitherto accepted truth. The characters enter and depart, growing ever more uncertain and puzzled. This was the first time that Pirandello had encountered nothingness—not the romantic, constellated abyss or the metaphysical doubts of before, but absurd and irreconcilable nothingness. It was a nihilistic relativism no longer on a theoretical level, but on the level of everyday life, of social life in the Italian provinces. Exactly a year before finishing the play he wrote to his son (17 April 1916): 'I am digging, digging . . . I have reduced myself to a well from which I can no longer escape. And why should I escape? For life now seems more and more like a comic and crazy phantasmagoria.'

About *Right You Are*. . . he wrote to his son again on 18 April 1917 that it was 'a great piece of devilry . . . a parable more than a comedy. I am pleased with it. Its originality is really striking. But I don't know what sort of success it will have owing to the extraordinary audacity of the situation. . . . According to my friends it's the best thing I've done yet. I think so too.' And he added: 'Ruggero Ruggeri may well stage

it next May here in Rome . . . it could have a huge success. . . . As you
see, the dramatic parenthesis is not closed yet. . . .' To Talli, who was
to perform it with Maria Melato and Annibale Betrone on 18 June at
the Teatro Olimpia in Milan, he announced his '*parable*, something
really original, new in its conception, very audacious in its form, and
destined—as far as one can judge from reading it—to have a very sure
effect owing to the intense and uncommon interest which it arouses
immediately. It arouses it in the first act and sustains it, gradually in-
creasing it, in the other two. And he drew the actor's attention to the
'last words of the play, which contain its deepest meaning: words put
into the mouth of a woman whose face is hidden by an impenetrable
veil, a *very alive* woman in the play, a symbol of truth.'

Pirandello was delighted with the performance of the play. 'Ten
days ago,' he wrote to Stefano on 29 June 1917, 'it was performed very
successfully. I was there. I managed to escape for four days from the
network of exam commissions. In Milan everyone received me very
warmly. Talli said that in over twenty-five years on the stage he had
never attended such a strange and interesting première as this. . . .
After Milan he will take it to Bologna, then to Genoa, then to Turin,
and, in Lent of next year, to Rome.' And on 17 June 1918 Pirandello
told his son of the success of *The Pleasure of Honesty* (*Il piacere dell'
onestà*).

However sad and anxious he was at heart, Pirandello was beginning
to savour the pleasure of success—a success which affected his narrative
works, to which, almost superstitiously, he still attached greater importance. Indeed, he continued to plan more works of narrative than
plays. Even *Six Characters in Search of an Author* appeared to him as
the idea for a novel—'a sad, sad form of strangeness', he wrote to his
son. '*Six Characters*, a novel to be written. Perhaps you can understand. Six characters in a terrible situation who follow me, to be composed in a novel, an obsession, and I want to have nothing to do with
them. I tell them it is no good, that I don't care about them or about
anything else. They show me their wounds and I chase them away . . .
and so, in the end, the novel to be written will be written.'

In 1918, while Treves was publishing another volume of short
stories, *A Horse in the Moon* (*Un cavallo nella luna*), two further plays
by Pirandello were performed, *It's Nothing Serious* (*Ma non è una cosa
seria*) on 22 November at the Teatro Rossini of Livorno by Emma
Gramatica's company and *The Rules of the Game*, performed on 6
December 1918 at the Teatro Quirino in Rome by Ruggero Ruggeri

and Vera Vergani. Both Emma Gramatica and Ruggeri gave good performances of the two plays. 'It appears,' Pirandello wrote to his son on 29 November 1918, 'that Gramatica's performance is admirable, so is Ruggeri's as Leone Gala in *The Rules of the Game* which acquired considerable strength during the rehearsals. Here and there I added an effective dramatic touch and the character emerges full of significance— very interesting. Ruggeri is in love with it and thinks *The Rules of the Game* my best play. Let's hope the public understand it; I do not expect the critics to do so. . . . Except for Ruggeri . . . none of them satisfy me, but we must adapt ourselves to what we find in a company that rests on the exceptional ability of a single actor. . . .'

The day after the first night he wrote: 'Yesterday evening was a battle day for me. I didn't win but I didn't lose either. *The Rules of the Game* was met with hostility, owing to the incomprehension of the audience after the first act. It picked up in the second act and at the third it aroused considerable discussion. I know I have written a serious work and all this hullabaloo has not bothered me at all. The morning and evening papers have, on the whole, been favourable to me. This evening the play is being repeated. But another play has already been announced for Sunday—a sign that the manager has no faith in a play which has already been compromised by the controversy about the first performance. Too bad!' Then, on 12 January 1919, in a letter to Ruggeri, he commented on the critics' reaction less optimistically: 'A batch of newspapers, all except one, fiercely opposed not so much to my play as to me, my theatre, the so-called *new theatre*. . . .'

As far as Pirandello's own attitude to the new theatre was concerned his ever closer friendship with Rosso di San Secondo was of consider- able importance. Rosso used to go and keep him company every even- ing and regarded him as a master, while Pirandello, who felt a deep affection for him, regarded him as a kindred spirit. In his youth Rosso had had the traumatic experience of seeing his mother go mad, and his brother had committed suicide. During the war Pirandello had written favourable reviews of Rosso's first plays *Ponentino*, *The Flight* (*La fuga*) and *Marionettes, What a Passion!* (*Marionette, che passione!*) and when, after the war, Rosso became editor of the literary supplement of *Il Messaggero della Domenica* Pirandello would go to his office every day from four to five o'clock.

The visits to the editorial offices of *Il Messaggero* served to break down Pirandello's former intellectual isolation, thanks to Rosso whose stimulating and adventurous attempts to participate in the European avant-garde prompted Pirandello to undertake his own theatrical revolution. He felt a strong desire to cut new ground, but he had so far shown an almost timid respect for traditional forms. He had been able, on his own, to create *Right You Are. . .* and *The Rules of the Game*, but neither of these works contain any radical innovations. Their audacities are still enclosed in a sheath of classical technique and realism.

Rosso di San Secondo, for example, had introduced Nordic expressionism into Italy and had shown Pirandello how characters 'fixed in their movements, turned into marionettes', (as Pirandello put it)[8] could appear on the stage. When Pirandello read *Marionettes, What a Passion!* in 1918 he slightly distorted its meaning and gave an entirely personal interpretation of the play according to an idea which he was developing for *Six Characters in Search of an Author*. 'Here,' he wrote, 'every logical preparation, every logical support has been abolished. We are suddenly hurled into complete exasperation . . . the characters are the various stages and grades of their own passions. . . . Apparent lack of logic . . . is in fact the supreme logic . . .' etc. In fact Rosso had inserted into his more modern style something which he had taken in part from Pirandello. And Pirandello, in his turn, found in Rosso's modernity a signpost towards the bolder aspects of his art which he had hitherto rigorously kept in check.

Rosso di San Secondo was closest to Pirandello but he was not the only writer who stimulated the revolutionary explosion of Pirandello's theatre or who helped to make way for the success of *Six Characters in Search of an Author*. In the war years Pirandello showed interest in the authors of the 'theatre of the grotesque' who revealed to him the potential of the theatrical pastiche, and informed him indirectly about some of the new methods of European art. Between 1915 and 1921 a number of works by Alberto Casella, Luigi Chiarelli, Luigi Antonelli, Enrico Cavacchioli, and Massimo Bontempelli were written and performed, enabling Pirandello to connect the new ideas with older romantic notions of his own. In an article which appeared on 27 February 1920 in *L'Idea Nazionale* he showed how he had moved closer to assimilating the grotesque almost in anticipation of *Six Characters in Search of an Author*. 'A fine definition of the most significant modern works of the grotesque is *transcendental farces*. . . . Hegel explained that the subject, the only true reality, can smile at the vain appearance of the world. It stipulates it, but it can also destroy it; it does not have to take its own creations seriously. Hence we have irony, that force which, according to Tieck, allows the poet to dominate his subject-matter. And, according to Friedrich Schlegel, it is through irony that the same subject-matter is reduced to a perpetual parody, a transcendental farce. . .'. 'The farce of the grotesque includes its parody and its carica-ture in the very same tragedy, not as superimposed elements but as its own shadow, a clumsy shadow of every tragic gesture. . .'.

Rosso di San Secondo and the editors of *Il Messaggero della Domeni-ca* put Pirandello in touch with other young exponents of the avant-garde: A. G. Bragaglia, and some of the futurists. In 1915 Pirandello wrote for *La Ruota* and in 1916 for *Cronache d'Attualità*, the two re-views run by Bragaglia who, in 1918, also opened an art gallery where De Chirico, De Pero, Boccioni, and Sironi held their first personal exhibitions and which became a meeting place for Prampolini, Mari-netti, Malaparte, and many others. Pirandello also frequented the gallery.[9] The futurists, their ostentatious break with tradition, their love of public scandal, and their 'synthetic surprise' theatre had a strong suggestive influence on the fifty-year-old Pirandello—so much so that later Romagnoli and other futurists, including Marinetti, claimed that Pirandello's innovations belonged, to some extent, to their movement. Indeed, Marinetti was to write:[10] 'Especially in certain alogical and unexpected scenes like the entry of Signora Pace in the play *Six Charac-ters in Search of an Author*, he was clearly futurist.' This may be an exaggeration, but it is true that Pirandello later wrote the script for a 'futurist' pantomime entitled *La Salamandra* (for which Bontempelli wrote the music), which was performed on 7 March 1928 at the Teatro di Torino by the Compagnia della Pantomima Futurista directed by Enrico Prampolini. Furthermore, Pirandello produced Marinetti's *Vulcani* in 1926 at the Politeama Nazionale in Florence with his own company.

In 1919 Pirandello collaborated with Nino Martoglio in directing the company Teatro Mediterraneo which came to life after numerous plans and discussions between Martoglio, Pirandello, and Rosso di San Secondo. It appeared at the Teatro Argentina. This was Pirandello's first experience of live and continuous theatre. Some years later he would become a manager and a producer, but by then he had learned a number of things from his work with the Teatro Mediterraneo, with actors committed to a modest repertory. It was for this company that Pirandello translated Euripides' *Cyclops* into Sicilian dialect (it was per-formed on 26 January 1919) and prepared a Sicilian version of Mor-selli's *Glauco* in order to help Morselli who could not find anyone to produce it. Pirandello withdrew his own version as soon as another company was prepared to perform it in Italian.

In the same year, 1919, three more plays of Pirandello were performed: *The Scion* (*L'innesto*) produced by Virgilio Talli on 29 January at the Teatro Manzoni in Milan; *By Judgement of the Court* in a Sicilian translation by Angelo Musco at the Teatro Argentina on 19 February; and *Man, Beast and Virtue* (*L'uomo, la bestia e la virtù*) by Antonio Gandusio's company at the Teatro Olimpia in Milan. In 1920 *Just As It Should Be* (*Tutto per bene*) was performed by Ruggero Ruggeri's company at the Teatro Quirino in Rome on 2 March; *As Before, Better than Before* (*Come prima, meglio di prima*) by the Ferrero-Celli-Paoli company at the Teatro Goldoni in Venice on 24 March; *Chee-Chee* by Armando Falconi's company at the Teatro del Casinò at San Pellegrino on 10 July; and *Signora Morli, One and Two* (*La Signora Morli, una e due*) by Emma Gramatica's company at the Teatro Argentina on 12 November. Then in 1921, came *Six Characters in Search of an Author*.

When Pirandello read *Six Characters in Search of an Author* to his friends they were overwhelmed by the degree of tension he had created. Arnaldo Frateili recalled the event:[11] 'As soon as Pirandello had finished writing *Six Characters in Search of an Author* he came to read the work in my house. There was my son Stefano, Silvio D'Amico, Alberto Cecchi, Mario Labroca (I think), and two or three others and we were shaken not only by the play but also by the passion with which Pirandello recited it. . . . He entered into the part of each character and lived their passions intensely, almost painfully—their love and hate, their joy and pain, their ecstasy and irony. . . . His voice heard from another room did not sound like the voice of one but of ten characters. . . . At the end, we argued about the work like maniacs. . . .'

These were the first discussions about a work which was to make the greatest theatrical impact of the 1920s. Pirandello entrusted the play to Dario Niccodemi's company which performed it at the Teatro Valle in Rome on 10 May 1921. Things started to go badly from the first, when the spectators came into the theatre and realized that the curtain was raised and that there was no scenery. The first protests were heard from people who were irritated by what they considered to be gratuitous exhibitionism—and though Pirandello had not yet caused any major outrage, he did not have a good reputation. The play began and the first oddities were noticed: a stage-hand in a green overall started nailing planks on to the stage; the producer looked out from the wings and sent him about his business; some actors dressed in their everyday

clothes strolled in chatting to each other; the manager of the troupe
started talking about this and that with his secretary. Then, once the
action had begun, there was an additional provocation when the manager said: 'What can I do if . . . we have to perform plays by Pirandello
which nobody understands and which never satisfy anybody, not the
actors, the critics, or the audience?' And finally there was the extraordinary arrival from the back of the auditorium, announced by one of
the doormen, of the curious six characters. All this was enough to en-
furiate anyone who had gone to the theatre to spend a pleasant evening.
The first catcalls were followed by shouts of disapproval, and, when the
opponents of the play realized that they were in the majority, they
started to shout in chorus, 'ma-ni-co-mio' ('madhouse') or 'bu-ffo-ne'
('buffoon').

Of course the play did not lack its supporters who endeavoured to
defend it, thereby creating an even greater confusion. As the commotion increased the play was strenuously performed by the actors, but
only very little of it could be heard, especially since, at one point,
members of the audience started to exchange blows and there was a
general riot. On the one side a group was formed by some of Pirandello's admirers, who included Mario Labroca, Maselli, Galeazzo
Ciano, and Orio Vergani who was an amateur boxer and particularly
committed to defending the play both because of his friendship for
Pirandello and because his sister Vera was acting the part of the step-
daughter (and had been one of the most enthusiastic supporters of
that first performance). At one moment a poet named Arnaldi was
seen to hurl himself into a box where a thick group of whistlers had
assembled.

Pirandello was sitting in a dressing-room with Lietta who was almost sick with fear. He displayed his taste for provocation, and perhaps
for humiliating himself, by appearing on the stage at the end of the
play—the first time he had ever done so. As soon as he appeared,
the din doubled. When the curtain fell, similar scenes took place on the
stage. All the usual crowd of people in the corridors and the dressing-
rooms, journalists, critics, and spectators, mingled with the actors, who
still had their make-up on and, taking no notice of the playwright,
continued to quarrel and to shout about the play. In the meantime the
audience went on rioting. Instead of dispersing outside the theatre they
assembled to greet the author with a last outburst of contempt. They
had to wait for a considerable length of time but they did not give up.
Pirandello remained for almost an hour in the theatre since he was

reluctant to face the crowd in the company of his daughter, and Lietta did not want to abandon him.

Orio Vergani gave a detailed description of Pirandello's departure:[12]

Pirandello looked calm. He thanked the actress who had weathered the storm and who, a month later, was to carry the play in triumph to Milan, Spain, and America. He did not go out through the main entrance, but went through the back door into a shabby little alley. From there he could get to the tramstop at Sant'Andrea della Valle. To call a taxi—they were very rare—would have aroused suspicion and attracted the attention of the audience waiting to hiss at him.

He came out arm-in-arm with his daughter. He was recognized by the light of the first lamp-post. His friends surrounded him to defend him. Beautiful ladies laughed and repeated with their painted lips: 'Madhouse!' Elegant young men with white ties leered at him and insulted him. His daughter, on her father's arm, trembled so much she could hardly move forward. Other people rushed up, laughing and whistling. Not even the policemen knew whether they should intervene on behalf of 'that lunatic Pirandello'. A taxi approached. In the light of the square Pirandello, with a barely perceptible smile of irony on his lips, received the insults. We couldn't start a fight before the taxi left. He opened the door for his daughter, got in in his turn and, through the window, we could see his face as he gave the driver the address of his distant, unpretentious house where he would return to work the next day. The elegant young men threw coins at him and so did the ladies, hurriedly opening their purses. I can still hear the sound of the coins on the pavement, the laughs and the insults.

The fighting and arguing in the streets and in the square near the Teatro Argentina lasted late into the night.

The play was performed again a few months later, on 27 September, by the same actors, at the Teatro Manzoni in Milan. This time the audience and the critics had a different attitude: they had had time to read the text published by Bemporad before the Milan performance and they listened to the play in religious silence. It ended in a triumph which soon spread to theatres all over the world. Between 1922 and 1927 it was performed in every major city in Europe as well as in New York, Buenos Aires, and Tokyo.

Few writers have been as physically obsessed by their characters as Pirandello—obsessed by their concrete presence. And there is a well-known anecdote recounted by Arnaldo Frateili about some workmen who were working opposite Pirandello's windows and who suddenly stopped work in order to watch the writer at his desk 'who had started to talk to himself, to wave his hands and flash his eyes and make the strangest faces in the world. Professor Pirandello seems to have been somewhat mortified by the episode which got round and astonished the neighbours.' But this obsession had been going on for many years and one of the first references to it is in a letter written by Pirandello from Rome to Luigi Natoli on 28 May 1904.[13] 'If material cares and social commitments did not distract me,' he wrote, 'I think I would remain from morning to night here in my study at the beck and call of the characters of my stories who are struggling within me. Each wants to come to life before the others. They all have a particular misfortune which they want to bring to light. I feel sorry for them. . . .' Then again in 1911, in 'A Character in Distress' ('La tragedia di un personaggio'), he wrote: 'I have two or three new visitors a week. And sometimes the crowd is such that I have to listen to more than one of them at the same time. And sometimes my mind is so split and dazed that it rebels against this double or triple uprising and shouts in exasperation that the characters must either appear slowly, one at a time, or must go straight back to limbo, the three of them!' At the beginning of the war vivid characters invaded his study and he almost threw a batch of newspapers at them in order to 'bump them off'. There was also his mother, who became a character as soon as she died.

Six Characters was born of Pirandello's contact with the characters of his imagination, but the play also represents the last stage of the history of his own nihilism. Even if the war did not bring about any great change in his attitude towards life and society it often caused him to protest violently against certain things which he would not have protested against before. He himself was to say one day: 'Mine has been a theatre of war. The war revealed the theatre to me: when passions were unleashed I made my own creatures suffer these passions on the stage.'[14] The war had overturned people's defences and had shattered the superstructures erected to defend many voluntary and involuntary, collective and individual, hypocrisies. It was the triumph of death, and for most people it was the revelation of death. Thus a quantity of individuals found that *Six Characters in Search of an Author* reflected faithfully the crisis that had taken place within each of them.

Pirandello did not attach much importance to the failure of *Six Characters* in Rome and, immediately after, he wrote *Henry IV*. He was aware that *Six Characters* was a great play and he consequently devoted himself to the new play in a state of creative euphoria which induced him to write his most monumental, if not his best work.

Four months before the first night, which took place on 24 February 1922, Pirandello had written self-confidently to Ruggeri who was going to perform the play: 'Without false modesty, the subject seems to me to be worthy of you and the power of your art. But before I get down to work I would like you to tell me something, whether you approve of it and like it. . . .' (and here he gave a summary of the plot). Ruggeri was extremely enthusiastic about it.

From an autobiographical point of view *Henry IV* is particularly interesting because it is the last time that Pirandello used the image of madness in his work. It was as though, now that he was living on his own, he wanted to free himself from the obsessive image of his mad wife. As long as she had lived with him—and despite his passionate love for her—he had studied her with the eye of a cold observer, with the eye of a writer listing the objects in his study. And, precisely because of his closeness to her, this must have weighed on his mind. In May 1924 a journalist asked him:[15] 'Did your wife's illness allow you to study the world of the mad, their psychology and their logic?' 'Not to study it,' Pirandello answered. 'Whoever suffers and lives the torment of a person he loves is unable to study it because that would mean assuming the indifference of a spectator. But to see life being transposed in the mind of my poor companion enabled me later to convey the psychology of the alienated in my creative writing. Not the logic. The lunatic constructs without logic. Logic is form and form is in contrast with life. Life is formless and illogical. So I think that the mad are closer to life. There is nothing fixed and determined in us. We have within ourselves every possibility, and suddenly, unexpectedly, the thief or the lunatic can jump out of any one of us. . . .' By 1924 the experience of madness was less intense but three years earlier, when Pirandello wrote *Henry IV* and erected a monument to madness which was almost oracular, he was deeply involved in this intimate problem of consciousness. Even if the character is not a true lunatic, *Henry IV* is an apology for madness and, implicitly, a public act of penance.

In Milan the 'responsible' critics did not want to yield to admiration of *Henry IV* without some reservations. In *L'Illustrazione Italiana* Marco Praga described it as a 'work of art of the sort that I do not particularly enjoy—or maybe I should say: that I am unable to enjoy, but which fascinates me, which I listen to in astonishment, and which amuses me in the highest sense of the word.' And Renato Simoni wrote: 'To my mind the tragedy lacks unity. My fault, no doubt; but also, partly, the fault of the tragedy. . . .' But Silvio D'Amico regarded it as Pirandello's most important work: '*Henry IV* remains Pirandello's masterpiece, above all because of the breadth of its vision.'

Pirandello was very pleased with the success. On 7 March he wrote to his daughter Lietta who was in Chile:[16] '*Henry IV* has been a triumph, a real triumph. Ruggeri acted magnificently and the performance was repeated on every evening that the Company remained in Milan, to the delight of enthusiastic audiences. It is the greatest success I have had so far: all the daily newspapers, of Turin, Rome, Venice, Genoa, Florence, Naples, and Sicily have devoted two columns to the event.' And the next day he wrote: 'I have received a telegram from the administrator Contento informing me of the resounding success of the play in Turin. Over eighteen curtain calls with cheers for Talli as well as for Ruggeri, that marvellous actor. The audience wanted me to appear, but they waited in vain.'

However, Pirandello did not manage to win over all the Italian critics before his success in Paris and he felt a hidden disappointment. He always declared, even after his success, that the critics' opinion was no concern of his and that they were unable to understand him. Nevertheless he complained about them. When he saw the critics becoming more favourable to him, often for reasons which had nothing to do with the value of the work, because of his success abroad for instance, his scepticism became chronic. He could still remember Tilgher's biting attacks on *Better Think Twice About It* ('Pirandello's art is one of leisure and amusement') [17] or Gramsci's attack on *Right You Are*. . . ('Pirandello's three acts are a mere fact of literature . . . they are a mere aggregate of words which create neither an image nor a truth . . . a monster . . . not a play').[18] And he now saw these same works become masterpieces for new critics or for the previously hostile critics. So when Gramsci and Tilgher and Renato Simoni and all the others started to understand at least part of his plays and to see them in a more favourable—or even an exalted—critical perspective, he continued, whenever he could, at every interview, in public and private, to flaunt his indifference and superiority to the critics. Only to Tilgher's exalted opinion did he appear, for a period of time, to attach importance. On the whole he wanted to display an ironic detachment towards the public destiny of his work as though he were no more than its necessary and modest mediator.

Now, after *Six Characters in Search of an Author*, it was as though he had tamed them all. Only the odd rebel resisted and wrote enraged,

A portrait by Pirandello of his wife

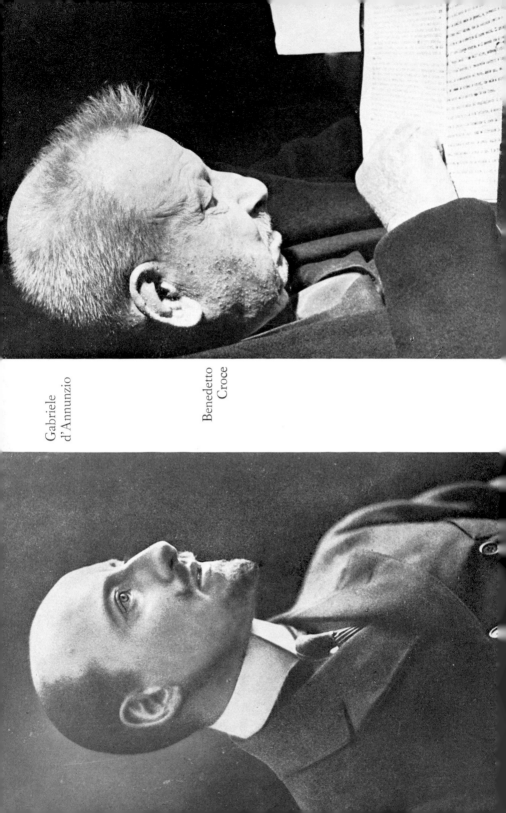

Gabriele
d'Annunzio

Benedetto
Croce

hysterical articles. Even if his works did not please the critics, indeed, even if they displeased them, the critics had to admit that Pirandello was, at all events, a writer worthy of great respect. They were forced to assume a more humble attitude: they had to begin to understand.

With *Henry IV* and above all with *Six Characters in Search of an Author* Pirandello had reached the high point of his art and had at the same time achieved the most certain expression of his own truth, the confession beyond which he would have no more story to tell. He was to write twenty-one more plays (he had written twenty-one before his two masterpieces), but of these no more than three or four were to be really distinguished and none of them moved the spectators as *Six Characters in Search of an Author* had done.

6

SUCCESS

The years until 1924 were extremely successful, but they were unhappy. Pirandello spent 1921 in the deepest misery. Life intruded painfully into works like *Six Characters in Search of an Author* and *Henry IV*. He was beset by new sorrows which gave him a greater sense of tragedy. Nino Martoglio, Pirandello's old and firm friend, died. He was found on the morning of 16 September 1921 at the bottom of a lift shaft which was being repaired. Pirandello wrote his obituary in *Il Messaggero*: 'I can't write about him . . . so much does it pain me to know that he died so suddenly and so tragically and to know that I shall never see him again . . .'. Martoglio's death wounded the writer deeply, just as he had been deeply affected by the death, the year before, of Federigo Tozzi who was not even thirty-eight.[1] From then on he retained the presentiment of a premature and sudden death which removed all sense from his plans for the future.

But a still greater and more violent shock was the separation from his daughter Lietta—and this was a wound that never healed. For years he had concentrated all his affection on her in order to make up for the desolation which his wife's madness, and then her absence, had left in the house. Lietta was the only female element who satisfied his need for love. He had loved her as though she had always remained a child to be protected (although he could not always do so) in that house which often filled him with horror. Even in the letters he wrote to her when she was twenty-five and a married woman he continued to use the most affectionate terms of address as if he were trying to continue a game between father and daughter for all eternity.

On 16 July 1921 Lietta married Manuel Aguirre, a Chilean officer at the Embassy in Rome, whom she met after the riotous first night of *Six Characters*. Seven months later she left Rome for Chile. She set sail from Genoa and her father saw her off. On his return to Rome he sent her a letter which reveals all the pitiful squalor into which he was plunged.[2]

My lovely little Lillinetta, I can't tell you how I felt in Genoa, in that icy wind, after your departure. Stefano and I rushed round the wind-swept town for over two hours, like a couple of lunatics. The hotel horrified me. . . .
(*In Rome, on my return, late at night*).
I was stricken with a worse anguish than ever when, after crossing Via Antonio Bosio with the frozen snow creaking under our feet, I turned down a muddy, almost country, lane lit by the moon. Suddenly under that moon, I heard your dear little voice say: 'Good night, Daddy!' as you used to when I looked out of my study window to watch you leave. And I was overcome by tears and almost collapsed. . . . Now I hear your voice saying 'Good night, Daddy!' every evening when I come home, and, every time, my eyes fill with tears and I feel a knot in my throat. . . . The house seems as empty to me as my life.

The next day, 12 February 1922, he wrote again:

Lillinetta mine, I received your first letter from Barcelona! I found it at five in the afternoon in the letter box as I was leaving the house. . . . But once I had reached the end of Via Antonio Bosio I had to return home so as not to be seen by the passers-by. I was crying like a child! Me! Yesterday evening, too, when Stefano and Fausto came home together just before dinner they found me seated at my desk in tears over your letter which I reread God knows how many times. I must take a grip on myself, but I can't manage it.

Lietta's distance was 'irreparable'. 'I am so afraid that this void will become ever deeper and swallow me up'; and, a month later: 'I am so full of anguish and bitterness because of the irreparable distance of my little Lilli that my satisfaction with the success of my work [*Henry IV*] was entirely superficial. It has not penetrated me at all, but I have re-turned sadder than ever to the black and miserable void of this unbear-able existence of mine.'

If his daughter could not come to him, Pirandello thought of going to Latin America to stay with her for some time. But the journey was

too expensive: 'A return ticket costs 20,000 lire! Where can I find it?'
he wrote on 10 July 1922. 'I have to work uninterruptedly every single
day since the obligations and expenses have increased rather than
diminished and increase still more from day to day. Amongst other
things, for over a month the expense of a nurse for grandfather every
night: twenty lire a night . . .'. He tried to get sent on a lecture tour to
South America: 'Three lectures on contemporary Italian culture to be
repeated in the various cities of Brazil, in Montevideo, Argentina, and
possibly even in Chile where I would come to spend at least a month
with you.' But the difficulties were superior to his capacity for intrigue,
'lacking in every practical sense' as he was. He wrote this to his
daughter, and added: 'Unfortunately you know what our country is
like! In France a writer with my reputation who suggested that the
Foreign Ministry send him to America to lecture on contemporary
French culture, art, literature, philosophy, criticism, would have had
every possible facility. I have not obtained anything! I have not even
managed to see Senator Contarini, the Head of the Ministry.' The
government granted him 'nothing! . . . and will never grant anyone anything.' He tried other channels but he did not manage to go to America.

When Lietta had her first child, Manolo, Pirandello wrote to her
affectionately: 'because you are no longer one but two in one.' He said
he wished 'every happiness' for her and for 'that other tiny, but at the
same time large part of herself, her son.' But he added at once that their
separation 'will not last long . . . and let us hope I can recover from it
for this short time. I have so often felt myself swallowed by the void
which has formed within and around me that I despair, and I spend
terrible moments sitting alone in the evening on the terrace of the
entrance hall, staring at the stars of the Bear just over my head.'

He learnt that his daughter's parturition had been 'very difficult' and,
not having received any letters for some time, he appealed again to
Cardinal Gasparri, who sent a telegram to the Papal Nuncio in Chile.
'And the Nuncio replied to Cardinal Gasparri two words only: "All
well". . . . You will have understood, Lillinetta of my heart, that not
the Pope but your father [che non il Papa, ma il papà tuo], who, in the
event, can make use of the Pope as of the King, wanted news of you,
was dying to obtain news of you . . . I am going mad with worry. . . .'

The following year, when Pirandello was at the peak of his success
and wrote: 'I have really reached the apex of my literary career,' he
still said that the only thing he really cared about was Lietta. 'How can
I resist this torment? . . . If you don't come back I shall die of despair!

What do I care about glory, profit, if you cannot enjoy it, children of mine, if I know you to be so far away and so upset. . . .'

In 1922, the year of *Henry IV*, three companies produced three plays by Pirandello: on 29 September Lamberto Picasso performed *At the Gate*, a one-act play written in 1916 and not originally intended for the stage. On this occasion the public seems to have lost interest in the theatre and hardly any seats were sold. Pirandello's other one-act play, *The Imbecile* (*L'imbecille*), performed at the Teatro Quirino on 10 October, did better, and *Naked* (*Vestire gli ignudi*), with Maria Melato playing the lead at the Quirino on 14 November was a great success.

The success and fame attained by Pirandello after *Six Characters* and *Henry IV* brought about an immediate renewal of interest on the part of his publishers. Bemporad decided to republish all his short stories under the new title *Short Stories for a Year*, so-called because Pirandello intended to write 365 of them. But he died before he could finish. The author wanted them to be contained in a single volume, but the publisher disagreed and finally decided on an edition in twenty-four volumes with fifteen stories each. Fourteen volumes were published in Pirandello's lifetime and the fifteenth appeared posthumously. Though Pirandello referred in the preface of the first volume to some *new* stories, he meant hitherto unpublished ones for he had no desire to write any more stories and was even reluctant to alter the ones he had already written.

Yet, until 1924, Pirandello remained at his desk and would have liked never to have to move. 'I must soon start writing again,' he wrote to Lietta on 11 June 1922. 'I can see no other solution to all the damage done me by life. The intervals of rest, between one chore and another, although they are never completely peaceful, produce this aggravation of all my sorrows and make my anguish deeper and more intense. . . .' 'The difficulties are many,' he wrote on 29 April 1922, 'the burdens on my shoulders are many, and I am so very tired of the work I have done . . . If I think about it I don't know how it is that I am still alive. But I am, and I work, and my heart is still that of a child, and so are my eyes. Who knows?' And then again on 7 March: 'The only reason that induces me to go on with the torment of my life is my longing for your happiness, children of mine. The more the fruits of my work grow, nurtured by all the tortures of my life, the better it is for you.'

He wanted never to move, never to move again. 'I am always reluctant not only to travel but even to go out of doors' (11 June 1922). 'I feel an almost insurmountable annoyance at the mere thought of having to go from here to Frascati or even of having to go out for one hour a day' (29 April 1922). When he was really successful he sent his daughter a packet of American newspapers which spoke of him in enthusiastic terms and a copy of the *New York Herald Tribune* 'with a large photograph of your old father.' 'I am doing all this for you,' he could not help adding, 'because, as far as I am concerned, I would just sit down on a stone in the middle of the road and never get up again, I'm so tired of everything. . . .'

Yet, little by little, success started to shake him. In his letters in 1923 one can perceive a crescendo of surprise and delight. 'The success abroad continues . . . the performances in New York are each more triumphant than the last' (5 January 1923). 'Invitations are raining in from all sides,' he wrote on 5 April, 'newspapers, reviews . . . salons . . . banquets, speeches! The Italian Ambassador! The Légion d'honneur!' Then on 28 April; 'I have come back from Paris not so much tired as troubled and moved by the really rapturous welcome given me, as you will see from some of the newspaper cuttings I am sending you and which I beg you to keep. It is the first and really exceptional case of an Italian writer. . .'. 'Even Spain has been conquered by my theatre,' he wrote on 8 December. 'Now only Latin America remains.'

By 1922 Pirandello's reputation had travelled beyond the frontiers of Italy. The spread of a work which arrives at the right moment is always very swift. Hitherto only a few short stories and *The Late Mattia Pascal* had been translated—the latter into German (in Austria) in 1905, and French (in Switzerland) in 1910. Purely by chance, the country that started the spread of Pirandello's work in the world was England, in other words the country that was later to be the least receptive to his plays. The Lord Chamberlain had already opposed the public performance of *Six Characters in Search of an Author* because he considered the work upsetting. And it was only owing to the great personal interest of George Bernard Shaw, an enthusiastic supporter of the play, that *Six Characters* was finally accepted by a private theatre club, the Stage Society, which performed it, with considerable success, at the Kingsway Theatre on 27 February 1922. Pirandello wrote to his daughter: '*Six Characters in Search of an Author* has had a colossal success in London. All the English newspapers have mentioned it, from *The Times* to the *Westminster Gazette*, the *Daily News*, etc., etc. A triumph. The tour abroad is off to a good start. And I hope for your sake that this will mean a great deal of money. . . .'

But after these initial successes, restricted mainly to intellectual circles, Pirandello did not have much recognition in England.[3] Between 1922 and 1933 his novels and a number of short stories were translated, but his plays were never popular. They were performed mainly in theatre clubs and at universities: by the Cambridge Amateur Dramatic Club, the Queen Mary College Dramatic Society, the Little Theatre in London; only very rarely were they staged in the commercial theatre. Yet, when Pirandello died, T. S. Eliot declared publicly that he had been a master of the theatre for everyone, even for the English.[4]

Pirandello's theatrical work accomplished its first successful world tour in 1922, moving from London to the Fulton Theatre in New York where *Six Characters* was performed in November, to the Kyvelis Theatre in Athens where, that same autumn, *The Pleasure of Honesty* was performed, and finally to Paris where Charles Dullin played Baldovino in the same play (on 21 December at the Théâtre de l'Atelier). But Paris remains the key to an understanding of Pirandello's fame in Europe between 1922 and 1924. On 10 July 1922 Pirandello wrote to his daughter Lietta that 'in October *Six Characters in Search of an Author* will be performed in Paris at the Théâtre des Champs-Elysées. The translator, Benjamin Crémieux, tells me that I will become *l'homme à la mode à Paris* this autumn and he begs me to be there for the welcome they will give me. . . .'

If Charles Dullin was the first person to perform Pirandello in Paris, it was George Pitoëff who, with deliberate audacity, launched *Six Characters*. In Paris and throughout the rest of the world Pirandello rose to fame by means of this masterpiece alone. His other plays, performed later, never had the same success: indeed, in many cases they bored and disappointed the audience.

George Pitoëff insisted on staging *Six Characters* in spite of the understandable fear of the director of the Comédie des Champs-Elysées, Jacques Hébertot,[5] who would willingly have avoided the experiment. Benjamin Crémieux had offered the play first to Copeau and then to the most important actors and impresarios in Paris, who had turned it down as unperformable. Finally he suggested it to Pitoëff who, together with his wife Ludmilla, read it in manuscript. He was deeply impressed by the play and immediately had a brilliant idea for the production. He wrote to Pirandello about it, and 'this,' he commented, 'was the beginning of a correspondence which enabled us to exchange views on the theatre that by no means always coincided.

Pirandello was immediately horrified by the plan for staging *Six Characters* which I suggested to him. He told me of his doubts, but I wouldn't listen to reason.'

Indeed, when Pirandello heard that the Six Characters were to be lowered on to the stage in a lift, it was too much for him. The play was striking enough as it was, without adding a further surprise, and the first night in Rome was still clear in his memory. Besides, he must have thought that the arrival of the characters from the sky in no way corresponded to his own basic idea of the play. His first meeting with the characters had been in a concrete, not a symbolic vision. They had appeared to him in the half-light of his study and had spoken to him, so it was perfectly logical that they should arrive through the theatre door and be announced by the doorman. The intellectual and abstract symbolism in which Pitoëff wanted to envelop the play was alien to him. So there was an exchange of numerous telegrams between Rome and Paris. Pirandello would wire: 'No, I don't want lifts', but Pitoëff would not admit defeat:

Every effort by Crémieux to reconcile our points of view was futile, and I started rehearsing the play. In view of my stubbornness Pirandello decided to come to Paris. We were in the middle of preparing the play and Monsieur Jacques Hébertot had some scruples about the effect Pirandello's opposition might have on the performance. So, as a good diplomat, he invited the Italian playwright to the dress rehearsal, but begged him to conceal his identity. He would thereby be able to assess the producer from his work. And we saw—or rather we didn't see—an author attend the birth of his play like an intruder, from the darkest corner of the theatre. You would have had to meet him to imagine the torture inflicted on him that afternoon! I myself only understood later what it was that literally pushed him on to the stage at the end of the performance. I can still see him holding out his hands to me and saying that that was exactly how he had conceived the play. . . .

As he was about to leave for Paris Pirandello had written to Lietta: 'The dress rehearsal of *Six Characters* will take place on the evening of the 10th at the Théâtre des Champs-Elysées, which is the most elegant and popular theatre in Paris. It will be a really exceptional event. I have heard about the awe with which the French are awaiting the performance and about all the various preparations for my arrival. . . . Invitations are raining down from all sides, newspapers, reviews like the *Revue des Deux Mondes* and the *Nouvelle Revue Francaise*, from La Société des Auteurs and the Société des Gens de Lettres, from salons,

Madame Aurel's famous one, etc., etc.' When he arrived in Paris he wrote again: 'I have been walking all day through this marvellous town . . . I write to you telegraphically because I am overburdened with visits, invitations to lunch and dinner, appointments, rehearsals, etc. . . .'

Pitoëff first performed the new work on 10 April 1923. All went well—except for a minor incident when the lift went wrong and stopped a yard above the ground. It was an awkward beginning but the audience did not notice. The next day Antoine wrote:[6] 'From the moment they enter the theatre the spectators are amazed. The curtain is raised. Nothing happens on the stage, illuminated only by rehearsal lights. Hasn't there been a mistake? . . .' When the time came the characters were lowered in a sash of green light; they were Ludmilla and George Pitoëff, Marie Kalff, Penay, and the two children. 'How astonishing it was,' wrote André Delhai, 'when first the feet, then the costumes, then the heads of those marionettes appeared, as immobile as dummies. It was even more astonishing when they got out of the lift at the end of the stage and suddenly started demanding from the manager of the troupe the right to perform the drama of their lives. . . .'

During the intervals, in the foyer, there were a few scuffles amongst the spectators and the work did not immediately attract a large audience. But the next day nearly all the Paris critics were enthusiastic. Lugné-Poe said that a new era of the theatre had been inaugurated. In *Le Temps* Brisson wrote: 'I saw Sardou's play and Pirandello's play on two consecutive evenings. I made a jump of fifty years—a jump that makes one think.' The performance did not play to a full house every evening, however, even if every member of fashionable and intellectual society went to see it. Yet Pirandello was satisfied: 'The two works [*Six Characters* and *The Pleasure of Honesty*] will be performed on countless occasions,' he wrote to his daughter. 'In the next season four or five plays of mine, *Henry IV*, *Right You Are (If You Think So)*, *Man, Beast and Virtue*, *Better Think Twice About It*, and *It's Nothing Serious* will be performed in Paris. Copeau of the Vieux Colombier and Gémier of the Odéon are already quarrelling about *Henry IV* and Dullin and Pitoëff about *Man, Beast and Virtue*. Requests for translations are arriving from all sides. Mortier wants to translate *The Life I Gave You* [*La vita che ti diedi*].'

After *Six Characters* other plays by Pirandello were performed in France, fourteen in all. The most famous productions were those of George Pitoëff and Charles Dullin. In 1924 the latter gave *Right You*

Are . . . (*Chacun sa vérité*) at the Théâtre de l'Atelier and acted the part of Laudisi, the sceptical and ironic character round whom the play revolves. The sets represented a long, dark cone and the characters appeared from the depths of it. When Dullin revived the play in 1937 for the Comédie Française he had a new idea. At the end of every act, at Laudisi's last line, 'And now, ladies and gentlemen, the truth has been discovered', all the lights were turned off and a projector lit up the actor's leering face, which appeared monstrous. Indeed, everywhere outside Italy Pirandello's works were performed with a succession of stage devices which suggested that the producers felt it necessary to add mystery to the plays, to integrate them into a different culture, and were unable to fit them into their own historical context. Even George Pitoëff, when he performed *Henry IV*, almost disguised himself as a marionette, making himself up heavily, and the sets shook as though there had been an earthquake each time Henry IV's solitude was threatened by alien visits, and settled down again each time he regained the refuge of his folly. He sometimes even had to hold up the walls which were about to fall on top of him.

Henry IV was performed at Monte Carlo on 3 January 1925, and then in Paris on 24 February.[7] Despite the box office returns the Paris critics were far from unanimous in accepting the work, though they praised the acting. Lugné-Poe sprung to Pirandello's defence for the second time and referred to the play as 'a work of superior quality which deserves to arouse our interest, or better still our passionate enthusiasm.' But Emil Mas called it 'another foreign work, confused, incoherent and boring . . .' and from then on the critics became increasingly hostile to Pirandello. They were irritated by the snobbery he aroused. After every performance he was attacked in the newspapers as a 'juggler', a 'virtuoso', a 'fraud'. Saint-Exupéry described him as 'a metaphysician of the porter's lodge'. The irony turned to venom after the first night of *Each in His Own Way* (*Ciascuno a suo modo*) (*Comme ci (ou comme ça*)) performed by Pitoëff on 3 May 1926. Lucien Descaves wrote in *L'Intransigeant*: 'Monsieur Pirandello, called to the stage with cries of irony, did indeed appear and greet the audience. That Monsieur Pirandello should have come from Italy to amuse himself at our expense is no reason why we should do the same to him. We must not forget that he is a foreigner and a guest. There is no need to insist: this will certainly be the last time.'

If Pirandello had to suffer the capricious humour of the Parisians he nevertheless retained a few faithful friends in Paris, like George Pitoëff.

According to Aniouta Pitoëff 'even if they met in the corridors of a theatre in Milan or Rome, in the Rue Henri Barbusse at the Crémieux' house or at a party, even if they had seen each other a day or two before, no sooner were they together than Pirandello and Pitoëff would embark on an interminable discussion. Pirandello would often come and sit at the long green table next to the children. When he liked someone Pirandello would be attached to his whole family, to his house. Ludmilla adored him.' But the Parisians did not find Pirandello sufficiently cool and elegant: 'he felt lost. He would not go anywhere without Marie-Anne Comnène (Crémieux' wife). He had to be dragged to parties, which he hated. He avoided the ones where there were over twelve guests. He disappointed people. They thought him lacking in wit, closed, provincial.' Indeed, from Paris he wrote to his daughter: 'I feel like a fish out of water. I want to be left in peace. . . .'

The time when Pirandello was given the Légion d'honneur[8] and when everyone pointed at him when he entered a café and said 'Pirandello, Pirandello!' was soon past. No longer, on his return from triumphant evenings in Brussels and Paris, could he tell Luigi Freddi, who was interviewing him for *L'Impero*,[9] that the President, Herriot, had come on to the stage after a performance of *Chacun sa vérité* to congratulate him; 'and the fact is all the more symptomatic since Herriot never goes to the theatre.' He would pass people modestly and shyly, smiling under his grey hat, recalled Adolfo Franci,[10] 'but he liked the manager or the doorman of the hotel to greet him on his arrival, calling him "Mon cher Maître".' He later became reluctant to return to France, even though he had to go there quite frequently. 'Paris does not understand me,' he said.[11] 'Paris has put a mask on my face.' And, when he settled abroad, after 1928, he preferred to stay in Berlin, where he spent more than two years. Only when Pirandello was awarded the Nobel Prize did the Parisians remember him; and they then fêted him more than the Italians.

Pirandello's hour of fame lasted in Italy until 1925–6. There was no other writer to compare with him, and, with the possible exceptions of Rosso di San Secondo and Roberto Bracco, Italian theatre of that period has little by which it is remembered. Even Pirandello's inferior works were superior to the average run of plays.

In 1923 the one-act *Man with a Flower in His Mouth* (*L'uomo dal fiore in bocca*) was given at Bragaglia's Teatro degli Indipendenti on 21 February and Pirandello collaborated in the production. *The House with the Column* (*L'altro figlio*) was performed by the Compagnia

Niccoli in the autumn at the Teatro Nazionale and, on 12 October *The Life I Gave You* was performed at the Quirino with Alda Borelli playing the lead. Pirandello was particularly fond of this play. In it he presented his romantic theory that the memory of the dead is stronger than death itself, and he said he even preferred the play to *Six Characters*.[12] Eleonora Duse had never acted in any of his plays and he wanted her to act in this one. He had her in mind when he wrote it. On 5 January he wrote to his daughter: 'I am working on the new tragedy *The Life I Gave You* which will be taken on tour by Eleonora Duse. I hope to have it ready by the 25th of this month.' But on 28 April Duse was still not ready. 'Duse, who is ill, has asked me to wait until October for the performance of *The Life I Gave You* which she is enthusiastic about. If I leave she will produce it and I will hear about it in America.' Even after Alda Borelli's performance Pirandello showed that he still wanted Eleonora Duse to act in it, and indeed, on the deck of the *Duilio*, when he was leaving for America, Pirandello told a journalist:[13] 'I would like to give *The Life I Gave You*, so well performed by Alda Borelli, to Duse whom I hope to see in New York.' But then for religious reasons (as Stefano Pirandello says), for moral reasons (as Silvio D'Amico suggests),[14] or merely for reasons of health, Eleonora Duse retracted and never acted in a play by Pirandello.

In America *Six Characters in Search of an Author* had had a great success. In January Pirandello had written to Lietta: 'There have been over seventy performances and they will go on for months and months. The impresario hired an even larger theatre because of the huge audiences. The newspapers are ecstatic. They say that Pirandello is very popular in New York, and other works will soon be performed in other theatres, *Henry IV*, *Right You Are . . .*, *As Before, Better than Before*, *It's Nothing Serious*. The first volume of the plays published by Dutton is a best-seller: they sold 500 copies in a week. The edition is splendid. *The Late Mattia Pascal* is coming out in the same format. . . .'

The Fulton Theatre, where *Six Characters* appeared in 1923, started a 'Pirandello season' and changed its name, as long as the season lasted, to 'Pirandello's Theatre'. Pirandello's departure for America was preceded by a publicity campaign. The chain of theatres belonging to the former actor, Savage, the Foreign Press Service directed by Arthur Livingston, Pirandello's translator, and Dutton the publishers, all had a financial interest in the success of Pirandello's plays. The main actor of the company, Arnold Korff (Henry IV), came to Italy on purpose to meet the playwright.

'All the newspapers have made much of this extraordinary event which has never happened before to a foreign playwright,' Pirandello wrote to his daughter. 'Even the French talk of it enviously.' He gave an interview to *Il Corriere della Sera* on 17 October and another to *L'Idea Nazionale* on 23 October, immediately after a meeting with Mussolini (see below p. 146). 'I told the Prime Minister,' he said, 'how my American season would go. It has been organized by the actor Savage who has now retired from the stage and owns three theatres. At one of these, the Princes Theatre, the first performances will be given before a select audience. The most successful plays will then be performed in the largest theatre which also belongs to Savage. . . .'

Pirandello left for the States in December 1923. The performances in New York were launched successfully on 1 October and went on until the beginning of 1924. The plays new to the Americans were *As Before, Better than Before* with the unPirandello-like title *Florian's Wife* and *Henry IV (The Living Mask)*. The welcome was truly American. The League of Vespers gave a banquet for him attended, Pirandello said on his return, 'by six hundred people, including some eminent personalities and Davis, who presented me with a medal coined in my honour.'[15]

The Americans continued to like him. Henry Ford thought he was a great 'popular' dramatist. It is strange how Pirandello managed to satisfy the tastes and interests of men who followed the most diverse ideologies—capitalists, democrats, fascists, some Catholics, and even Bolsheviks. 'The communist academy of Moscow,' Tomaso Napolitano was to write in *Quadrivio* on 18 November 1934, 'has published in a very fine edition the best part of Pirandello's theatrical production, and the Communist Party has favoured the spread of his works. . . . The case of Pirandello is unique and, one would have thought, impossible, for here is a member of the fascist Italian Academy honoured in Soviet Russia as the courageous promoter in a bourgeois country of the moral values of a new antibourgeois and anticapitalist society which has been identified with the classless society of the proletariat.'

Pirandello's work was a machine of relativism which always worked, whatever the point of view of the spectator. Henry Ford had apparently said (or so Croce asserted in his essay on Pirandello): 'I don't know much about literature, but I do know that he's an excellent business proposition. His works can suit a large public. Pirandello is a man of the people, or at least that is what I think. He is not for the intellectuals, which is why I have decided to finance his American tour. I want to prove that one can earn millions with him.' But nothing came of Ford's bet. Pirandello was probably not such a good business proposition after all.

When he returned to Italy Pirandello replied to the journalist who asked him what he thought of the Americans:[16] 'I shall tell you very sincerely: the life of the Americans is usually lacking in spirituality; they hardly ever have a sense of politics. All the American vitality is resolved in a vast automatism which, when carried to excess, ends by destroying itself. . . .' And, a month after this declaration, he told another journalist:[17] 'America did not fill me with enthusiasm. And I told the Americans so. I don't like mechanical progress. It adds nothing to life. It ought to enrich it, instead it impoverishes it. . . .' In other words he had found in America a confirmation of the intuition he had expressed eight years earlier in *Shoot* concerning the alienation brought about by a machine civilization. And in *Shoot* Pirandello had denounced the prevaricating demon of humanity hidden in the machine. If the old domestic mirror had been enough to deprive the human presence of reality in his eyes, he accepted in his novel the far more stimulating provocation of the machine and revealed its social danger. Of course, Pirandello was born well before the motor car, just as he was born before the electric light, the cinema, and the radio, and he had difficulty in adapting himself to them.

Yet, barely four years after his trip to America, when he was under the influence of Adriano Tilgher and was about to make a further journey to the United States, he revised his views. In an article which appeared in *Il Corriere della Sera* on 16 June 1929, he wrote: 'Everyone who has heard me talk of my travels knows how much I admired America and how much I liked the Americans. What interested me most in America was the birth of new forms of life. . . . To see them being born is an incomparable intellectual joy. In Europe it is the dead who go on recreating life. . . . In America life belongs to the living. . . .'

America did indeed make a strong impression on him. It assumed in his memory a fantastic dimension. It became a wholly symbolic place with a Kafka-like quality. In the last years of his life he wrote three short stories with an American subject, 'A Challenge' ('Una sfida'), 'The Nail' ('Il chiodo'), and 'Tortoises . . . For Luck' ('La tartaruga'), in which a new atmosphere prevails in a falsely rational, empty, absurd, but still tangible, space. The gestures performed by the characters are meaningless. The solitary protagonists, victims of evil or furnished with the weapons of evil, are examples of protest and of innocent rebellion.

In January 1924 Pirandello went to Spain where *Cap and Bells* had
been performed at the Catalá Romeo theatre in Barcelona in November
'with great success', as he told his daughter. 'All the papers are enthusiastic: they say that the arrival of my kind of theatre on the Spanish
stage is a landmark. . . .' In Barcelona, too, he held one of his lecture-
dialogues with the audience. In April he was in Sicily for the performance of some of his works at the Teatro Bellini, and for the first time he
took a play to Agrigento, *Right You Are*. . . . The journalist who interviewed him quoted his words in the *Giornale di Sicilia* on 10 April
1924: 'I have not been to Palermo since 1912. . . . You can imagine how
anxious I was to see my native Sicily again. . . . At that time my theatre
had not come to life. What's more, I didn't think it would ever come
to life.'

In May, in Milan, *Each in His Own Way* was performed by the
Compagnia Niccodemi with Vera Vergani and Luigi Cimara.[18] On the
first night, wrote the gossip columnist of *L'Ambrosiana*, 'the auditorium was full of the most elegant and aristocratic people in Milan, at
first all agog, at the end muttering comments.' The critics were divided.
The text of the play had been harshly criticized before it appeared and
Pirandello went as far as to write, in the form of a letter to *Il Corriere
della Sera*, a reply to Domenico Lanza's attack in *La Gazzetta del
Popolo*. Pirandello's reply was attacked in its turn by an anonymous
critic in the socialist paper *Il Secolo*. On the whole, however, the critics
were favourable and the play was a success.

It was about this time that the relationship between Pirandello and
the critic Adriano Tilgher reached a point of crisis. Tilgher meant a
great deal to the writer. He dominated him like an evil genius, and his
presence in Pirandello's life and work since 1922 was decisive. To start
with, there was a chronological coincidence between the drying up of
the live springs of the dramatist after the creative outburst of *Six
Characters* and *Henry IV*, and the injection of critical and intellectual
dynamism by Tilgher. Pirandello adapted himself to Tilgher's formula
in order to make up for a lack of inspiration. But he was still to write
more than one work which was all his own and freely inspired—such
as *Tonight We Improvise* (*Questa sera si recita a soggetto*) and all the
new short stories which owe nothing to Tilgher, the last of which
surpass Pirandello himself. But apart from these exceptions the personality of the prestigious Neapolitan critic was clearly reflected in the
technical and cerebral elaboration of Pirandello's work.

Adriano Tilgher was an authoritative and militant critic of literature and the theatre. He followed, not without eclecticism, Simmel's theories on relativism. And, with his integral anti-historicism, opposed both to Croce and Gentile, he proved the most suitable man of culture in Italy to plumb the depths of Pirandello's work for philosophical significance.

Pirandello had written his novels, his stories, and nearly all his plays without a conscious philosophical scheme, but inevitably they reflect his rather rickety hypotheses on relativism, and his scepticism. Pirandello himself described this process:[19] 'My works are born from live images which are the perennial source of art, but these images pass through a veil of concepts which have taken hold of me. My works of art are never concepts trying to express themselves through images. On the contrary. They *are* images, often very vivid images of life, which, fostered by the labours of my mind, assume universal significance quite on their own, through the formal unity of art.'

Tilgher tried to organize this mental labour, transferring it from the confused psychological sphere to a more theoretic sphere, and simplifying it according to ideas gleaned from Schopenhauer, Bergson, Dilthey, and Simmel. Tilgher's interpretative formula is best expressed in his own words:[20] 'The philosophy implicit in Pirandello's art revolved round the fundamental dualism of Life and Form: Life, perpetually mobile and fluid, which cannot help developing into a form, although it deeply resents all form; and Form which determines Life, by giving it rigid and precise borders, and freezes it, suppressing its restless motion.'

Elsewhere Tilgher continues his explanation of Pirandello's relativism:

His thought is not abstract and merely theoretic, it is formed with passion, is impregnated by it. . . . And since, of the two rival elements, Life and Form, it is not Form that creates Life but Life that creates the Form in which it can flow or stagnate, the reason for Pirandello's relativism becomes clear. Pirandello is a relativist. He denies the existence of objective reality and truth, and maintains that for each one of us Being and Appearing are identical, that there is no such thing as knowledge but only opinions (*Right You Are (If You Think So)*) and that every opinion is as good as any other (*Each in His Own Way*) precisely because, for him, all our affirmations and theories, laws and norms, are nothing but ephemeral forms within which life is momentarily trapped and which are ultimately devoid of truth and consistency.

The first edition of Adriano Tilgher's *Studies in Contemporary Theatre* (*Studi sul teatro contemporaneo*) appeared in 1922. When first Tilgher read Pirandello's work he found nothing of interest in it. Consequently he had bitterly attacked *Better Think Twice About It*. But later, after *Right You Are . . ., Just As It Should Be*, and *As Before, Better than Before*, Tilgher, who was then contributing to a number of papers, *La Stampa*, *La Rassegna Italiana* and *Il Tempo*, started to write of Pirandello first with interest and then with enthusiasm. And when *Six Characters in Search of an Author* appeared in 1921 Tilgher made a careful analysis of the play, and earned the playwright's gratitude. On 29 August Pirandello wrote to him, referring to the appendix of the latest edition of *The Late Mattia Pascal*: 'Believe what I say at the beginning of the piece about you for it is the truth: in other words, dear Tilgher, I am very grateful to you.' In the same letter he urged the critic, who had announced a forthcoming essay on his plays, to wait 'before writing about me' for the appearance of *One, None and a Hundred Thousand*. 'It contains a great many of the things I have read recently in those essays of yours which I so much admire.'

Pirandello was probably aware that Tilgher was trying to stake out his own personal territory and that his interpretations were highly tendentious. At almost the same time he told an interviewer:[21] 'These problems were mine alone, they came spontaneously out of my mind; they imposed themselves naturally on my thoughts. Only after my first plays appeared was I told that they were problems of the times, that others, like myself, were tortured by them. . . .' Soon the war of attributions would break out: what did Pirandello owe to Tilgher? Pirandello tried to protect himself. But when the long essay about him in *Studies in Contemporary Theatre* appeared, the playwright was dazzled by it and was swept away by enthusiasm for the critic. Amongst other things Tilgher had revised his former opinion of *Better Think Twice About It* and now defined it as an 'extraordinary work' full of 'a bitter, open, lucidly logical violence.'

Even if he did not explicitly say so, it is evident that Pirandello saw *clearly* (too clearly) into his own work for the first time as a result of Tilgher's interpretation, and he was immensely grateful. In April 1923 Pirandello was delighted that Tilgher should have been invited to Paris for the first night of *Six Characters*[22] and, on 20 June, he wrote: 'My dear Tilgher, you cannot imagine how pleased I am with the translation into French of your admirable study of me and my work. I would have no difficulty in declaring publicly all the gratitude I owe you for the incalculable and unforgettable good you have done me, for having explained so perfectly to the public and the critics who opposed me in every way not only the essence and the character of my theatre but also the endless travails of my mind. . . .' The critic, however, retained a mental reservation which was still ill-defined but which was aggravated by the embitterments of his own life. Tilgher stated in 1940, a year before he died, that the formula 'of form and life' *did not appear in any of Pirandello's works before my essay* (1922) and I alone coined it in these terms. Of course I did not produce it out of nothing. If I expressed it in these terms, adapting Georg Simmel's terminology to the world of Pirandello, it was because I thought (and still think) that that was the best way to characterize synthetically and perceptively the heart of the Pirandellian world. I found an underlying connection in scattered phrases of Pirandello but the formula is mine and not Pirandello's. . . . Yet Pirandello adapted this formula and made it his.'[23]

In fact Pirandello had been using the formula (though he had not expressed it in such precise terms) for many years, not only in literary texts[24] but also in other writings. In his letter to his son Stefano, dated 20 February 1917, he wrote: 'There are within you many possibilities of being. It cannot be easy to give yourself a form. Unfortunately you will have to adapt yourself to one which does not immediately entail the sacrifice of all the other possibilities. . . .' After Tilgher's intervention, however, the formula often turned into a rigid pattern in Pirandello's work and Pirandello referred to his plays all too frequently in lectures, interviews, and articles with words borrowed straight from Tilgher. As late as 1934, to Mario Missiroli who was interviewing him for *L'Illustrazione Italiana*,[25] he said: 'When I speak of a theatre suited to the spirit of our time I mean a theatre which is aware of the irreconcilable antithesis between life and form, so clear to contemporary thought. Life should obey two opposing laws: that of moving and that of persisting in some form. If it always moved it would never consist of anything; if it always persisted in some form it would never move. . . .' Pirandello never mastered the philosophical jargon and was always a little amateurish, empirical, and clumsy when explaining his thought. Later this philosophy became a fixed means of interpreting reality, from the political reality of fascism to the sociological reality of America, from the reality of family life to that of his private feelings for Marta Abba.

In 1922 and 1923 Pirandello felt great friendship for Tilgher and, whenever he could, he helped him, for example he helped to get *Studies*

in Contemporary Theatre published in France. But in 1924 the relationship changed. Tilgher had moved from *Il Tempo*, which had closed
down, to *Il Mondo* where he courageously joined Giovanni Amendola
whose anti-fascist views he had long shared. When, after the murder of
Matteotti, Pirandello applied to join the fascist party and was violently
attacked by Amendola, Tilgher thought it his duty to take Amendola's
side, even if he tried to avoid making any public declarations against
Pirandello who was still his friend.

It was Amendola who made the friendship difficult to sustain and
probably ruined it completely. In an article in his paper he wrote that
Pirandello's rise to fame was due solely to Adriano Tilgher who had
created him and acted as his 'most generous interpreter'. Many other
journalists now insinuated the same thing, or accused Pirandello outright of being influenced by the critic. From then on, consciously or
unconsciously, Pirandello's self-defence began and, until his death, the
playwright constantly repeated that he had never depended on anyone
for anything. Tilgher hit back in his turn. 'It would have been much
better,' he wrote many years later,[26] 'if Pirandello had never read my
essay. It is never good for a writer to be too conscious of his inner
world, and my essay fixed Pirandello's world in such clear and well-
defined terms that Pirandello must have felt imprisoned in it, hence his
protests that he was an artist and not a philosopher . . . and hence his
attempts to escape. But the more he tried to escape from the critical
pigeon-holes into which I had placed him the more he shut himself into
them.'

Tilgher went too far. Pirandello immediately regretted the incident
—the implicit attack on Tilgher in Interlandi's paper *L'Impero* (see
below, p. 155)—which had caused their quarrel and, on the first occasion that presented itself, a meeting with Tilgher's wife, he said so.
Tilgher then wrote him a letter[27] to which Pirandello replied:[28]

Dear and illustrious friend, your loyal and affectionate letter filled me
with joy and I am most grateful to my fortunate encounter with your
noble-minded wife who enabled us to perceive the misunderstanding
which so many people have treacherously endeavoured to aggravate.
I have no need to come closer to you again since, in my mind, I have
never really left you. Silvio D'Amico can vouch for this. I remember
one evening, as we were leaving the house of Fausto Maria Martini, as
if you foresaw what was going to happen, you advised me always to
stay close to you since too many people would enjoy it if we quarrelled
and broke with each other, just as too many feared and envied our

friendship. Well, my dear Tilgher, although the tempestuous vicissitudes of Italian political life have kept us apart since that evening, I repeat that in my mind I never left you, nor did I feel any less gratitude for you or esteem for your great intelligence and your exemplary character. . . .

At this point, however, Pirandello took advantage of the affectionate tone of the letter to put across some fascist propaganda and he was inept enough to say: 'A man like you, my dear Tilgher, cannot and must not be excluded from national life. You who understand things so clearly cannot fail to understand the historical necessity by which Italy has been led to the present state of affairs. . . . There is no point in my adding that I do and will do all I can for you. . . .'

We do not know to what extent such confident advice may have exasperated Tilgher who, precisely because of the advent of fascism, had seen himself unjustly 'excluded from national life' at exactly the moment when he had attained an enviable position of authority. What is certain is that Pirandello now became a target for his polemics, and that he was not moved by Pirandello's further efforts, in 1924 and 1925, to ask his advice humbly and in the name of his 'unaltered affection and esteem'. Pirandello asked him about the repertory to be adopted in his Arts Theatre which was about to be inaugurated[29] and begged him to collaborate in the foundation of a drama school to be attached to his theatre.[30] When Pirandello's allegory about Life and Form, *Diana and Tuda* (that creature of Tilgher's and Pirandello's), was published by Bemporad in 1926 Tilgher no longer wanted to support it. He attacked it in *L'Italia che scrive* in March 1927 and still more venomously in *Humor* of 1 June 1927.

After the attack in *Humor* there could obviously be no question of friendship between the two men. They went their separate ways and Tilgher retained a feeling of considerable bitterness. In 1927 he publicly stated that he had played an important part in Pirandello's destiny as a writer and set himself up as a wise amender of Pirandello's recent errors. He attacked *The Wives' Friend* (*L'amica delle mogli*), a play which appeared in 1927, and *The New Colony* in 1928,[31] after which he ceased to write about Pirandello's plays.

However, Tilgher ended up by taking Pirandello's advice about understanding 'the historical necessity by which Italy has been led to the present state of affairs', whether he liked it or not. On 1 April 1928 *La Stampa* published his laudatory words about Mussolini. 'With Mussolini romanticism has come to power. He is now trying to construct the definite, precise, classical form in which the romantic soul will finally be able to rest in tranquillity. . . .' But Tilgher was never reconciled with fascism and according to Leonardo Sciascia there were more policemen than friends at his funeral in 1941.[32]

At that period of his life, Pirandello liked to think of himself as the inventor of a sophisticated truth. According to Vitaliano Brancati, his so-called 'diabolism' was an ingenuous dissimilation. 'It is enough to look at a photograph of him,' wrote Brancati,[33] 'to realize how attached he was to his diabolical expression. Rarely was a picture taken without his raising an eyebrow and adopting a deliberately infernal look. In some photographs we see Pirandello sitting at a typewriter, his hair on end, writing something dictated to him by a Pirandello who is standing up and raising his finger menacingly. . . .' Other people felt seriously troubled by Pirandello's expression, since they felt that it displayed an introverted and visionary quality which could not be fully defined. It was impossible to spend any length of time with him without feeling slightly awkward. Arnaldo Frateili, referring to Pirandello before his success, recalled:[34] 'As one sat with him . . . it was impossible to overcome a certain sense of unease, the sort of feeling one might have standing in an excessively bright light next to a whirling machine which might sweep us away.' And André Rousseau observed that 'his eyes were not only lively, but penetrating, with an expression of almost unbearable sharpness. . . .'[35]

Pirandello's daughter Lietta remembers him as[36]

an incandescent forge. It was as though he had shut within himself a whole secret world which was yearning to be revealed. His brain never stopped working. He was always looking 'beyond', as though to find a deeper reality beyond the transience of appearances. He discussed his characters with us as though they were real people, more real than living people. He read us everything he wrote, as he wrote it, to me, my brothers, our closest friends who came to the house, and his imagination was so fertile, his talent so colossal that we were sometimes deeply troubled, almost dazed by it. . . .'

Pirandello was both flattered by these diabolical attributions and diffident about them. In 1922 he told a journalist:[37] 'What everybody sees is only the negative side of my thought: I appear to be a destructive devil who removes the ground from under people's feet. But surely it's the other way round? Do I not advise people where to put their feet

when I am about to pull the ground away?' And in the same interview
he lamented the fact that the public distrusted him: 'My dealings with
the public have now become somewhat difficult. ... The public is
prepared to surrender itself to other writers, and virtually asks: "De-
lude me!" But with me it reacts differently. It remains diffident, almost
on the defensive. I say a word ... book, for instance. ... And the
public immediately thinks: "You're not hoodwinking us ... you say
'book', but who knows what you really mean!"'

Allusiveness, of course, is another aspect of Pirandello's art, but very
few contemporaries were in a position to notice the countless facets of
the man and the work. One of the most illuminating testimonies is that
of T. S. Eliot. 'Pirandello,' he wrote,[38] 'is a dramatist to whom all
dramatists of my own and future generations will owe a debt of gratitude. He has taught us something about our own problems and has
pointed to the direction in which we can seek a solution to them.'

FASCISM

The years in which Pirandello wrote *Six Characters in Search of an Author* and *Henry IV* were the years of the post-war political crisis and the triumph of fascism. The anti-democratic rebellion of the blue-shirted nationalists, of d'Annunzio's followers, of all the black-shirted stragglers whom Mussolini had assembled in the *Fasci di combattimento* and then in the Fascist Party must surely have appealed to the playwright's more anarchistic and destructive side.

In its first period fascism appeared to be a purely irrational, senseless, almost nihilistic movement, even if it was put to a calculated use by the interested parties. In the movement's overall programme there were elements of republicanism, anti-clericalism and even of anti-militarism, all points which Pirandello, republican, anti-clerical and, in peacetime, anti-militarist, approved fully. But there was also that unconscious love of destruction which Nino Valeri, the great historian of fascism, sensed in the legionaries of Fiume:[1]

A feverish hatred, amongst the most determined of them, for the hard, grey life of every day, a contempt for the established order, a lack of interest in past and future, contempt for morality, for savings, for the family, for ancestors, for religion, monarchy, and the republic; a nihilistic aspiration to put a fine end to this useless and stupid life in a sort of heroic orgy. These were the feelings which lay buried in the hearts of many middle-class Italians but which were normally repressed and condemned in the name of respectability. The wild explosion of these feelings was perhaps the most important characteristic of the legionaries who accompanied d'Annunzio to Fiume in 1919 and the sign of an intrinsically revolutionary political situation.

Pirandello was probably attracted by this implicit, and sometimes even explicit, will for destruction and by the violently anti-social, anti-institutional aspect of the punitive expeditions. But he was fascinated by the repeated declarations of Mussolini who claimed that the doctrine of the fascists was action and that preconceived organic ideology was to be rejected. This appealed to Pirandello; but, during these years of intense theatrical productivity and misery at home he was only vaguely committed to the movement. He no doubt approved of what he read in Mussolini's paper *Il Popolo d'Italia* and in *L'Idea Nazionale*, the paper of the nationalists, who, under the auspices of Enrico Corradini, were to ally themselves formally with the fascists in 1922. He was later to say on several occasions that he had admired Mussolini for some time. Moreover, he shared the ideas of *Il Corriere della Sera* to which he contributed regularly and which viewed the fascist movement with a certain amount of sympathy. But he was still far from feeling the need to commit himself outright.

Of this there is proof enough. For example, in a letter to his daughter Lietta dated 29 October 1922, written the day after the march on Rome, he was apparently not aware of the event, at least he did not accord any importance to it. In the letter he complained of continuous sciatica, of the difficulties of producing *Naked*, but he did not refer to the last democratic prime minister, Facta, to the fact that there had almost been a state of siege, or to the fascists' presence in Rome. The march on Rome took place between two productions of Pirandello's plays, *The Imbecile* given at the Quirino on 10 October, and *Naked*, given at the same theatre on 14 November. Both plays, as well as later ones, serve to mark the immense distance between external events such as the development of fascism and the inner chamber in which Pirandello's creation took place.

Pirandello, who proclaimed himself an anti-democrat, was in fact one of the most democratic playwrights ever to have lived. In one sense his theatre is the hypostasis of democracy. In his plays the laws of equality and of freedom of expression are sovereign, and everyone has the possibility of holding a personal assembly. Pirandello had no taste for organized society but his work does show pleasure in the anarchistic extremes existing in a democratic structure. Each of his characters is entitled to stand up and proclaim his private opinions. In some of his plays Pirandello appears to be more the son of anti-dogmatic and democratic Protestantism than of a Catholic society accustomed for centuries to submit passively to integralist and authoritarian regimes. His characters often appear to be part of a Protestant sect, strictly moralizing preachers defending themselves against a Catholic siege. But Pirandello was as Catholic as he was Protestant, as anarchist as he was moderate, and finally he became fascist too.

Mussolini received Pirandello for the first time at Palazzo Chigi on 22 October 1923. We do not know who arranged the meeting, but Pirandello had a number of friends who could have served as intermediaries, from the journalist Telesio Interlandi to the critic Ugo Ojetti. Mussolini himself, who had heard about the famous playwright's sympathy for fascism, must have wanted to effect a personal meeting with a man whose works had been performed in London, New York, Athens, Paris, Cracow, and Prague, were about to be performed in Amsterdam, Warsaw, and Barcelona, and who had just been invited to New York. He must have wanted to attract him, for it was worth his while keeping this new-born national glory on his side. And indeed, he does appear to have attracted Pirandello. So flattered was Pirandello at being summoned almost officially to the Foreign Ministry like an Ambassador by the Head of State that he suddenly seemed ready to shed his political reserve and become a faithful follower of Mussolini.

Six days later, in *L'Idea Nazionale* of 28 October 1923, a number devoted to the first anniversary of the march on Rome, there appeared an enthusiastic homage by Pirandello to Mussolini. The Duce was transformed by Pirandello's words into a somewhat 'Pirandellian' character, along the lines of Tilgher's recent scheme. Pirandello's signature appeared together with those of a number of nationalists who sympathized with the new regime, Federzoni, Corradini, Gentile, Alfredo Rocco, Francesco Coppola, and several others, though his article, entitled 'Created life', was slightly eccentric when compared with the other contributions:

Mussolini can receive only blessings from somebody who has always felt the immanent tragedy of life which . . . requires a form, but senses death in every form it assumes. For, since life is subject to continual change and motion, it feels itself imprisoned by form: it rages and storms and finally escapes from it. Mussolini has shown that he is aware of this double and tragic law of movement and form, and hopes to conciliate the two. Form must not be a vain and empty idol. It must receive life, pulsating and quivering, so that it should be for ever recreated. . . . The revolutionary movement inaugurated by Mussolini with the march on Rome and all the methods of his new government seem to me to be, in politics, the necessary realization of just this conception of life.

Pirandello now appeared to be open to the imposition of tighter social controls and he does not seem to have been displeased by the climate of 'normalization'. He agreed with the statement by Luigi Federzoni in the same number of *L'Idea Nazionale*: 'Social peace, public security. . . . The march on Rome's main accomplishment was to confirm the victory of national order over subversive attempts, a victory which found its practical confirmation in the cessation of internal conflicts, the disappearance of the epidemic of strikes, the restored continuity of public services, and the renewed prestige of the Army and the Navy....'

This was at the end of 1923. Success and a greater measure of confidence in his own work had removed Pirandello from his previous anarchistic solitude. That is to say, success had removed him from the most probable cause of his sympathy for the fascists of the immediate post-war years. By following the evolution of fascism he came closer to acquiring a taste for bourgeois order even if he still kept his distance from it. He had more sympathy, too, for the superficial rhetoric which had passed from the anti-democratic nationalists to the demagogic fascists, who, in that first government of Mussolini's, were influenced by the ideology of the conservative right wing. The coalition of moderate fascists with Salandra's liberal nationalists, with elements of the Catholic *Partito Popolare*, and with the nationalists, including such symbolically patriotic personalities as General Diaz and Admiral Thaon de Revel, signified for many people—and also for Pirandello—a restoration of the myths of the Risorgimento and the authority of the state.

For the first time Pirandello yielded to vanity. To O.V. (Orio Vergani?) who interviewed him immediately after the meeting in Palazzo Chigi for *L'Idea Nazionale* of 23 October 1923, he said with some complacency: 'Before I left, the Honourable Mussolini cordially wished me luck, on his behalf and on the government's, for my theatrical tour in America, which will indeed be an ordeal. And he told me he would be very glad to demonstrate the satisfaction of the government— "which is a new government, as you know," he added—in my work as a writer by offering me a high dignity in the order of Santi Maurizio e Lazzaro. . . .'

He was also pleased about Mussolini's personal opinion of him and his work. 'The Prime Minister,' he told O.V., 'whom I had never met before today, immediately informed me of his great liking for me and for my plays. Then he added that he would tell me briefly, as a layman, what he thought of some of my works—of those which he had seen recently. My finest work, the one he likes most, is *Six Characters in Search of an Author* and then *Henry IV*. He told me that he was moved by the idea behind *The Life I Gave You*, but that he did not like *Naked*. He then asked me when I was leaving for the United States. . . . He wanted to know which of my plays were being performed abroad and particularly in northern Europe and Scandinavia. I told him that by the winter *Six Characters in Search of an Author* will be performed in Sweden, Norway, and Finland. He asked me if anything of mine had been performed in Russia. . . .'

In these interviews Pirandello displayed a certain ingenuous pleasure —the pleasure of the man who has made it. From his solitary walks in Via Nomentana, from his time spent at the Magistero and in the company of a few friends, from his sedentary and ill-remunerated work, he suddenly and quite unexpectedly reached an exceptional level of fame. He was lauded to the skies in Paris, invited to America, summoned by the Head of State. Neither his self-control nor his vanity could resist, and he yielded. The political progress of Mussolini and fascism coincided with his own success and fame. It was as though fortune had decided to bless and to exalt these two incongruous figures at the same moment. For the fascists such an idea was a convenient pretext for a form of double adulation. Both at the time and many years later they were to resort to this extraordinary conjunction between two 'national geniuses'. In *L'Impero* of 19 September 1924, for example, Telesio Interlandi wrote: 'Here are two exquisite interpreters of the troubles of our times, two indomitable navigators of the stormy tide of life, Mussolini and Pirandello, who are taking each other by the hand.' And when Pirandello died Carlo Ravasio wrote:[2] 'Pirandello, a national genius, felt that above the facts and mishaps of everyday life, that other genius, Mussolini, was pressing forward with history.' The comparison with Pirandello did not bother Mussolini, for it served to enhance his own personality.

As for Pirandello, he concluded the interview with the reporter from *L'Idea Nazionale* with the words: 'I have always had the greatest admiration for Mussolini and I think I am one of the few people capable of understanding the beauty of his continuous creation of reality: an Italian and fascist reality which does not submit itself to anyone else's reality. Mussolini is one of the few people who know that reality only exists in man's power to create it, and that one creates it only through the activity of the mind.' However, the plays he wrote at the time, *The Life I Gave You* and *Each in His Own Way*, do not display the same confidence.

Pirandello spent the end of 1923 in America, in New York, where some of his plays were being performed. When he returned his political views were unchanged. Indeed, contact with American society had strengthened his aristocratic (in this case fascist) concept of political life. On 8 May 1924, in the course of an interesting interview with Giuseppe Villaroel for *Il Giornale d'Italia*, he began by saying shamelessly: 'I am apolitical. I simply feel like a man on earth, and as such very simple and humble. If you like, I could even add "chaste".' But then he went on to specify his political ideas. 'The basic error on which the whole of American life is based is, in my opinion, the democratic concept of life. I am anti-democratic *par excellence*. The masses need someone to form them. Their needs and aspirations do not go beyond practical necessities. Well-being for the sake of well-being, riches for the sake of riches, have no significance or value.' And here, out of pure chauvinism, he said something curiously senseless: 'Money seen in that light is no more than dirty paper. Here, however, it would serve another purpose and arouse other energies. In Italy wealth would have a spiritual value.'

It was Pirandello's Sicilian chauvinism which aroused his indignation over the behaviour of the great Belgian playwright Maurice Maeterlinck who had dared to speak ill of Sicily a few months earlier. On his return from America, in an interview given in Palermo with *Il Giornale di Sicilia* of 10 April 1924, Pirandello said: 'Monsieur Maeterlinck is an old boor. As a person he made a disastrous impression in America. Amongst other things he learnt off by heart a lecture in English which he delivered at a meeting of intellectuals without his listeners being able to understand a single word. He aroused general mirth and the most biting of comments. He has shown that he understands nothing of Sicily and that he has a tiny little mind which can be troubled deeply by a couple of snotty little ragamuffins.' In the same interview Pirandello recalled a banquet given in his honour in New York when he was asked about his views on 'the League of Nations in which the Americans believe blindly.' 'I gave all my most crushing opinions from a practical point of view,' he said, 'and though my words were like a cold shower they were listened to with great interest.'

During the interview with the *Giornale d'Italia* Pirandello expressed a further opinion of Mussolini.[3] 'I have the greatest esteem for him. He confers reality on things because he has a power of feeling and a lucidity of intelligence which are remarkable.' This was followed by a criticism: 'I would like him to be more consistent in the actions which he should and could perform,' but then he modified this criticism: 'Perhaps if I were in his position I too would see difficulties of which I am now unaware. Maybe these difficulties prevent him from carrying his ideals to their ultimate conclusion. Nevertheless he has the supreme merit of having established Italy's importance.'

With his political ingenuousness and his eagerness to solve all problems, Pirandello would have liked Mussolini to be less Machiavellian and inconsistent in his authoritarianism, and more brutal, speedy, and self-confident in his elimination of the democratic opposition. The only reservation he displayed in this period towards Mussolini was based on the Prime Minister's apparent respect for the opposition. Pirandello considered this to be a tactical error. But Mussolini thought it more opportune to proceed without alarming public opinion. He seemed to be gradually losing the sympathy of the liberals who had supported him hitherto. Even if the Chamber, elected in April 1924 with the new electoral law and in a climate of intimidation, was largely favourable to the fascist government, the opposition, who controlled forty per cent of the seats, showed more fight. The moral force of men like Matteotti and Amendola, and now of Nitti and Albertini, not to mention Salvemini, Gramsci, Gobetti, and others, was becoming increasingly felt. Then, on 10 June 1924, Giacomo Matteotti, the socialist deputy, was murdered by Mussolini's extremist followers.

Pirandello joined the Fascist Party as ostentatiously as he could. He did so at a moment when the fascists were frightened and demoralized, and he did so in order to oppose the anti-fascist reaction, to give proof of an exemplary loyalty and courage, and to give Mussolini a helping hand when he was in danger. Mussolini afterwards retained a feeling of gratitude towards Pirandello. He allowed him a measure of freedom to protest and he protected him from the hostility of other fascists.

The day after the crime the moral revulsion throughout the whole of Italy imperilled Mussolini. The fascists disappeared from the streets or hid the badge they had formerly flaunted in their buttonholes. The fascist militia itself was on the verge of being dispersed. Thirty or forty deputies, fascists and fascist sympathizers led by Raffaele Paolucci, were on the point of asking Mussolini to resign. Amendola was accompanied in triumph by the crowd from the Chamber of Deputies to the offices of *Il Mondo*. Francesco Saverio Nitti, the former Prime Minister, wrote to the king:

Now that the Chamber has been reduced to a miserable assembly of violent and ignorant men [the socialists had withdrawn from parliament], now that the king's function has been reduced to acknowledging the daily violation of the statute, Italy has become a prison. The constitution has been abolished. All the parties are against the government, all the most distinguished men, all the intellectuals, all the free thinkers. . . . Thousands of workers and peasants have been massacred, tortured, beaten up. . . . Most of the newspapers are against fascism and the fascist press has assembled the fugitives from all parties, the traitors of all causes. But the papers that defend fascism are supported by all the profiteers. . . .

To one of the most fanatic fascist papers, *L'Impero*, Pirandello gave a copy of the letter he wrote to Mussolini asking to join the Party. It was printed on 19 September 1924, and it caused a considerable stir. 'Your Excellency,' the letter ran, 'I feel that this is the most propitious moment for me to declare a loyalty which I have hitherto observed in silence. If Your Excellency finds me worthy to join the Partito Nazionale Fascista I will consider it the greatest honour to become one of your humblest and most obedient followers. With utter devotion.'

This time the tone of modesty towards Mussolini and of provocation towards everybody else was deliberate. Pirandello knew perfectly well that at that moment his gesture was of great importance. Indeed, he was later to say, in an interview with *Il Piccolo della Sera* of 21 October 1924, that his 'recent decision to join the party was taken in order to help fascism'. And to Telesio Interlandi, who went to his house the day after he joined to ask him the reason for his gesture, he replied 'with a single word: "Matteotti".'[4] Interlandi explained:

The obscene speculation over the corpse of the socialist deputy, the *industrialization* of that corpse which was carried to the most revolting extremes, the campaign of lies and falsification flourishing on that macabre terrain, the partially successful attempt to reduce fascism from a historical phenomenon to a phenomenon of political criminality, the clear perception of the terrible risk involved in abandoning the country to its poisoners; all this induced Pirandello to give a concrete form to what had always been an attitude of mind. Anti-rhetorical and opposed to all that is superfluous, he used as few words as possible—and words of the greatest humility—to make his faith known publicly. Nor must we overlook, amongst the reasons which determined Pirandello's decision to pronounce himself a fascist, the need to react publicly against the verbose and inconsistent political manifestations of certain men of letters. . . .

Pirandello's gesture was immediately exploited by the fascists. It was interpreted as it was intended to be interpreted. *L'Impero* states:

Pirandello's letter requesting to join the Partito Nazionale Fascista is an act of courage and faith. At a time when the Partito Nazionale Fascista is going through what we might call a 'crisis of courage', when a country, dynamic by definition, is marking time for one reason or another, Pirandello's letter assumes a significance which perhaps not even the fascists have understood. It is a stone thrown into a pool where the formerly rough fascist water seemed about to subside. For if Pirandello, a man of letters, a mind far removed from partisan rivalry, a man who attained world fame some time ago, sated with and perhaps almost intolerant of applause and honours, free of any sort of external pressure, if Pirandello, I repeat, has decided to join the most violently resisted party of today, there must be a reason—a reason which can illuminate many things. . . .

L'Impero's editorial on Pirandello's gesture comments:

If the most tortured mind of the present age, in his violent negation of any certainty, sees fascism as the only doctrine which can continuously create an ever new contingent reality, able to provide a great people with hope for a future of power, fascism must be an historical fact of capital importance.

Telesio Interlandi reported on his long conversation with Pirandello of 22 September.[5] 'We went to see Pirandello in his lonely house,' he wrote. 'Anyone who knows the great playwright knows that he is an anti-democrat by nature, a declared enemy of every ideology consisting of "eternal principles". We went to hear why he had requested to join the Fascist Party, an act which disconcerted the adversaries of fascism and especially those who talk of an incompatibility between fascism and intelligence. . . .' Interlandi's report is occasionally something of a parody with respect to the plays and ideas of Pirandello but it is not apocryphal: it is a faithful reproduction of the writer's words. Pirandello was later to sanction it. He only denied having made one of the statements imputed to him, and his denial was somewhat confused. Interlandi continued:

From this conversation we derived the conviction—obvious to anyone acquainted with Pirandello's thought—that the great playwright was the man most suited to understand and to value the activistic essence of fascism. Pirandello's sense of public life is substantially *fascist* (and was so even before fascism was defined) in so far as it denies the concepts of the absolute and affirms the vital necessity of the continuous creation of *illusion*, of relative realities. . . . Indeed, fascism denies the absolute standard of ideologies which were the relative realities and noble goals of yesterday. . . . Fascism affirms that the life of a people cannot freeze into a form which, because it is a *form*, can no longer be life, an impetuous, restless process of becoming. Fascism creates for itself, and imposes on those who are unable to create for themselves, a new reality towards which we must strive and which we must overtake as soon as we reach it. This implacable striving towards new forms, this process of becoming, is the life of people, is *Life*. And what adversaries and weak minds call *normalization* is nothing other than *Death*, the submission to a tomb from which it would be impossible to escape. In this sense Pirandello sees Mussolini as a formidable creator of contingent realities, a superb animator and architect of life. Not all human beings are capable of creating an illusion to aim at: the spirit is not equally distributed amongst these human *forms* which we men are. Some people have such a minute quantity of it that they cannot create for themselves the slightest reality on which to rest their feet before leaping forward. They need someone to impose his own reality on them. And the people is the sum of the many beings incapable of creating their own reality: they require it from a great leader. Mussolini's task is to impose his own reality on the Italian people: and that reality, today, is fascism. In view of the incompatibility of an absolute, immutable truth, acceptable with one's eyes closed, Pirandello sees some colossal pillars looming up—dead things which cannot be denied since they constitute elementary necessities. *Necessities* is what Pirandello calls them. Such necessities, in the political field for example, are the Monarchy, the Unitary State, the Family, the Church: static blocks which do not live since they would encounter death in life. So we ourselves, *out of necessity*, have placed certain relative realities out of reach of the overpowering tide of life so that they will not be overturned and destroyed. . . .

Here Pirandello's readiness to accept a conservative, or even reactionary compromise was aggravated by sophistication, and there is a close concurrence between his later theatrical works and his final, equivocal attempt to return to religion. The article continues:

Pirandello views the situation today as follows: on the one hand there is a party which has in its favour *facts*, and on the other there is an agglomeration of people endeavouring to destroy these facts with

Massimo Bontempelli

Rosso di San Secondo

Adriano Tilgher

Pirandello wearing a Fascist black shirt, *c.* 1930

words. These people have no new *reality* to impose on the nation since they represent only the reality of yesterday, past and therefore dead. However, these people say that they do not want to govern the country, so whom or what can one substitute for fascism and Mussolini? Mussolini and fascism have committed the error of respecting their adversaries. Pirandello will never forgive this, especially not of the Duce. . . . Mussolini has lost many chances of solving a situation which cannot be resolved through a parliamentary compromise. Whatever Mussolini does, fascism will fulfil its aims. For it is not a political party guided by one or more wills towards this or that objective: it is an historical phenomenon which, with or without Mussolini, is destined to accomplish its ends. Not, certainly, by working out a programme, but by carefully observing the evils by which the country is oppressed. Pirandello thinks that the crisis of today can only be solved by doing away with all the verbiage (above all with the verbiage of the opposition press, or at least by opposing it with an equally well equipped fascist press); by suppressing the Chamber of Deputies, a superfluous institution which is both damaging and a contradiction of the fascist idea of the State; by turning the Senate into a mixed Assembly of technicians and representatives of the basic institutions of the State, formed half by royal appointment and half by provincial delegations which alone can introduce into public administration the authentic voice of the provinces; by avoiding every weakness and every perplexity; and by accelerating the liquidation of what is dead in the State and has become an obstacle. . . . As you see, Pirandello's view of the present crisis is very clear. It enables us to express our satisfaction about the numerous similarities between his and our view of the solution.

Pirandello's letter to Interlandi was printed in *L'Impero* of 24 September:

Dear Interlandi,
  In order to make my views clearer I should point out that I did not say as decisively and crudely as it appeared in your interview that I was in favour of 'doing away . . . with the opposition press'. I said that since the law concerning the press was passed, as an exceptional measure to prevent a macabre and obscene propaganda campaign of partisan hatred, very little has in fact changed, with the result that the application of the decree appears pointless and damaging. Pointless because the campaign of hatred bore disastrous fruit in the killing of the Honourable Casalini, and damaging because it has been, and is, an easy pretext for protesting against 'suppressed liberty'. A fortunate country ours, where certain words are puffed up with vanity, and strut about gurgling and fanning out their tails like so many turkeys! And

yet everyone knows that good only comes of things when, without shouting or even raising a fist, simply but resolutely, these words are answered. They then flee with their tails between their legs and their faces pale with fear.

Yours affectionately, Luigi Pirandello.

Pirandello's letter is interesting because in it he appears to be saying that the law passed against the press on 10 July 1924 was too mild a measure against men who were shouting 'like so many turkeys' for certain *words* like 'suppressed liberty'. When the opposition press was completely suppressed a few months later, Pirandello did not disapprove, and continued his support of the regime.

The man who felt most wounded by Pirandello's declaration was Giovanni Amendola, whom Pirandello had described as 'a mediocre politician'. On 25 September 1924 the title of an article in his paper *Il Mondo* called Pirandello 'a vulgar man'. Amendola then went on to accuse Pirandello (unjustly, it would appear) of publicizing his allegiance to fascism in order to distract people's attention from his failure to be appointed senator—and, in the same article, he implied that Pirandello was Tilgher's creation:

And so this poor writer, who wandered for twenty years in search of fame—like one of his characters in search of an author—and who at last found his author and his most generous interpreter . . . today projects his own feelings on to his neighbour and, blind and deaf to the reality surrounding him, solemnly proclaims that, without the publicity given it by fascism, the opposition would not exist. No, dear character who has found his author, we are the men who make newspapers, not like you, who are made by newspapers. Never mind: your Duce and your fascism never created us: they would rather have destroyed us.

The row exploded. Politics became confused with literary polemics and the matter degenerated on to the level of pamphleteering. Pirandello was not altogether free from responsibility for this, since he had been the first to form a conjunction between his (and Tilgher's) irrational philosophy and the myth of Mussolini. The venom increased and spread to the whole Italian press, even to the provincial papers. *Sicilia Eroica* thought it worth reminding Pirandello of the statement printed a few months earlier: 'I am apolitical: I simply feel like a man on earth.'[6]

Pirandello found numerous defenders. Five of his friends, Antonio Beltramelli, Massimo Bontempelli, Alfredo Casella, Silvio D'Amico, and C. E. Oppo, headed a public protest. The letter of protest, which was signed by numerous writers, said: 'Luigi Pirandello's display of loyalty to fascism is the consequence of convictions which have always been his. By rejecting *a priori* any honour which might appear to be a reward for his unprompted gesture he has enabled certain political pamphleteers to insult the integrity of this distinguished man whose work is attracting the attention of the entire literary world. We who live for an ideal, for art and for philosophy, oppose this grimly partisan manifestation. We oppose it as something supremely immoral. . . .' Tilgher was invited to sign the protest, but he did not reply. In *L'Impero* of 27 September there appeared a note which pointed out that, after Amendola's 'revolting article', one would have expected Tilgher to set things right, 'but Tilgher must be very busy.'

Tilgher replied in *Il Mondo* the next day. 'Gentlemen,' he wrote, 'let us dot our i's. It is not the mere fact that Pirandello favours fascism but his violent attack against the opposition—or, to be more precise, against the head of the constitutional opposition whose ideas *Il Mondo* follows—which earned him the attacks you deplore and which are not directed against Pirandello as a playwright but against Pirandello as a politician. Now, whoever dives into politics, especially in hard times like these, is offering his whole body to his adversaries and cannot claim to be spared any blows.' 'In view of the names of its ringleaders,' Tilgher added, 'the manifestation' seemed 'to be more political than artistic'. Tilgher's reply was followed by a further attack by Amendola, answered, in its turn, by Telesio Interlandi in *L'Impero* of 29 September. Pirandello, who thought it better not to take further part in the argument, wrote a letter in *L'Impero* of 3 October to all those who had signed the protest. These included Beltramelli, Bontempelli, Casella, Alberto Cecchi, Silvio D'Amico, Arnaldo Frateili, Mario Labroca, Ada Negri, Ugo Ojetti, Oppo, Respighi, Malaparte, Ardengo Soffici, Orio Vergani, and Giuseppe Ungaretti.

My dear friends,

If those of you who organized this protest, for which I am indeed grateful, had told me of it before following the generous impulse of your indignation I would have done all I could to prevent it in order to stop your names being dragged with mine in the mud of this silly and cowardly polemic. Whoever knows me knows that I am not a vulgar man. Whoever does not know me could well believe that, more than a vulgar man, I am an incredibly stupid man if, out of the vanity of seeing myself included in the list of new senators, I joined the Partito Nazionale Fascista the day before the list was issued. I consider myself entitled to regard as stupid those who were unable to appreciate such an obvious point and who could believe such a silly tale. On seeing me be insulted so idiotically for a sin of the pettiest vanity, at the very moment when I renounced such a vanity absolutely (and it was no sacrifice for me to do so), it would have been enough for you, my dear friends, to express your disgust to me in private, as so many did.

With grateful affection, your Luigi Pirandello.

Shortly afterwards Pirandello again declared his lack of interest in politics. To a reporter from *Il Piccolo*, Trieste (21 October) who interviewed him, he said: 'My life is nothing but work and study. My works, which some people consider unpremeditated and written off the cuff, are the result of a long period of spiritual incubation. I am isolated from the world and have only my work and my art. Politics? I have nothing to do with them, I have never had anything to do with them. If you are referring to my recent act of allegiance to fascism, I can tell you that it was done to help fascism in its task of renovation and reconstruction...'

But on 4 November, in *L'Impero*, a conversation with Pirandello was reported: 'Pirandello affirms that the recent attacks on him have not shaken his faith in fascism, "nurtured and always served in silence". He is firmer and more resolute than ever in this faith of his, and he admits that in his Art there is something which approaches the audacious and renovatory concepts behind fascism. He refers to the apathetic mentality of many intellectuals who look down on politics without understanding that politics, too, are an art—and one of the most difficult forms of art—that politics are a fact of life and that nobody, especially an artist, is entitled to withdraw from the often sad but always necessary conflict of ideas.'

In the meantime Mussolini showed as much esteem for Pirandello as the playwright showed for him. For even if the Duce had displayed his contempt for intellectuals and had declared that, as far as he was concerned, a militant fascist, a *squadrista*, was worth more than a writer or a philosopher, he was always delighted when a writer or a philosopher came down on the side of fascism. Pirandello, in his endeavour to assimilate fascism in his own intellectual convictions, resembled many Italians of that period who, as Nino Valeri observed, 'tried, in ever greater numbers, to fit fascism into an historical context.' 'Fascism accepted, even if with evident contempt, any form of cultural manifestation, provided it served to reinforce the regime in some way, or at least to tranquillize a bourgeosie frightened by novelty.'[7]

Mussolini wanted to offer Pirandello some material assistance when,

in 1925, he and other writers and actors decided to found an Arts
Theatre. 'How could "pure" art be realized without the government?'
wrote Nardelli.[8] 'Pirandello went to the Duce. The Duce received him
kindly, listened to him, agreed with him, questioned him. The financial
side required about 300,000 lire. The Duce accepted the idea and
promised his assistance. He even made over 50,000 lire at once so that
Pirandello and his friends could set to work immediately.' When the
theatre was inaugurated at the Sala Odescalchi with Pirandello's work
Our Lord of the Ship (*La sagra del Signore della Nave*) on 4 April 1925
Mussolini was present. Nardelli continued: 'The Duce took in the
moral importance of the matter at a glance and christened the plan: the
Theatre of the Regime. But when he got up to leave he heard that the
installation was to cost 700,000 lire. And Pirandello had to break the
news to him. . . . The government never lost interest in the Arts
Theatre. Indeed it provided all possible assistance in the face of almost
impossible requests and, in time, it paid for everything.'

The following year on 12 June 1926, Pirandello made a further
declaration. To a journalist of *Il Pensiero* of Bergamo he said:
'I am a fascist. And not a recent one: I have been a fascist for thirty
years. . . .' And so ended the period of Pirandello's greatest commitment to fascism. The next was of relatively minor importance since he
was far removed from any real political participation. He appeared to
be guided by contradictory feelings: by a desire to behave consistently,
by a desire to protest, and by opportunism. We can say that Pirandello
truly participated in fascism only in these first years and that he merely
acquiesced in it later.

The suppression of the freedom of the press, the special tribunals,
the renewal of the death penalty, the foundation of the O.V.R.A. (the
fascist secret police), and all the laws announced in 1926, must have
begun to disturb Pirandello's moral consciousness and he began to
want to stand on his own. He started to behave inconsistently towards
fascism. On the one hand he felt strong enough to state courageously
his own independence as an artist and as a man, on the other he continued to adhere to the day-to-day practice of the regime, and accepted
the honours which the government parsimoniously bestowed upon
him. But then, as Corrado Alvaro said, Pirandello had nothing of the
conspirator about him. And it should not be forgotten that fascism had
become a patriotic myth for him, one of his rhetorical dreams that had
never matured.

The first episode in which he proved his desire to remain aloof from politics and politicians and not to tolerate intimidation took place in 1927 during and after the tour made by his company in Brazil. In Brazil, says Corrado Alvaro,[9]

he encountered some Italians in exile who were printing a newspaper of their own. When Pirandello was questioned he came out with the curious declaration that 'abroad there are neither fascists nor anti-fascists: we are all Italians'. Once he was back in Rome he was summoned by the Party Secretary [Augusto Turati] who had on his table a vast collection of press cuttings assembled by Enrico Corradini who then aspired to the role of national playwright. The press cuttings referred to Pirandello's attitude abroad. Pirandello reacted unexpectedly: he took his party card out of his pocket, tore it up and threw it on to the Party Secretary's desk; he wrenched his badge from his buttonhole, flung it on the ground and walked out in fury. They had to run after him, calm him down, and apologize.

The incident proved, amongst other things, that Pirandello had a number of enemies in the party (led by Farinacci and Corradini) who made things difficult for him whenever they could.

Nevertheless, in March 1929, he was in the first group of intellectuals appointed to the Italian Academy (together with Gioacchino Volpe, Francesco Orestano, Pietro Mascagni, Marcello Piacentini, Antonio Beltramelli, Marinetti, and Alfredo Panzini.) His political attitude became increasingly contradictory. On the one hand he hated having to wear a cocked hat and to be photographed in that strange uniform, on the other he used the assembly ('a parade of skeletons' as he called it)[10] in order to deliver a speech on Verga which turned out to be a highly unorthodox attack on d'Annunzio. His audience was appalled. This same speech, which he had delivered in Catania in 1920 and which had been an implicit defence of his own style as a man and as a writer, now, at a public session of the Italian Academy, became an outspoken and almost defiant means of revenge for those thirty years of fame which d'Annunzio had usurped from him:

There are two human types which probably every nation produces: the constructors and the adaptors, the necessary intellects, and the beings who are merely a luxury. . . . Inattentive observers, whether Italian or foreign, are easily taken in by the noise, the pomp, the flashy manifestations of those I 'call mere spinners of words' and they think that only this type exists in Italy. Indeed, Italy seems to have been made specially for them, to emphasize, and to give colour and meaning to their abundant displays, their fine words and gestures, their decora-

tive passions and solemn evocations. So much so . . . that it is almost
impossible for a foreigner not to imagine the Italians all living like this,
drunk with sun, light, colour, and song, all playing on easy instruments, adventurers, actors, made for love and luxury even if living in
misery; and their best representatives are imaginative writers with a
sonorous language, magnificent decorators. . . . Of course it is not like
that. There are others in Italy, too: those who show off less and produce more: these I have called 'spinners of things'. . . .

'D'Annunzio,' recalls Alvaro,[11] 'was regarded as the champion of
the regime. In the hall, and amongst the Academicians, were many of
his political friends. Some could no longer remain in their seats and
they paced the adjacent rooms nervously while Pirandello spoke on
implacably. The ladies in the audience were dazed. It was an accusation
against the whole of Italian society. A gesture of protest was feared
from one moment to the next and it might well have occurred if the
fear of a far worse scandal had not advised caution.'

Pirandello's political enemies even went as far as to sabotage his
work for the theatre. His plays found fewer and fewer companies ready
to perform them—a fact that was only marginally connected with the
change of taste and the decline in standard of Pirandello's plays, but
was closely connected with other events. Pirandello was now always
travelling and for many years lived abroad, in Berlin and in Paris. He
preferred his works to have their first performances abroad, in Hudders-
field, Koenigsberg, and Prague, or even in Lisbon and Buenos Aires
rather than in Italy. On 24 March 1934, at the Teatro Reale dell'Opera
in Rome, *The Changeling*, put to music by Malipiero, was hissed off the
stage by a group of Farinacci's followers a few days after Hesse's
Ministry of Culture, on behalf of the Nazi government, had forbidden
the opera to be performed because it was 'subversive and contrary to
the principles of the people's German State.'

In fact it is hard to understand the reasons for the German censor-
ship. In January Hitler himself had attended a thoroughly successful
performance of the opera. According to Pirandello[12] the *volte-face* was
due to a racist reaction since the opera contained a fairly specific exalta-
tion of southern and Mediterranean sun and vitality against 'the dark
and cold lands of the north, where there is bitter fury.' Or it may
equally well have been due to a reaction against the 'atonality of the
music and the cultural defeatism' which the Nazis claimed to find in it.[13]

Nevertheless, the playwright whose life, far from his family, grew
increasingly lonely, finally yielded to Mussolini's insistence (for the

Duce regarded his absence from Italy as an act of hostility to the regime) and returned. He adapted himself to a vague compromise with the regime, which occasionally degenerated into insincerity and adulation of Mussolini. Some of the most sickly praise he lavished on the Duce, accompanied by private complaints about him, gives us an idea of his state of mind.

The course of events in these years was as follows. A few months after the failure of *The Changeling*, from 8 to 14 October 1934, Pirandello presided over the Fourth Convegno Volta which was devoted to the theatre. On this occasion, to Mario Missiroli who was interviewing him for *L'Illustrazione Italiana* of 7 October 1934, he praised a 'corporate arrangement which endeavours to discipline the interests of all' such as existed in fascist Italy. At the same time he directed d'Annunzio's play *Jorio's Daughter* (*La figlia di Jorio*) at the Teatro Argentina with Ruggero Ruggeri and Marta Abba acting in it. We do not know whether he volunteered to do so or whether he was asked to, but it is certain that his decision to direct the play clearly signified an official reconciliation with d'Annunzio. In private, of course, his views remained the same as ever.

We have an exchange of letters[14] between Pirandello and d'Annunzio concerning the event. The tone is ceremonious and official. D'Annunzio wrote to Pirandello and the letter was printed in the papers. 'I am very pleased that, at such a distance, you should suddenly give me this fraternal proof of affection in preparing and inspiring a new performance of *Jorio's Daughter* which is nothing if not a great popular song in dialogue. Do you not hear the accents and the cadences of the stupendous songs of Sicily? I say that nobody will be able to intonate the verse of my play as you can and as you will teach the actors to do.'

Pirandello replied that he was sorry he could not go and visit him and added: 'I too regard *Jorio's Daughter* as a great song to be accented regionally, powerfully, and clearly. I shall do all in my power to prevent the actors from adopting the sort of literary preciosity which they so enjoyed on other occasions. ... I embrace you. ...' This was followed by a message from d'Annunzio:

My miserable infirmity prevents me from inviting you to the Vittoriale not so much to discuss *Jorio's Daughter* as to talk about many other things, and to effect the meeting which I have long desired. Perhaps you are unaware that I was close to you even when you were a young man and dear Ugo Fleres used to talk to me about you. ... I have full confidence in you and in the actors chosen by you. I beg you to send me a list of them so that I can give each of them a token and a souvenir of myself. Your treatment of the human spirit shows me that you are a penetrating magician. If only you could conceal my presence by magic I would be able to master my troubles and attend the first brilliant performance of my tragedy, staged by my admired rival.

Alvaro reveals how Pirandello reacted in private to d'Annunzio's letters and gifts. 'On Pirandello's table, next to d'Annunzio's letter, lay a silver box with on it one of d'Annunzio's mottoes. The box was full of cigarettes. Pirandello offered them to his guests, lit one himself and threw it away in disgust. They were scented with a strong rose essence. "The same as ever," he said, referring to d'Annunzio. The message and the gift had been brought by someone, for d'Annunzio did not seem to know of the postal service. ... We talked about d'Annunzio. Pirandello had known him in his youth in Rome, or rather he had known him by sight.' When he was young Pirandello had found d'Annunzio's style and character 'extraordinarily ridiculous' and had wondered 'whether, despite the glorification of Gabriele d'Annunzio ... as the foremost writer of our day, people might not laugh about him in three centuries' time just as we, today, laugh about the famous Don Valeriano Castiglione, the embellishment of the library of Manzoni's incomparable character Don Ferrante....'[16] D'Annunzio, for his part, does not appear to have been any better disposed towards Pirandello.

In November 1934 Pirandello was awarded the Nobel Prize and in December he went to Stockholm to receive it. Before he left for Sweden Benjamin Crémieux interviewed him for the Paris paper *Le Journal* (1 December 1934), and, in the course of the conversation, Pirandello said: 'People have asserted that I was one of the precursors of fascism. I think one can say that I was a precursor in that fascism represents the refutation of every preconceived doctrine, the will to adapt to reality, the will to modify one's actions in accordance with the mutations of reality. ... There must be a Caesar and an Octavian for there to be a Virgil.' The Nobel Prize must have gone to Pirandello's head for him to compare himself to Virgil and Mussolini to Caesar or Augustus. (In private, on the other hand, he had criticized Emil Ludwig for daring to say that his was a fascist art.)[17] As for Pirandello as a precursor of fascism, there had indeed been some superficial flatterers who had described him as such. The author of a study of his work, Pasini, had written: 'Reasonable people must admit that if fascism had any precursors Pirandello should be regarded as one of them and not the least influential. Even before the World War he was aware of the Roman Tradition.'[18]

On his return to Rome from Stockholm no official celebration was held in Pirandello's honour. 'Was it really rumoured,' wondered Gian Gaspare Napolitano,[19] 'that Mussolini was a candidate for the peace prize as a promoter of the Four Power Pact? This would certainly explain certain areas of silence, embarrassment, hesitation. . . .' When Pirandello arrived from Stockholm nobody was at Rome station to meet him except for

Massimo Bontempelli who went to fetch him early on that cold and foggy morning. Paola Masino accompanied him. There were no journalists or photographers awaiting him, nobody. And when he got off the train and embraced his friends in the fog, Pirandello's fantasy suddenly ran away with him. 'Look,' he said to Bontempelli, 'there are only the three of us in the world, only the three of us.' A few days later Bontempelli organized a dinner for Pirandello at the Trattoria del Buco next to the Collegio Romano. In the back room a table in the shape of a horseshoe, adorned by a few faded carnations, had been prepared. But something must have gone wrong because far fewer people came than had been invited and, at the last minute, when the late-comers could no longer be expected, several places were hurriedly removed so that Pirandello should not be aware that anyone was missing.[20]

A little later Corrado Alvaro arranged a party of a few friends for Pirandello, but most of them looked as if they were simply congratulating someone who had been exceptionally lucky. Finally, however, Mussolini received him officially. In L'Italia Letteraria of 5 January 1935 we read the brief communiqué: 'The Duce received Luigi Pirandello who arrived back in Rome after his tour in the north and expressed his delight that he should have been awarded the Nobel Prize. The academician told him about the manifestations in Stockholm and Prague (where No One Knows How (Non si sa come) was performed for the first time) and suggested to the Duce that he create a National Prose Theatre in Rome as a permanent company using the Teatro Argentina.' And indeed, one of Pirandello's tacit intentions in approaching Mussolini again was to obtain the assistance necessary for founding a State theatre—his old and ever frustrated ambition.

After the interview Pirandello returned home somewhat annoyed. By this time he had fallen in love with Marta Abba, his favourite actress. Corrado Alvaro tells us that he said of Mussolini:[21] 'He is a vulgar man', and that he told him how Mussolini had reproved his self-control and had said to him: 'When you love a woman you don't beat about the bush, you throw her on to the sofa.'

When the war was declared on Ethiopia Pirandello, just back from a stay abroad, told 'C.B.' who was interviewing him for *L'Italia Letteraria* of 27 October 1935: 'I returned to Italy a few days ago: I did not want to be far away at such a delicate moment. . . .' A little later he gave his country, together with a number of other gold objects in his possession, his Nobel Prize medal—a gesture which, according to Manlio Lo Vecchio-Musti, 'aroused the indignation of Swedish hypocrites and imbeciles. Of course he cared nothing for them.'

On 29 October 1935 he delivered a speech in Mussolini's presence at the Teatro Argentina.[22] Of the Ethiopian campaign he said: 'The world should look on it with admiration but, instead, it spies on it suspiciously, unaccustomed to a spectacle of real and great beauty. We who are producing this spectacle and living through it at this moment, know how much pain, anxiety, and vigilance, how much daily obedience and moral discipline accompany its beauty, and how much we must exert ourselves not to yield to laziness or cowardice. . . .'

Mussolini had, it appears, at last given his assent to the State Theatre, and this speech was intended as a public act of gratitude and an inducement to him to keep his word—and it was also the last proof of Pirandello's allegiance to fascism. Pirandello continued:

The Author of this great feat [the African campaign] is also a Poet who knows his trade. A true man of the theatre, a providential hero whom God granted Italy at the right moment, he acts in the Theatre of the Centuries both as author and protagonist. And, each time, he knows how to say the right word to everybody, he knows the right reply, whether his voice be heard beyond the borders of his Country, whether in his Country, he is addressing the regiments leaving to conquer a small portion of land in the sun for the Italian people who are entitled to it, or whether he talks to the farmers, . . . or whether he addresses poets, in his desire for the people to be admitted to the theatre—not, certainly, to attend ephemeral and empty scenic games, but to nourish and sharpen their minds with works worthy of these times of awakened senses and very serious commitments. . . . Let us hope, gentlemen, that the measures already taken and the greater and more effective ones still to be taken, will soon give some foundation and decorum to our theatre and let us in the meantime salute, with a faithful, ever devoted heart, our Duce.

This is an ingenuous attempt on Pirandello's behalf to be Machiavellian. Lost in his cult of the theatre, he tried, naïvely, to adapt certain political forces to the purpose of his own theatre. He thought for a moment that they could be adapted to his desires, but they turned out to be useless and even hostile. Pirandello's approach to Mussolini, which had once been full of trust and enthusiasm, ended by being a calculated approach to a powerful man who could subsidize a State Theatre for him. Pirandello cherished this illusion for some time, but again he was wrong.

A year later Pirandello died, but his funeral was not conducted according to fascist custom. Indeed, the refusal, expressed in his will, of any official ceremony was of some embarrassment to the regime. Alvaro, who was present, recalls:[23]

The Government representative arrived and read that half page in amazement. He read it and reread it . . . he copied it out and wondered how he could present it to the Duce. A great man, a famous man, leaving like that, shutting the door behind him, without a word of greeting, without a thought, without homage, asking to be buried in little more than a winding sheet and not in a uniform, not in a black shirt as was customary, leaving like a pauper, with no commemoration, no celebration. . . . He said: 'He left slamming the door'. . . . It is interesting to know that in those twenty-four hours indignant fists were hammering on the desk of the most powerful citizen, and that an official order was given denying the great playwright anything more than the usual report in the papers. . . .

A journalist of the period, Marco Ramperti, on the other hand, protested in *L'Illustrazione Italiana* of 20 December 1936: 'A pauper's hearse! Ashes thrown to the wind! Nonsense! Today Luigi Pirandello joins the glorious dead of the Italian Empire and, in their hearts, forty million Italians follow his hearse with their heads bowed.'

To conclude this account of Pirandello and fascism it is perhaps as well to recall that he was always eager to distinguish between art, which he considered idealistically pure and autonomous, and politics. He knew from his own experience that whenever he wrote he reached a sphere which had absolutely no connection with the official, external life to which he adhered in other respects. At the Convegno Volta in 1934 he had some very precise things to say on the subject, things that certainly did not concur with the times:

Art can indeed anticipate life, but it is difficult for art to assess the quality of life today, to view it *sub specie aeternitatis*. . . . To do so deliberately . . . even with aims which are very noble but extraneous to art, is to do politics, not art . . . it is a betrayal of art. . . . The mystery of artistic birth is the mystery of maternal birth. It is not something that can be fabricated on purpose, but something that must come to life naturally . . . it needs to live for its own sake, with no other aim than to be pure in itself, free of every interested motive. If it were not so, it would no longer be a work of art, and would therefore be condemnable not only because of its distortions, but above all because it has sullied the very name of art.

8

THE ARTS THEATRE

Towards the end of 1924 Pirandello's son Stefano, together with Orio Vergani and a few other friends, decided to found an arts theatre in Rome. It was the work of the young, undertaken with enthusiasm, at first under Pirandello's indirect guidance and then under his immediate control.

There were no real repertory companies in Italy just then. Before the war there was the Compagnia Stabile Romana at the Teatro Argentina until 1910, and again from 1913 to 1917. The Stabile Milanese had performed at the Teatro Manzoni, also until 1917, and the so-called 'minimum theatres', Martoglio's in Rome, Nani's in Turin, Papa's in Milan, Dondini's in Rome, and Lucio D'Ambra's Teatro per Tutti.[1] It is worth keeping the examples of Nino Martoglio and Lucio D'Ambra in mind (D'Ambra also directed a Teatro degli Italiani after the war), because it is probable that Pirandello was influenced by them. His friends may well have reawakened his vocation as a director which suddenly took possession of him and which turned into a veritable passion.

After the war there was no theatre ready to undertake a modern repertoire of quality. The experimental theatres of Milan, the Teatro Lirico and the Convegno, Bragaglia's Teatro degli Independenti in Rome, and Lorenzo Ruggi's theatre in Bologna, acted irregularly and performed an eccentric repertoire of plays like the 'synthetic futurist theatre' and one-act plays by Malaparte, Campanile, Spaini, and Alvaro. The young men who now assembled round Pirandello were in search

of something else: a theatre half-way between the theatre of the avant-
garde and the old-fashioned theatre of the travelling companies which,
according to Pirandello, served up 'the usual meat balls of Franco-
Italian cuisine'. The ideas of Pirandello were clear enough as far as the
repertoire was concerned, but there were a number of practical difficulties to be overcome.

To start with capital was needed, at least enough to hire a theatre in
which to perform the plays. Thus a sort of cooperative of eleven
friends was formed (twelve with Pirandello) who contributed 5,000
lire each. Besides Stefano Landi (i.e. Stefano Pirandello, who vainly
tried to escape the shadow of his father by using a pseudonym) and
Orio Vergani, the associates were Massimo Bontempelli, Giovanni
Cavicchioli, Giuseppe Prezzolini, Antonio Beltramelli, Leo Ferrero
(writers); Lamberto Picasso, Guido Salvini, Maria Letizia Celli (actors
and designers); and Claudio Argenteri, a publisher.

The theatre they finally decided to rent was the theatre in Palazzo
Odescalchi. They paid 3,300 lire a month but the theatre had to be
redecorated and transformed into something attractive and welcoming.
Though Pirandello set little store by the beauty of his own house he
followed closely and with great interest the plans and the work of
the architect and decorator Virgilio Marchi. According to Nardelli
the building was turned into an auditorium 'small but warm, with the
stalls well lit. . . . It was perfect: it had a flavour of scented drawing-
rooms, but with modern modifications, harmonious colours, comfortable soft seats of yielding velvet and a fairy-tale-like atmosphere in the
foyer. . . .'

Pirandello and his son read hundreds of scripts in order to choose the
repertory. He even asked Tilgher for advice. The writers he decided on
in the end were Bontempelli (*Our Goddess*) (*Nostra Dea*), De Stefani
(*The Shoemaker of Messina*) (*Il calzolaio di Messina*), and Giovannetti
(*Paulette*) amongst the Italians; and Dunsany (*The Gods of the Mountain*), Vildrac (*The Pilgrim*), Evreinov (*What Matters Most*), and
Ramuz (*L'Histoire du Soldat*, with music by Stravinsky). For the first
performance Pirandello chose his own *Our Lord of the Ship*, a one-act
play written the previous summer during a holiday in Monteluco and
based on a short story written in 1915.

On this occasion Pirandello wanted to present a spectacle which was
both splendid and evocative—an inaugural feast. Of the numerous
characters envisaged in the text 130 acted in the play. Pirandello had
worked indefatigably until the last minute together with his son, Orio

Vergani, and Guido Salvini. He urged on the decorators, the carpenters, the electricians, and himself took up hammer and nails in order to hang the last piece of drapery in the box of honour where illustrious guests were about to sit. On the first night the royal family was there, and Mussolini dressed, according to one witness,[2] in riding boots, with a whip in his hand.

Pirandello had not missed a single rehearsal, 'seated in a low chair, his face craned forward, his hands playing with his white beard', as Adolfo Franci tells us.[3] 'On the first night he was in the wings, half smiling, half serious. ... As happy as if he were in heaven.' The 130 actors were in a theatre with a capacity of 300 seats. The Sicilian costumes were very colourful, and a long procession, coming from the back of the theatre, crossed the auditorium to the beat of distant and evocative drums growing ever nearer. The curtain was designed by C. E. Oppo who had painted on it an *ex voto* with the image of the Lord blessing a boat in danger. The play, performed largely before an invited audience (only fifty tickets were sold), took place in a cordial but cool atmosphere. In *L'Idea Nazionale* the next day, however, Silvio D'Amico wrote that 'the play had contained an impressive mass of actors and various kinds of music. A symphony of colours was performed by a refined and complicated orchestra of lights the likes of which (we are told) exist only at the Scala. Here there is no question of improvisation and approximation—only loving care, consummate experience, and scrupulous accuracy. . . .' At the end, when Pirandello was called on to the stage, he appeared smiling and, according to Franci, 'full of childish joy'.

For the new productions of the Arts Theatre, which was also called the Teatro degli Undici or dei Dodici, Pirandello needed a leading actress. He required a particularly talented actress since the forthcoming works in the repertoire, Giovannetti's *Paulette* and Bontempelli's *Our Goddess*, each contained a difficult female part. Pirandello liked Emma Gramatica, but he thought she had too marked a personality, and since she had already had companies of her own it was unlikely that she would prove suitably cooperative. So when Pirandello read an article by Marco Praga praising a young Milanese actress called Marta Abba, who had acted 'astonishingly well' with Talli in Chekov's *Seagull* at the Teatro del Popolo in Milan, he sent Guido Salvini to sign a contract with her without further ado. Marta Abba thus entered his theatre and his life.

Pirandello did not regret his new acquisition. When he rehearsed her for the first time he listened to her in amazement and repeated: 'Very good, very good.'[4] The girl appeared to be very self-confident and showed that she was relatively well read. The daughter of a small trader, she had been acting in a local amateur theatre in Milan when Luigi Antonelli discovered her and told the critics about her.[5] They went to see her and from then on her career advanced rapidly. From acting in Roberto Bracco's play *Maternità* she passed on to Chekhov's *Seagull* and thence to the plays at the Odescalchi.

However energetic her character[6] she complied meekly with Pirandello's ideas about acting. She knew, as he put it, how to 'sink' into a character. In order to please Pirandello still more she would sometimes put the name of the character she was acting on the door of her dressing room instead of her own name—and this must have touched the playwright who once said that he no longer saw the actors, only the characters.

Marta Abba's first role with the company was in *Our Goddess*, the fourth of the plays performed at the Odescalchi, written by Bontempelli in imitation of Pirandello, but in that light, poetic, 'magical' style of his own.[7] In it the female protagonist changes character and heart according to the dress she wears, and Marta Abba was excellent. Even if her next play, *Paulette*, was a failure, she had conquered both the audience and the manager. Pirandello had spoken of her with enthusiasm from the beginning. 'Talking about Abba,' said Guglielmo Lo Curzio recalling an evening in 1927, 'talking of the meticulous and passionate study she made of every part she acted, he said: "You see, that woman has a jewel here, a jewel", and he pointed the thumb and forefinger of his right hand, yellow with nicotine, at the centre of his flushed forehead. . . .'[8]

One of the most important works performed at the Odescalchi was Ramuz' *Histoire du Soldat* with music by Stravinsky, and in 1926 the Odescalchi also put on the ballet *La Morte di Niobe* with libretto and music by Alberto Savinio and sets by his brother Giorgio De Chirico. The theatre had one success after another (the first Roman season lasted from 2 April to 10 June), but it was impossible to make ends meet. Mussolini had given Pirandello 50,000 lire but it was far too little. The debts increased and the manager even signed bills of exchange in other people's name. With the royalties he had recently earned in Italy and abroad he had commissioned Nardelli to build him a house in Via Onofrio Panvinio, near Sant'Agnese. But he was unable to pay the workmen since he had given precedence to the decorators of the Sala Odescalchi, which in fact had only been rented. One evening, therefore, the builders of Pirandello's house had to force the money out of the cashier of the theatre.

Through the intermediary of Antonio Beltramelli the government promised, and provided, a new subsidy. Guido Salvini, who was the administrator of the theatre and in charge of the lighting, set off round Rome to procure money and managed to persuade the engineer Puricelli to provide the most urgent sum, which would be returned to him by some Milanese industrialists whom Mussolini asked to subsidize Pirandello. But ends still did not meet and the situation started to worry the playwright. Yet the fact that Pirandello had a theatre of his own aroused curiosity and interest abroad and he and his company were soon invited to London, Paris, and Germany.

As a producer Pirandello is of particular importance in the meagre history of Italian stage production. He did not leave behind him a school or tradition, partly because he never actually specified his own ideas on production and acted purely on instinct. But his theatre was exemplary in Italy, owing to its repertoire and the rigour with which the actors were directed. Pirandello devoted himself to searching for a style of acting somewhere between the traditional Italian style, undisciplined, based on improvisation, but frequently brilliant, as in the case of individual actors like Tommaso Salvini, Zacconi, and Eleonora Duse, and the new school of European stage production which had developed enormously, from Meininger to Antoine's Théâtre Libre, the Deutsches Theater in Berlin, and the Moscow Arts Theatre, and which was based on infinitely painstaking preparation by the actors.

Once he had his own company Pirandello began to take an interest in the new European methods of acting and production, particularly in Russian and German techniques. Of course, in his new function he had to give up some of his former ideas about acting—ideas which were very dear to him. As late as 1918 he was formulating views on theatrical interpretation which were as pessimistic as they were abstract. He said that the actors were a 'necessary evil' and unreliable 'translators' of the 'dreams of the poet'.[9] 'So many actors and so many translations, more or less felicitous but, like every translation, always necessarily inferior to the original. . . .' He adhered to the sort of aesthetic premise which required art and the theatre to be a perfect, absolute paradise. Consequently he suffered because of irreconcilable antinomy between the concept of a work as sacred and its desecration by those impure instruments, the actors. This antinomy coincided with his own secret aspirations and lay behind one of the most important ideas of *Six Characters in Search of an Author*: the idea that contrasts the pure and eternal characters of fantasy with the actors who should, but cannot, bring them to life on the stage. If Pirandello had retained such an attitude his attempts at theatrical production would have taken place on a treacherous and ultimately impracticable terrain. He had to gain confidence in the actor. So in these years he passed from the idea of the actor's 'insufficiency' to the idea of his 'complementarity'. In other words the actors assumed for him the absolute importance of the poet's integrators.

Perhaps the most important aspect of his new attitude to acting was his often repeated suggestion that the actors should 'sink' into the characters. A. G. Bragaglia recalls Pirandello's referring to actors 'sinking into their parts' as if they were divers. It was an idea which, has had a strong influence on European stage production in the last thirty years. It is connected with Antoine's concept of the truth, spontaneity, and naturalistic 'obedience' of the actors and with Stanislavsky's doctrine by which the essential moment was the moment of 'identification' with the character—a moment which could be arrived at in any way, rational and irrational, in order to reach that 'circle of attention' in which nothing extraneous should interfere.[10] Guido Salvini, who was a pupil of Reinhardt and who collaborated with Pirandello at this time, recalled that at the Arts Theatre the playwright began by giving his actors a lesson about the system of acting taught in the modern Russian theatre.[11]

On the other hand, Pirandello had in him a genuine, inborn 'theatrical faith', which Stanislavsky considered a necessity. Pirandello was not joking when, in the interval between the first and second act of a performance of *The Scion*, he pointed at Lamberto Picasso, who walked past the dressing room where he was sitting, and said: 'You see that man? He will shortly accept as his own son the offspring of a monster.'[12]

Pirandello was the first to 'sink' into both his own characters and those created by others. Like other great actor-writers of the past, like Molière and Shakespeare, he himself was an actor in his own way. He acted as he read the scripts, acted as he directed or simply watched plays. There are countless testimonies of this and I shall cite only a few of them.

'No actor,' wrote A. G. Bragaglia,[13] 'will ever manage to transfer himself into the character as he did. Pirandello had the power to make his characters alive and real.' 'His face,' Niccodemi recalled,[14] was of an incredible mobility. It reminded one of a crowd of faces in motion. He repeated and imitated the contraction on the actors' faces. His mouth, covering the entire range of its expressive possibilities, turned into numerous mouths. His chin trembled convulsively, his nerves were stretched to breaking point; his face was streaked with lightning. ... The scene grew larger, fiercer ... two, three, four characters were introduced and Pirandello was those two, three, or four characters. He followed the crescendo, multiplying the resources of his expression; he accentuated it with a gesture ... with the tortured movement of his entire person. He murmured the bitter words with incredible violence, dropping his chin on to his chest and grinding his jaws. ... But he was most effective of all when he was silent. There was more movement in him when he was seated than in anyone else. ...

Ruggero Ruggeri said that once, when he was uncertain which expression to assume during a rehearsal, he simply took it from Pirandello's face. George Pitoëff observed that he was a 'magnificent actor':[15] 'When we knew he was coming we would invite our friends to watch him following the rehearsal and to see all the passions enacted on the stage pass over his face.' Pirandello behaved similarly when he was watching plays written by other people. According to a reporter from *L'Idea Nazionale* (3 April 1925) he was like 'one of those one-man bands ... carrying an astonishing number of instruments and capable of playing them all at once. ... With a multiplicity which sometimes went almost too far, he threw himself with his blood, nerves, and breath into living the life of the characters.'

Pirandello came under Russian influence mainly through Nikolai Evreinov whose theories, a sort of 'pantheatricality', fascinated him, so closely did they correspond to his own views. A book of Evreinov's had appeared in Italy in 1913. It was entitled *Theatre in Life*. Many years later, in an article printed in *Il Corriere della Sera*,[16] Pirandello wrote: 'My friend Evreinov, the author of a play which even the Americans applauded, goes so far as to say and to demonstrate in a book of his that the whole world is a theatre and that not only do all men act a part which they have assigned to themselves or which others have assigned to them, but that every animal, every plant, the whole of nature, acts.'

True to the principle of the identification of the actor with his character Pirandello had a profound loathing for the prompter. He expressed himself in picturesque terms about the presence of this 'alien' on the stage. Niccodemi reports Pirandello's view that:[17]

The actor must be the character of the play. . . . He must be a reality in himself, not a relative but an absolute reality, not the false truth of the stage but the positive and irrefutable truth of life. But this is no longer possible. The actor is now mirrored in the prompter . . . he says his lines with more or less talent or brilliance, but he says them mechanically, repeating the words whispered to him from the prompter's box . . . and the prompter does not just say the words: he has inflections of his own, he makes grimaces of his own which can influence an actor lacking in confidence. The prompter acts in his box. One must see him in action. He is like an imprisoned lunatic, twisting and turning, clenching his fists to give greater emphasis to his words, cupping his hands round his mouth to make it a more audible megaphone. In a word he directs the play according to the state of his nerves, his mind, or his humour. 'One must abolish the prompter,' Pirandello would say, and would make a gesture as though he were hanging a man.

It was not easy for him to extirpate the evil of the prompter from the stage. The actors were appalled by this novelty, but he succeeded in the end and, in due course, he was copied by other Italian producers. He directed the actors passionately. He started off by reading the script aloud to them. Dario Niccodemi, who remains the best witness of this aspect of Pirandello's life, recalled a reading of *Six Characters in Search of an Author* on the stage:[18]

What violence in his reading, what a tornado, what a tumult of words, sounds, shouts! It was irresistible. Without ever looking up from the script, his hands gripping the table as if to prevent it from fleeing with terror from such a racket, his eyes glistening with a truly superhuman intoxication, his burning brow furrowed as if by lightning, pouring with sweat, dealing violent punches on the page as if to emphasize certain words to make them sink into the minds of the listeners, as one bangs a nail into a piece of hard wood, Luigi Pirandello appeared to read more for himself than for others. He seemed to be alone with the passion of his characters, with their will dominating his own. He read the whole act in one breath and when he raised his face, bright with intelligence . . . he seemed surprised, harrowed as he was, to see the semicircle of people who had listened to him in amazement. . . .

Pirandello did not condition the actors slowly and gradually. He did not have much time and he was not a patient man. He preferred the method of direct and rapid suggestion. Guido Salvini said that he 'violated' the will of the actors and that rehearsals were short but very intense. 'It is enough,' Pirandello would say, 'for the actor to look me in the face for me to know whether or not he has entered into the character.'[19] 'It was very tiring. Pirandello was not a normal man. He was violent, given to extremes, overexcitable. . . .'[20] And the actors acted in a similar way, nervously and jerkily, in direct contact with the style and the specific rhythm of the play—'a rushed scansion, with certain anguished silences,' recalls Caprin.[21] Besides, the fear of appearing cerebral induced Pirandello to play down the rational parts of the dialogue, which had to be spoken quickly, in a rush, while the emotional and passionate lines had to be given as much emphasis as possible.

This passionate participation did not prevent him from 'doubling himself', from observing himself and from explaining the characters to the actors. 'He can explain the obscurest things with marvellous clarity,' said Niccodemi.[22] 'Indeed, the more obscure they are the more clearly he explains them. He knows how to sink to the full into certain psychic abnormalities and how to make them manifest. But a curious process of doubling takes place in his own person. He is both the author who guides and teaches, and the spectator who watches and enjoys himself. . . .'

He admired his actors and they had the deepest respect for him. For many of them the period they spent in Pirandello's company was like a second training. Others, younger ones, had their first theatrical training from him and some later became famous. Pirandello influenced the development of Italian theatre in the twentieth century as a producer as well as in his role as playwright. He was succeeded, especially after the Second World War, by a far more modern school of production, but he was undoubtedly a necessary bridge between the theatre of the early twentieth century and that of today.

The tours of Pirandello's company abroad were regarded by foreign audiences mainly as curios. Only in Germany, where they lasted longer and where the performances were repeated in many cities, did they arouse a more serious response. The first city which the Arts Theatre visited was London. Cochran, who had invited Pirandello to the New Oxford Theatre, wanted him to perform a repertoire of his own works and not of those given at the Teatro Odescalchi. Pirandello's company therefore performed, between 15 and 28 June, *Right You Are . . .*, *Naked*, *Henry IV*, and *Six Characters in Search of an Author*. The performances had a certain *succès d'estime*. 'The leading politicians in England,' wrote a reporter from *Il Tevere* on 31 July 1925, 'were amongst the most assiduous frequenters of the London season . . . the finest names of English social and artistic circles. ... The audience frequently brought along translations of the plays. ...'

In Paris the performances took place in July at the Théâtre Edouard VII. Because it was not the theatre-going season the public took little notice of the plays, even though the press made much of Pirandello's arrival. Since Pirandello took care to perform plays already familiar to the Parisians the critics noted that the acting was 'more alive' than the ritualistic style of the Pitoëff company. They compared Ruggeri's fluent, flexible performance of *The Pleasure of Honesty* with that of Dullin who had played the part of Baldovino not many years before, with 'his opaque, dry voice, his feverish gaze and his immobile body contorted into theatrical poses—but he had learnt that from Copeau.'[23]

Pirandello's most memorable tour was in Germany. The season was more favourable, October and November, after the company had rested and had then rehearsed intensively for over a month—all of them except for Ruggeri, who did not go to Germany. Germany was a country in which there was a veritable cult of the theatre. Pirandello was welcomed with every possible honour. With the special permission of the government the state theatres were officially opened to him although they were closed to foreign companies by law. In Berlin, says Nardelli,

the Hotel Adlon wanted to put up Pirandello's company free [in fact it was at the expense of the State]. When Pirandello arrived at the sumptuous hotel in Unter den Linden he saw it covered with flags. Masses of footmen were standing outside the door in full array. Pirandello thought they were there to greet some important figure and, so as not to spoil the show, he went through the servants' entrance. Once he was in the hotel, however, he was told that the gala was in his honour so he had to go out again and come in through the main door where his arrival was studiously filmed by the UFA.

The tour had started with *Six Characters in Search of an Author* in Switzerland two days earlier, in the town of Basle, and it ended in Münster in Westphalia with the same play on 7 November. At a truly unbearable pace the Company crossed Germany in every direction: they were in Berlin on 12 October, in Frankfurt on the 15th, in Bonn on the 17th, in Cologne on the 19th, and then in Düsseldorf, Kassel, Dresden, Leipzig, Halle, Magdeburg, Hanover, Hamburg, Bremen, and finally Münster. There were only three or four evenings off, and the days were spent travelling. The play performed most frequently was *Six Characters in Search of an Author*, but they also gave *The Pleasure of Honesty*, *Right You Are . . .*, and *Henry IV*.

Pirandello and his actors were rewarded by great success. But the critics of Berlin were cautious and had reservations, mainly because of the comparison with Max Reinhardt's recent production of *Six Characters* at the Komödie with Max Pallenberg, an extraordinary leading Ractor. einhardt's production had had an immense success and had been performed 131 times. Some critics thought the play had been improved by Reinhardt's interpretation and they considered the producer the real poet of the evening. Reinhardt had managed to create 'a nightmare atmosphere which had shaken the audience, a ghostly atmosphere, oscillating between reality and unreality. . . .'24 It had been an ultraromantic interpretation of *Six Characters* with an expressionistic slant, so now the critics of Berlin repeated unanimously, and with a remarkable presumptuousness, that: 'the productions of Pirandello the theatrical producer did not correspond to the views of Pirandello the dramatist. . . . The Italian production seemed to emphasize the purely game-like character of the play, as though it wanted to warn the audience not to take things too seriously and to show that what was happening on the stage was mere theatricals. The acting and the lighting of the Italians were considered too elementary for the psychological profundities of the text. All they acknowledged was that Pirandello had given his plays a quick and precise rhythm which was most effective.'25 In other words the Berlin critics concluded that 'only the northerners could give the requisite form to *Six Characters*'.

Pirandello had little time to take much notice of the critics. And besides, the public was enthusiastic, especially in the provincial towns. In Bonn, where *Henry IV* and *Six Characters* were performed at the Stadttheater on 17 and 18 October, the former university student was given a particularly warm welcome. He recounted it with great emotion two years later to Giuseppe Caprin.26 The college of professors, dressed in their togas, ordered a solemn sitting in the Great Hall, with all the students present, wearing their peaked hats and the ribbons of the student corporations. Numerous 'grave and cordial' speeches were given in Pirandello's honour and the Vice Chancellor delivered an encomium of the former student who had risen to fame. Pirandello himself told the students: 'I swear that I would give all my work and my reputation to be young with you again and to sing our old Rhine songs with you.' And then those 'sentimental bears played a trick on him'. From the back of the hall a deep voice broke into song and all the students joined in. 'They made me cry,' Pirandello confessed.

When he returned from Germany Pirandello, who had savoured the efficiency of the German theatre, was full of ideas for the future. He thought of founding a permanent 'State' theatre which would be generously subsidized and drew up a plan for it with Paolo Giordani. He envisaged a company with three bases, in Milan, Rome, and Turin. The main actors would circulate while the others remained permanently in their own city. He wanted to sign up four main actors and four main actresses in order to give each actor a suitable part. Here again his ideas partially coincided with those of Stanislavsky for whom each character should correspond to 'tall or small, fat or thin, sad or grey, contemplative or clownish actors.'[27]

But the plan was never taken seriously. Pirandello obtained a subsidy of 300,000 lire from the government which was to be given to the Teatro degli Undici, nominally still in existence, for three years. But the 300,000 lire were far from being enough. In the second season he lost over 500,000 lire of his own (well over fifty million lire today). But Pirandello was now interested in money only for the sake of his theatre or to help one or other of his children. He was no longer able to shut himself into his study and spend all day writing, seated in his medieval chair. He had left his house and he no longer wanted to return to it. In November 1926 he confessed:[28] 'I am a man who has burnt all his boats. Break away. Why have a house? I would like to get rid of the one I bought in Rome. To grow old somewhere? One can only grow old with one's wife. And for me . . . emptiness, emptiness. One's children obviously need to lead a life of their own. But it isn't true that I am detached, empty, inside . . . I have a sentimental life of my own, a complex one, all of my own. . . . Travel. I am a traveller with no luggage. . . .'

But Pirandello's 'complex sentimental life' gave him no consolation. He was looking for something outside himself—acting, reducing himself dynamically to another dimension, trying to realize himself beyond the written page, in the external, objective field of the theatre which was a fluid, collapsible, insubstantial reality. The man of the theatre had come out of his chrysalis. Pirandello revealed a new and strange vivacity which astonished everyone who had known him before, when his life had had a different rhythm. But his vitality was sometimes interrupted by fatigue and moments of sudden distraction. 'All of a sudden all that irrepressible human force would collapse as if stricken to death.

His body would remain motionless, his hands hanging at his side, his face colourless, his eyes lustreless.'

But despite such moments of fatigue, Pirandello's passion for the theatre lasted until the end of his life. His activity as a short-story writer, on the other hand, ceased for many years. Until 1933 he wrote an average of no more than two short stories a year, in some years just one, and in other years, 1928, 1929, 1930, none at all. For a man who used to write fifteen or more stories a year in addition to novels, newspaper articles, and critical essays, this indicated a veritable metamorphosis in the sphere of his creative work. Instead, he wrote ten new plays and adapted three or four stories for the theatre in ten years. 'I elaborate my work as I go along,' he said.[29] 'When the time comes I write them quickly. I wrote the first act of *Diana and Tuda* in a hotel in Leipzig. . . .'

His former friends hardly recognized him. 'Not even we could say exactly when the transformation took place,' wrote Frateili.[30] 'He was a little older, his hair thinner, his beard whiter, but he had a youthful, active, sometimes even hostile twinkle in his eye which we had never seen before. . . . Pirandello now had a secretary. He received visits from journalists and writers from all over the world. On his rare stays in Rome his study turned into a drawing-room. . . . I used to meet him in Rome, Berlin, Viareggio, Castiglioncello, San Remo. . . . He was always cordial and affectionate, but he had changed.' And the other great friend of his youth, Ugo Fleres, now called him a 'disdainful Dulcamara' as though he were alluding to a deliberate sophistication of this new Pirandello and had not realized that a necessary transformation had taken place in the shy, bashful, unknown Italian writer of the past.

Pirandello wrote to his daughter Lietta in 1923: 'The fame of your poor old father has increased and has become international in these two years of your absence. . . .' It would be foolish to think that a man whose fame had so rapidly become universal would remain unchanged. He underwent a transformation which affected him both as a man and as a writer. His new solitude, the absence of his wife and children, spurred him on to a different life. His immobile, impatient anguish turned to desolation in perpetual motion. But there was also the new and very important fact of finding himself in a different social sphere. He had left the world of the Roman petty bourgeoisie, of his friends and relatives, of the school rooms of the Magistero and he was endeavouring to be integrated on a higher level. He had to answer ever more demanding international critics who had recently declared, in France and Germany, that they doubted the value of his work and that they were afraid of having overvalued it.[31] From 1926 onwards, therefore, Pirandello turned his hand to new types of plays—myths, philosophy, or the autobiography of a great man. He had lost contact with the petty bourgeosie, and his participation in contemporary Italian society was an uncomfortable affair. He tried to detach himself from it, to find important new symbols which would have meaning for everyone and which may have won him the Nobel Prize, but which actually suggest a certain aridity.

In November 1926 Pirandello left his company for a week to go to Zürich to attend the first European performance, in German, of *Diana and Tuda*. He gave a lecture before the performance and allowed the audience to ask questions. In this case the lecture consisted of reading the preface he had written to *Six Characters in Search of an Author*. He explained the meaning of *Diana and Tuda*—the familiar paradox of life and form. The questions asked by the audience were far from elevated. 'A middle-aged lady asked him: "Why is your work so sad, Professor Pirandello? Aren't there good and beautiful things in life too?" Pirandello replied that it wasn't his fault, that he didn't invent the characters, that he took them as life sent them to him, ready made.'[32] Then, in defence of *Diana and Tuda*, which was considered too philosophical, he answered: 'I am not a philosopher . . . I'm an artist, working in the concrete. My creatures are so concrete, so human, that I could tell you what each one's voice and fingernails are like.'

Pirandello's exchanges with audiences were sometimes of considerable interest. On another occasion, in Buenos Aires,[33]

with ministers, ambassadors, and even the President in the audience . . . Pirandello said: 'But Signora Morli could not do otherwise. That was her nature and there was nothing to be done about it. . . . Those wretched creatures obsessed me. . . . Where could I have let them live if not on a stage, the natural place for characters? . . . I shall tell you of a dream I had: I saw a deep courtyard with no exit, and from this terrifying image was born *Right You Are (If You Think So)*. The idea of *Henry IV*, on the other hand, was taken from an English print representing a cavalcade of ladies and gentlemen.'

The Arts Theatre continued their tours in Italy and abroad. In 1924 they went to Austria, Hungary, and Czechoslovakia; in the summer of 1927 to the Argentine and Brazil. On their return, in November, they inaugurated the new season in Naples with Ibsen's *Lady from the Sea* (another part for Marta Abba). At the same time other new works by

Pirandello were performed: the one-act play, *Bellavita* by the Compagnia Almirante-Rissone-Tofano in Milan. *Scamandro*, an old Graeco-Trojan farce written in 1905, was given on 19 February 1928 at the Teatro dell'Accademia dei Fidenti in Florence. And the futurist pantomime *La Salamandra* was performed with music by Bontempelli.

The last Italian tour of Pirandello's company was not a success. It started in the provinces. Pirandello again went to Sicily, to Catania, Palermo, and Agrigento, never losing his vitality or his will-power, but tired and disappointed nevertheless. The theatrical season dragged on until August and the last performances were given in Viareggio. Lucio D'Ambra described Pirandello at the time:[34]

At night. In Viareggio. A night-club. (Pirandello was seated at a table with a bulldog he was looking after for a famous actress). . . . He was melancholy. He may have been satisfied with the world, but not with Italy. . . . In one evening, after four years' struggle, his dreams as the manager of a theatre company were destroyed in a final performance to an empty house of Ibsen's *Lady from the Sea* . . . His company died in his arms, a company that, for four years, had been his whole life, his martyrdom, and his passion. Pirandello was stunned . . . And, stunned, sad, and tired, he let himself be dragged everywhere by everyone. The Mayor of Viareggio wanted to give a banquet in his honour and give him a gold medal. So he went to the banquet. Society women wanted to meet him and invite him to their houses. So Pirandello went. . . . He paid no attention to where he went. Where had his spirit gone?

Pirandello dissolved his company but he did not abandon the theatre. The stage was to obsess him until his death.

THE LAST SEASON

In the year 1928 Pirandello wrote another 'myth', *Laʒarus* (*Laʒʒaro*), which he read in Viareggio to his friends, Leonida Repaci, Lucio D'Ambra, and others, exerting the same fascination on his listeners as ever. 'As he read it,' said Lucio D'Ambra 'our deepest feelings were moved by the formidable force of the play. . . . I, a friend of thirty years' standing, embraced Pirandello. The younger men kissed his hands with tears in their eyes . . . a masterpiece was born.'

Laʒarus was not, however, a masterpiece: it was ambitious but lacked originality. Pirandello was still the greatest playwright alive, and was always a great technician, but he often chose his subject-matter badly. For example, it was merely to create a part for Marta Abba that he dramatized his short story 'The Wives' Friend', and only for the sake of writing a play, quite irrespective of its quality, that he dramatized in 1929 another short story, 'Somebody's or No One's' ('O di uno o di nessuno').

With the notable exception of *Tonight We Improvise*, Pirandello moved ever further away from autobiography and became increasingly attached to 'myths' with which, he told Alberto Cecchi in 1928,[1] he wanted to address 'all mortal creatures'. He added that 'tragedy [he was referring to *The New Colony* which was about to be performed] is always mythical. It has its beginning and its end on the stage. The origins of myths are these: the elementary events of earthly cycles, dawns, sunsets, births, deaths.' In myth one can represent the origin of profit and trade which are both born of need, one can recreate the story of

every primitive civilization, confirm the value of maternity, demonstrate the necessity and consequently the law of the family, the husband,
the leader, or the king. 'The family is the basis of every society, of
every morality.' A year later, in 1929, Pirandello wrote an article in
Il Corriere della Sera (16 June) in which he stated:

As long as forms remain alive, that is, as long as the vital force lasts in
them, they constitute a victory of the spirit. To destroy them simply to
replace them with other forms is a crime. . . . Some forms are a natural
expression of life itself. It is therefore impossible for them to become
obsolete, or to be replaced without destroying life in one of its true and
natural manifestations.

With these words Pirandello showed that he had given up contrast-
ing life with form, and identifying form with death. But this development may have been an entirely superficial phenomenon. It may have
been due to a need to comply with the demands of the present moment,
or to a sudden fear of the chaos of contradictions which Pirandello had
previously broached so adventurously.

Pirandello's attempt at conformity dates from 1924, the year which
marked the peak of his success as a dramatist and the year in which he
joined the Fascist Party. *L'Impero* of 11–12 November 1924 reported
a key interview with Pirandello when he revealed his fear of the truths
which he had confronted courageously not long before:

For a long time I have been considered a pessimist, perhaps because
my works reveal an anti-traditional and reactionary mentality. But I
have been misunderstood. My art is free of the pessimism which
engenders lack of faith in life. And I am not even a negator since, in the
spiritual activity which torments me and which animates my works,
there is an incessant desire *to create life*. . . . I feel a sort of joy in creating
the ground beneath the feet of my characters. . . . Of course, one needs
courage to renew oneself. There is a whole moral code in this statement. By no means everyone is capable of creating reality for himself,
and reality is so ephemeral that it can disappear at any moment. So
there must be a creator, a giver of reality.

Pirandello's 'myths', however, are confused and contradictory, and
they failed. There was a strong desire in Pirandello to find some fixed
value in life, but he failed to do so. His resulting exhaustion and despair
parched the sources of his poetry.

In the summer of 1928 he decided to leave Italy in a sort of voluntary
exile. He left for Germany and his visits to Italy became increasingly

rare. He travelled until 1933, stopping for longer periods of time in Berlin or Paris, cities where he stayed in almost total solitude, seeing few acquaintances and living in a hotel or a two- or three-room flat. Even after his return to Rome in 1933, to his old house in Via Bosio, he continued to travel.

Before leaving, as he was dissolving his Arts Theatre, he pronounced the bitter words reported by Lucio D'Ambra:[2]

Yes, I'm leaving. Now that my company has been dissolved I have nothing more to do in Italy. I shall take refuge in the cinema. . . . But abroad, in a hotel room, I shall still be able to write. . . . People look at me as though they are reproaching me for the fact that Italy has given the world a writer. But the sequence was different. If I am not mistaken, my greatest fame came from abroad, the best performances of my work are given abroad, the longest and most objective studies of my work are written abroad. So perhaps people should say that the world has given Italy a writer. . . .

Pirandello had become unpopular in Italy for his outspoken criticism of others. In Germany, however, he was invited by a German cinema company to adapt three of his plays for the screen. One of them was *Six Characters in Search of an Author*. He collaborated on the script with Adolf Lantz, but later, owing to production difficulties, the film was abandoned. He had intended to stay in Berlin for six months but he remained until 1930. He lived 'in splendid isolation,' wrote Pietro Solari.[3] Yet his isolation was sad rather than 'splendid', for his star had set in Germany too. Since April 1926 none of his plays had been performed. His last work given at the Kammerspiele, *Naked*, had been regarded by the Berlin critics as a 'sophisticated and affected play, made obscure by a poor form of dialectics . . . and the consensus of opinion amongst the critics was that, despite Pirandello's formidable experience of the stage and his knowledge of his own possibilities, the thinker in him had taken a lead on the poet.'[4]

In Berlin Pirandello would shut himself up for hours on end in his fourth-floor flat in Lützow Platz and work on his new plays—above all on *Tonight We Improvise* which is clearly based on theatre life in Berlin. He went to the theatre often, every evening if he could—and Germany, or rather Berlin, was a paradise for a theatre lover. There were dozens of brilliantly run theatres, and the plays were often produced by such prestigious individuals as Max Reinhardt or Erwin Piscator. Pirandello felt both attracted and repelled by Reinhardt. He was grateful to him for the famous production of *Six Characters* at the Komödie,[5] but he could not stand his cavalier attitude to the text and the fact that the spectacle became an end in itself. Yet Pirandello must also have been stimulated by Reinhardt's abundant exploitation of stage technique and by the way he would turn any space into a theatre—a square, a castle, a church, even a circus. A. G. Bragaglia recounted that one night in Berlin Pirandello was swept away with enthusiasm by the idea of writing 'a play for an arena, with Girardengo or Carnera, a great sporting drama to be performed partly on a mechanical stage and partly on a sports pitch.'[6]

From this mixture of attraction and repulsion towards contemporary methods of production Pirandello derived the idea of *Tonight We Improvise*. A realistic incident, which Pirandello had already recounted in 1910, in a short story entitled 'Leonora, Farewell' about passionate jealousy, is combined with a theatrical pastiche which features a German-style producer, Hinkfuss (based on Reinhardt), together with a number of Italian-type actors. The audience was invited to participate in the play, to protest, to shout, to say what they thought. Pirandello finished the play in Berlin on 24 March 1929 and it was performed for the first time in Koenigsberg on 25 January 1930. It was well received by a provincial and fairly ingenuous audience. But when a different company performed it in May at the Lessing Theater in Berlin with mediocre actors (except for Elisabeth Lennartz) in an inadequate production, it appeared weak and arbitrary, and flopped totally.

Pirandello's idea of writing an easily recognizable satire on Reinhardt's school of stage production was regarded as lacking in taste by Reinhardt's admirers. So when Hinkfuss came out with lines which seemed to condense and poke fun at theories dear to the master, the audience protested and the performance degenerated into the worst disaster Pirandello had known since the first night of *Six Characters* in Rome. Oscar Büdel recalls that this performance was:

the greatest theatrical outrage Berlin had ever known. . . . In the first and second acts there was already tension in the air. When, in the last act, Elisabeth Lennartz appeared on the stage where Mommina was singing arias from *Il Trovatore* to her daughter, it exploded. A little earlier, during a quarrel between Dr Hinkfuss and the actors, on hearing lines such as 'Go away! Get out! Get out!' the audience started shouting: 'Schluss! Schluss!' The producer, Hartung, had reacted by yelling at the audience: 'Respektlose Bande!' The actress was in tears, but, despite the catcalls and the ever more insistent demands to end the play, she carried on until it was over. . . . Herbert Ihering, one of the

Marta Abba

Pirandello in 1934, with his grandchildren

most distinguished critics in Berlin just then, considered the commotion fully justified. He described the play as 'a confused nonsense trying to be profound' and concluded that 'the fashion for Pirandello is definitely over.'[7]

Pirandello was very embittered by the whole episode. According to Pietro Solari 'he suffered the full humiliation of a beginner over that mortification . . . but he was even more offended by the furious opposition to his concept of art as expressed in *Tonight We Improvise*. . . .' Here Pirandello may have been wrong, for his theory of art was the idealistic theory which had been current in Italy for at least fifty years but which, when presented in a theatre in Berlin in 1930, could easily encounter a hostile reception. 'Art,' he said in the prologue of the play, 'is true creation in that it is freed from time, from cares, from obstacles, for no other end but itself. . . .'

Owing to the unpopularity he had aroused Pirandello could not remain in Berlin (although he went back for *The Changeling* in March 1933 and for the Eleventh Congress of the International Confederation of Authors and Composers in October 1936). He went to Paris, where he stayed for a considerable length of time and where he returned frequently, until the year of his death.

In Paris Pirandello felt dazed by so many years of failure and bitter solitude. He took to writing short stories again, and in one of these, 'One More' ('Uno di più'), written in Paris in 1931, he tells of a five-year-old child who dies because she is surrounded by hatred and by the wickedness of others. In another, 'Breath' ('Soffio'), we find a man who has discovered a means of killing anyone who passes in front of him. The letters he wrote to his distant children are further evidence of his bitterness. On 15 May, on his return from Hollywood, in a letter[8] to all three of his children, he wrote:

My life is now empty. I no longer have any of the things I wanted and, not having anything, I live for others and no longer for myself. Your father will have to spend his few remaining days alone, with no house or fixed abode anywhere. Besides the fact that his mind can no longer resign itself to any routine, this existence is a necessity, since a hostile destiny has so aroused the enemies of his talent that he can no longer return to his own country. He has to earn his living abroad, wherever he can. I hope to die on my feet so that I do not end up in a hospital in France or America. But I don't care. I now think of nothing but work and I shall work as long as I can. Death does not frighten me because I have been prepared for it for a long time, as I have for everything in life. It is a very bitter peace, achieved at the cost of accepting everything. I no longer see any liberation, not even in death. . . .

But he did nothing to conciliate the enemies which 'hostile destiny' had 'aroused' and, whenever he could, he gave destiny a hand, as he did that same December in his courageous speech against d'Annunzio.

In another letter of that year he again alluded to his nomadism. He said that he had been to London, that he had changed his address in Paris, and added:[9]

If you could see my mind, its lack of peace or hope of any possible restoration or improvement, you would be afraid. . . . You already have so many problems of your own and I, as a father, am unable to console you. Nor can you, my daughter, console me. A house, a country, are no longer for me. My soul is now alienated from everything and no longer has any contact with anything or anyone. I cannot bear my ideas to have any order, nor can I see that my life has any coherence. And so I go on from day to day. Here today, somewhere else tomorrow. I don't know how much longer I can hold out in this state, or why it still goes on; but any other would be impossible for me. That is how it is.

The relationship between Pirandello and Marta Abba does not seem to have been of much solace to him. If anything it simply increased his misery. His anguished, platonic love looked impossible in a life that had ended in total solitude. As he was glancing through one of Pirandello's drawers Corrado Alvaro found a slip of paper on which Pirandello had written: 'The end of youth, a body racked by years, and therefore the end of love.'[10] It was in these circumstances, moved by the frustration of old age, that Pirandello wrote *When One Is Somebody* (*Quando si è qualcuno*) in the summer of 1932. It tells of a great man about whom other people form a fixed idea. They consequently deny him the possibility of growing younger, of loving as his perennially young heart would want.

Pirandello's love for Marta Abba, which lasted seven or eight years, manifested itself in a thousand attentions, in a kind and helpful devotion which some people even considered undignified. They regarded it as unsuitable for a great man to run after a young woman, to cater to her whims, to adapt himself to all her changes of humour. Somebody remembers him at Agrigento, searching for 'old gold' together with the actress in all the goldsmiths' shops in town, and in the Cathedral of Catania at Christmas, standing behind Marta who was kneeling near the altar. Corrado Alvaro relates:[11]

I remember that, though he could be extremely generous, he was childishly avaricious about matches and a special sort of water which he drank at table and never gave to anyone. Once, when Marta Abba was at lunch, he poured out some of this water for her, telling her to drink it because 'it did one good'. . . . On another occasion, when I went into his study, I saw her lying on a sofa. She had taken off her shoes and her bare feet were exposed. She was tired. It was spring. I felt that Pirandello was embarrassed. Before that springtime exhaustion he behaved as though she were a little girl, as though she were the little animal, cruel and primitive, which he had always seen within woman.

On 25 November 1926 Pirandello made out a will with which he intended to 'punish' Lietta, probably for some lack of understanding shown towards Marta Abba. When he died, having very likely forgotten that he had ever made it, this same will was to be the cause of endless litigation and of some far from negligible consequences for his copyright.[12] 'Half of all I possess,' he said, 'must be divided into three equal parts between my three children, Stefano, Lia, and Fausto. The other available half must also be divided into three equal parts, but the third, as a punishment, must not go to my daughter but to the daughter of my choosing who, with her noble and pure love, comforted the last days of my errant life. She was rewarded with the basest and most revolting spite: I am referring to Miss Marta Abba. To compensate her for all the ill that came of the good she did me I also want her to have all the royalties accruing from performances in Italy and abroad for those works which I would never have written without her, starting with *Diana and Tuda*. So far there are two of them, *Diana and Tuda* and *The Wives' Friend*. Soon, with *The New Colony*, there will be three. There might be four or five in all. . . .'

Subsequently Marta Abba gave up the hereditament, but the litigation over the copyright began immediately after the war. According to a sentence issued by the courts of Rome in 1957 Marta Abba was entitled to the copyright of nine of the last fifteen plays written by Pirandello and Pirandello's children were ordered to inform Marta Abba if, by their initiative, any collection of his complete works was published. Furthermore Marta Abba has in her possession the letters written to her by the playwright. 'Some of these letters,' wrote a reporter from *Il Giorno*,[13] 'contain pejorative judgements by Pirandello about his children. Marta Abba undertook to remove any sentences which might cause offence to them in the event of publication.'

Alvaro tells us that Pirandello 'was in love with the actress until the

year before he died. . . . In his last years he assumed the role of someone who gives what he knows is a gift: friendship, warm admiration
and affection, protection and experience. . . .'[14]

Despite Pirandello's temporary desire to punish his daughter, his
love for her remained intact. Indeed, in his last letters, Pirandello wrote
to Lietta (and not Lia, as he called her in his will) with affection,
though not with the same abandon as before. In 1936, recalled by 'a
foreboding' of her father's imminent death, Lietta left Chile to be with
him during the last days of his life.[15]

There was no company in Italy ready to perform *When One Is
Somebody*, either because of the obtrusive autobiographical element or
because it had no appeal—we do not know which. So, on 18 March
1933, Pirandello wrote to his daughter: 'One of the plays I wrote last
summer at Castiglioncello, the play I cared most about, *When One Is
Somebody* . . . has not found a company ready to shoulder the expense
of performing it, and, at least for this year, remains in my desk drawer.'
This happened at the very moment when, as he showed in the play,
Pirandello had a high opinion of himself. He regarded himself as a
great man, and, in his dream in the second act, he found himself surrounded by Dante, Ariosto, Foscolo, and Leopardi who had assumed
the shape of gesticulating characters of his own creation.

Pirandello's restlessness continued. On 11 June 1932 he wrote to
Lietta:

I have left Paris for three months. I have a great deal of work to do,
two plays to finish, one for America, one here; one for Ruggeri who is
returning to the stage in October. . . . Towards the end of September
I shall return to Paris to see *As You Desire Me* at the Théâtre Mont-
parnasse with Baty at the beginning of October. It is my destiny to run
round the world without resting, until the day when I die on my feet,
as I hope will happen soon since I can no longer remain in one place.
Despite my efforts my own country cannot employ me or hold me.

In March 1933 he wrote again:

The further I go and the closer I get to the extreme limit of life, the
harder it is for me to fix a date, establish a programme, trace an itinerary,
foresee what I will do tomorrow, where I shall go, if I shall stay. I tell
everybody that I don't know. And I really don't want to know. Since
I no longer feel at home anywhere this constant sense of precariousness
enables me to bear my brief stays here and there. A stay can be pro-
longed, provided it never occurs to me that it might become permanent: if it does I flee. It was for this reason that I fled from Berlin after

two and a half years and from Paris after two years. I don't think I shall be staying long in Rome either.

When One Is Somebody was first performed on 20 September 1933 at the Odeon in Buenos Aires, with Pirandello and Massimo Bontempelli present; and it was at last performed in Italy by Marta Abba and her own company at the Teatro del Casinò Municipale in San Remo in November. According to one critic the success of the performance was 'an artificial apotheosis'.[16] It was 'exaggeratedly' attacked (according to the same critic) in Rome and Naples, and met with a cool reception in Milan.

Pirandello's dealings with the cinema began in 1913. From his initial lack of interest during the first phase of the cinema Pirandello passed on to aversion and declared contempt for the period marked by films like *Quo Vadis?* and *Cabiria*. Arnaldo Frateili, who spent a great deal of time with Pirandello when he planned or actually wrote filmscripts, said that 'the writer's critical and hostile attitude towards the cinema never changed despite his involvement with it.'[17]

In 1913, however, because of his financial straights, Pirandello decided to approach his friend Martoglio, director of the Morgana Film Company. He wrote to Martoglio:[18] 'Verga, Bracco, Salvatore Di Giacomo. . . . Full steam ahead! Couldn't I do something too? I have so many subjects, of every sort. You know that!' On 27 May of the same year he insisted: 'I know that Lucio [D'Ambra] has mentioned my intention of suggesting some detailed projects to you. I already have one, "Bull's Eye" ["Nel segno", a short story which appeared in *Marzocco* in 1904], very fine and almost ready. I could prepare another one in a few days' time and I would also be ready to sign a contract, at a decent fee for each film. What do you say to that? Tell me where and how we can meet. . . .'

He wrote a script for Martoglio which should have been performed by Giovanni Grasso but which was never produced since the Morgana Film Company soon ceased to exist. At that time Pirandello lived at 10, Via Alessandro Torlonia. Almost directly beneath his house, in a large meadow, stood the studios of the cinema company Film d'Arte Italiana of which Ugo Falena, a friend both of Lucio D'Ambra and Pirandello, was the arts director and Lo Savio the administrator.[19] Orio Vergani remembered that from Pirandello's windows 'one could see actors and actresses gesticulating in front of the cameras through the glass doors of the studios. And then the shouts of the cameraman, "Shoot!", reached the writer's observatory.'[20]

More than once Pirandello visited these studios with Lucio D'Ambra who later said that Ugo Falena often used to call on his two friends to ask them to lend him a chair or a kettle for use on the set. Once Pirandello promised that, within a week, he 'would give him a rough script of Ippolito Nievo's *Confessions of an Octogenarian* which nobody, fortunately, ever saw.'[21]

Even if Pirandello did not succeed in writing for the cinema at the time, the crowd under his windows—actors and actresses, producers and cameramen, the most extraordinary collection of people—finally aroused his imagination and induced him to write a novel about the cinema. In 1915 he had *Shoot* ready for *La Nuova Antologia* which published it from June to August. It was his penultimate novel. In order to represent the film world accurately he wanted to learn about everything. He went to visit the studios of the Cines Company, and Arnaldo Frateili said that the offices of the Kosmograph described in the novel were very like those of the Cines Company.[22] He learnt the technical terms off by heart; he took an interest in the process of cutting and fixing the film; but gradually, as the book developed, the whole universe of the cinema turned into a mass of symbols.

Today the cinema jargon used by Pirandello looks curiously archaic. But the book conveys the atmosphere of that period, the observation of a life which never fulfilled itself. In the secret chamber of the author's imagination the central symbol of the novel, the camera, is transformed into 'a spider which sucks and absorbs the live reality of the actor and turns it into an evanescent appearance,' a vampire-like image and the umpteenth symbol of depersonalization.

Pirandello's judgement of the cinema was severe. The cinema was a swallower of life and the films 'tapeworms'. The life of a film was 'not life' but 'fixed life', or death. Besides, if the cinema 'is a mechanism, how can it be art? It is like entering one of those museums of living statues, of waxworks, dressed up and painted.'

Notwithstanding the humiliation he must have derived from it, Pirandello continued, a few years later, to sell his stories to the cinema. Indeed, according to Frateili, 'he welcomed every occasion of seeing some work of his on the screen.'[23] In 1919 Mario Gargiulo directed *The Collapse* (*Il crollo*) from a short story of his, and adapted *Sicilian Limes*. The following year Ugo Gracci directed *The Light of the Other House* (*Il lume dell'altra casa*). Also in 1920 Pirandello collaborated with

Frateili on the script of *Black Panther* (*Pantera nera*), and *It's Nothing Serious* appeared with a script by Frateili and directed by Augusto Camerini. In 1921 three films were based on short stories by Pirandello, *Adriana Takes a Trip* (*Il viaggio*), *The Rose*, and *The Brazier* (*Lo scaldino*), directed respectively by Gennaro Righelli, Arnaldo Frateili, and Augusto Genina. After his theatrical successes in Paris the French cinema, too, showed an interest in his work and bought the rights of *The Late Mattia Pascal* (1925) which was directed by Marcel L'Herbier with Ivan Mosjukin acting the title role. The film had a considerable success and the following year a film of *Henry IV* was directed in Berlin by Amleto Palermi. In a letter written from Berlin in May 1930, shortly after the failure of *Tonight We Improvise*, Pirandello said that in August he would set sail from Hamburg for the United States where he would sign a contract with Paramount.

In the meantime the cinema was improving. When Pirandello was born it did not exist. He was a grown man when it had passed from its experimental phase to its industrial phase. In the end the writer witnessed the first experiments with sound track. He was in two minds about them, feeling more and more that cinema was the mortal enemy of the theatre. He declared that he was certain of the superiority of the theatre and of its perennial quality, but he could not help taking part in the debate about the new invention and, in *Il Corriere della Sera* of 16 June 1929 he wrote an article entitled, 'Will the talking film replace the theatre?' Here all his former aversion came to the surface.

In Italy no sound films had yet been produced and some people feared that the arrival of the talkie would provoke the final crisis of the theatre. Pirandello sprang to the attack. 'At this time of universal infatuation with the talking film I have heard the following heresy: that the talking film will replace the theatre; that in two or three years' time the theatre will no longer exist; that all theatres . . . will close because everything will be devoted to the cinema, to the talking film.' But, 'the theatre is not striving to become cinema, it is clearly the cinema which is striving to become theatre.' The industrialists of the silent film must be panic stricken, for, 'like old fish . . . they have wagged their fins and their tails in the stagnant waters of a silent marsh for too long. . . .' For Pirandello the talking film had a ghost-like quality: it was a sequence of meaningless, talking photographs. 'The lips of these great images in the foreground move emptily, since no voice ever emerges from their mouths. It emerges from a machine, as the grotesque voice of a machine, not as a human voice, but as the vulgar muttering of a ventriloquist. . . .' It was like the vain peacock which 'opened its mouth for all to hear and made everybody laugh.' In short, the benefits of scientific invention were provoking the suicide of the cinema in favour of the theatre.

Pirandello was not alone in condemning talkies: Chaplin, Murnau, King Vidor, and René Clair would have agreed with him. But Pirandello also offered a solution to the problem. The cinema

should free itself from the word, that is from literature, and immerse itself in music. . . . There: pure music and pure vision. The two aesthetic senses *par excellence*, the eye and the ear, united in a single pleasure: the eye that sees, the ear that hears and the heart that feels. . . . *Cinemelography*, that is the name of the true revolution. . . . Think what a prodigious mass of images can be aroused by the whole musical folklore, from an old Spanish *habanera* to the 'Volga, Volga' of the Russians, or the 'Pastoral Symphony', or the 'Eroica', or even one of the Nocturnes or one of the 'Valses brillantes'. . . .

What a pity that Pirandello as a prophet was only heard in Disneyland!

In 1930, however, one of Pirandello's short stories, 'In Silence', was made into the first talkie to be produced in Italy. The film was called *The Song of Love* (*La canzone dell'amore*), and was issued simultaneously in Italian, German, and French versions. Later, around 1932, Pirandello intended to devote himself to an arts cinema, and, in collaboration with his son Stefano, he provided a subject, *Play*, *Peter* (*Gioca, Pietro*),[24] which was eventually made into a fine documentary by Walter Ruttmann, under the title, *Steel*. Unfortunately it had no commercial success.

Meanwhile, Pirandello started to work for Hollywood. He was present at the shooting of *As You Desire Me* which had been turned into a sentimental film, directed by George Fitzmaurice. It soon became famous on account of its stars, Greta Garbo and Erich von Stroheim. M.G.M. had paid Pirandello 40,000 dollars for the film rights, but he later complained[25] that the American agent, the European agent, and other middlemen had taken almost the entire sum and he had only one tenth of it left. This was his only film produced in the United States during his lifetime, but, on the wave of his success, he had a number of offers from Hollywood and made further plans for films. Indeed, he made a journey to America specifically to supervise the adaptation of other works and to write some original screenplays. M.G.M. commissioned him to write a script for *Six Characters in Search of an Author* (after the other version, planned in Germany in 1929 with Adolf Lantz, had fallen through). It would have been directed by Irving Thalberg who was 'seriously interested' in the project, Pirandello wrote to his daughter in June 1932. The film was not made, however, just as, some years earlier, a further film version of *Henry IV* had not been made since the producers wanted the story to end with Henry IV's marriage to Matilde Spina.[26] Pirandello planned a story for the Barrymore brothers whom he greatly admired, but the project fell through.[27]

This time, therefore, Pirandello returned from the cinema world of America without having concluded anything. Yet, in October 1935, after receiving the Nobel Prize, he had further plans for Hollywood: he told a journalist that Edward Robinson, 'who, as you know,' he added, 'is one of the greatest actors alive in America', had been given the part of Baldovino in *The Pleasure of Honesty*.[28] Pirandello was in the United States for a few months in 1935 but the film never got as far as the studios.

In 1935 Pirandello collaborated in Italy on the adaptation of *Better Think Twice About It* in which Angelo Musco played the lead. And he was constantly working with his son Stefano and Corrado Alvaro who were making the film of *No Man's Land* from two of his short stories 'Romulus' ('Romolo') and 'Give Them Eternal Rest, O Lord' ('Requiem aeternam dona eis, Domine'). Corrado Alvaro tells us[29] that Pirandello adapted himself reluctantly to the functional necessities of the film script and thought of the scenes in too literary a manner.

In the last year of his life Pirandello made a final attempt on the American film world. This time it was at the invitation of Max Reinhardt who had fled to Hollywood owing to Nazi persecution of the Jews, and who wanted to film *Six Characters in Search of an Author*. Pirandello planned the adaptation together with Reinhardt. He explained the new plot to a journalist. Its quality appears very dubious The journalist reported:[30]

The film will take place on three levels: that of reality, that of art, and on a third level in which art acts on reality, influencing and determining it. Pirandello himself, the Author, is at the centre of the film. One evening, impelled by curiosity, he followed a woman in mourning (the Daughter) and saw her meet another woman in mourning, the Mother. He saw the despair in their faces and gestures. Peeping out from a window he saw a child who was even sadder and more desperate than the two women. . . . When he left them he could no longer forget these characters, into the mystery of whose lives he had so unexpectedly entered. His fantasy had taken possession of them. He started to sketch acts, incidents, and the Six Characters come to life. But when he follows them in life Pirandello sees with terror that they really are alive and that they are performing the drama he had thought out for them. Irrevocably, as though ordered by his imagination, all that he had thought out takes place. The Child he has doomed to die will die. Pirandello steps back: he is suddenly faced with his responsibility as a man. If that child dies he will have killed him. So Pirandello abandons the Six Characters. He does not conclude the work and nobody dies. The unfinished characters no longer have an author or a goal, but they no longer have peace either. Fixed, nailed for ever to their drama, eternally deprived of catharsis. This is the outline of the film. Reinhardt is to do the rest and he will certainly do it well.

Fortunately this *Six Characters—Twenty Years Later* was never produced and Reinhardt never could 'do it well' at the expense of an aged Pirandello who yielded to other people's suggestions and who would certainly have worn ill the clothes of a cinema actor under the glare of the Hollywood lights. Instead we admire more the Pirandello who, in the last years of his life, battled bravely on against the cinema in favour of the theatre. At the Convegno Volta in 1934 he suggested drastic measures be taken so 'that there be only one evening performance in cinemas at a fixed time' and so that 'the closed theatre of every evening' be saved—'a question of civilization for every country that wants to be civilized.'[31]

The year of the Nobel Prize, 1934, began by bringing Pirandello new disappointments, but it ended in fame and glory, pacification and satisfaction. In this same year he applied himself to a new, essentially moral problem, and recovered part of his shattered confidence. Writing *No One Knows How* he was convinced that he had recovered his true medium, and the disappointment of the critics was drowned by the clamour of the Nobel Prize.

In March *The Changeling* had been banned in Germany and had been hissed off the stage at the Rome Opera House. In October Pirandello presided over the Fourth Convegno Volta, under the patronage of the Italian Academy, on the subject of dramatic art. On 8 October, in his inaugural speech, addressing authors, producers, critics, and students of the theatre from several countries, he expressed faith in the theatre. He affirmed that the theatre was the only certainty in a period of 'anguished waves of doubt'. 'The theatre cannot die. It is a form of life itself, we all act in it, and if theatres were abolished and abandoned, the theatre would continue in life.' Besides, said Pirandello (and his words shed some light on his last phase—that of a moralist concentrating on the problem of man's absolute responsibility), 'the theatre offers to the judgement of the audience human actions as they really are, as an example and a warning in the confusion of everyday existence. It arouses a free and human judgement which effectively recalls the consciences of the judges themselves to an ever more elevated and demanding moral life.'

No One Knows How, the last work Pirandello finished,[32] was performed for the first time in France at the Théâtre National on 19 December 1934, in the presence of the author on his return from Stockholm. It had a *succès d'estime*. The play deals with the insoluble problem of moral responsibility: is man responsible for the evil he does if he does it without knowing why? It was an endeavour to solve the feeling of guilt which lay at the basis of Pirandello's whole life, and we can here see clearly how radical was his concept of original sin, inculcated into him by his Catholic education and combined with a personal myth of the fall, applying to the entire metaphysical destiny of man. In *No One Knows How* the answer was dogmatic, but Pirandello had raised a problem which was very real in the spiritual conscience of the times. In its existential sense, at a moment of greater cultural lucidity, it was to be taken up by Camus in *The Fall*. But Pirandello's mistake, an inevitable mistake in view of his background and his education, was to resort to an essentially Catholic morality (even if he may also have been stimulated by the new influence of Freud).[33] The sin of the flesh, adultery, was regarded, as in the Garden of Eden and in the puritanical nineteenth century, as the paradigm of guilt.

At the time, *No One Knows How* appeared to brand Pirandello more as a reactionary than as a precursor. Yet he was very pleased with the play. 'It may be my strongest work', he said. 'It is certainly the one that tackles the most serious problem: that of will and responsibility.' At which Mario Missiroli, who was interviewing him,[34] asked: 'So, after having discussed the problem of knowledge in your former works, there now comes the problem of action? After pure reason, practical reason.' And the playwright replied: 'In a sense, yes. My former work must be regarded as the logical premise of this last one.'

But it was not so much a question of 'a logical premise' as of sharing the same psychological territory. In his old age Pirandello wanted to differentiate himself from what he had been before, to give a proof, to himself rather than to others, of an evolution of his own. In a letter to

Pietro Mignosi on 11 May 1935 he wrote: 'It is enough for me to know
in my heart ... that I have been a pure instrument in the hands of
Someone above me and above everybody. The rest is of no importance. ...'[35]

There had indeed been an evolution. It was as though Pirandello
really had grown older and the forces of protest and rebellion had
stiffened within him and lost their impetus. He seemed to be in search
of an external support for certain traditional metaphysical incentives.
That he was returning to Catholicism (even if he remained half-way, in
an almost Jansenist position) seems clear. In the interview with Mario
Missiroli he fully accepted the Christian and Catholic dogma of the
expiation of sins for which one is not responsible:

I have undertaken to demonstrate [in *No One Knows How*] that one
never avoids the penalty, or rather the expiation, even in those cases in
which the will of man is almost surprised in its sleep and crime appears
to be a mere *occurrence*, rather than a deliberate action. What stronger
denial is there of scepticism? ... To be aware of something does not
mean that one knows how one happened to do that particular thing.
Remember Tolstoy's *Kreutzer Sonata*. It is one of the many antinomies
which cannot be reduced to abstract thought and which are resolved
exclusively in practice. In the same way as our knowledge is gained
amid the illusion of the senses and one can never make the relative
coincide with the absolute, nature with the spirit, *reality* with truth, so,
in the moral world, conscience is awakened as a very severe and in-
transigent judge in the mind of whoever has broken the law, even if he
does not know how. Crime belongs to nature but the really dramatic
moment is the moment of justice and it is all the more dramatic if the
tribunal is invisible, in other words if it resides in one's conscience. ...

This is the conscience of a Christian. Some time later, shortly before
he died, Pirandello indicated still more explicitly the connection between the Christian and Catholic moral code and his own contraposi-
tion between 'the man who is free' and 'the man who is not free'.
Speaking on this occasion[36] of *Lazarus*, written eight years earlier, he
said:

In *Lazarus* I give the clearest reply to the dissidence [between life and
form] in all my plays in as much as it is a religious and social phenomenon. If you remove form from the man who is not free he immediately
lapses into animality, because form is a spiritual link; and the first act of
his so-called liberty is a rifle shot against another man, against the new
Adam living in peace with his Eve. The son then sacrifices himself,

re-enters the order, dons the sacerdotal garb for those who need it. His rational faith led to ruin and that too was only form. Christ is *charity*, love. Only for the love that understands and can observe the golden mean between order and anarchy, between form and life, is the conflict resolved. I am also pleased that no religious authority has condemned me. None of my works are on the Index. *Civiltà Cattolica* discussed my work in detail in three articles which constitute a veritable volume, and it agrees about my perfect orthodoxy. Perfect orthodoxy as far as the presentation of the problem is concerned. And these problems can only have a Christian solution.

In actual fact *Civiltà Cattolica* attacked Pirandello severely in its articles and it is surprising that he never uttered a word of protest, and instead seemed rather pleased about the whole matter. Besides, certain Catholics took advantage of this tendency to return to Catholicism, however confused, contradictory, and superficial, and attempted to claim for the Catholic Church a writer who was substantially secular, or who was, at least, far from any dogma. Mignosi's sensational book, *The Secret of Pirandello (Il segreto di Pirandello)*, which appeared in 1935, represented Pirandello as an exemplarily devout writer. *Six Characters in Search of an Author* was interpreted in a Roman Catholic key, with the author as God. A violent polemic ensued among Catholics as to whether or not Pirandello would save his soul. Giancarlo Vigorelli, then a young man, writing in 1937[37] when Pirandello was dead, denied the existence of grace in Pirandello's work, while Giovanni Papini wrote that 'Pirandello was a great, productive and original writer, but he never managed to meet the Supreme Author. . . .'[38]

The Jesuits, for their part, paid a great deal of attention to Pirandello and sometimes gave a moderate verdict, at least until *Lazarus*, for 'thank God, Pirandello did not concern himself much with theology and this was praiseworthy of him'.[39] But even after *Lazarus*, the most tolerant of them, like Hubert de Leusse,[40] did not want to condemn him too severely. The reaction of the Vatican, on the other hand, was less liberal and less generous. *L'Osservatore Romano* went as far as to justify and support the Nazis' banning of *The Changeling* in March 1934. It was not difficult to understand, it wrote, the reason for the intervention of the State in view of that 'filthy fable which offends the principles both of morality and of authority.'

As for the Jesuits closest to the Vatican, the polemic which started on 19 May 1923 continued in *Civiltà Cattolica* until 2 January 1937, that is, until after the writer's death, revealing a constant concern and irritation amongst the hierarchy of the Society about the phenomenon of Pirandello. To start with, Pirandello was treated as 'an eccentric', 'one of the few men who assume the philosopher's pallium and distort life, reducing it to an arbitrary caricature and then, taking the poet's lyre, laugh and joke bitterly and stridently and like to call themselves humorists.' Then, when *Lazarus* appeared, the attacks by Pirandello's Jesuit enemy, Domenico Mondrone, grew more bitter. He described Pirandello's plays as 'the most odious and absurd defamation of the fundamental truths of Catholic education and Christian faith: the very existence of a personal God and of a miraculous fact like the Resurrection.' When Mondrone pronounced Pirandello's epitaph two weeks after his death he said, with reference to Pirandello's claim never to have been put on the Index, 'just as all lunatics are not interned in an asylum so all damnable books have not been expressly condemned by the Index.'

In Rome, on 9 November 1934, Pirandello received the telegram from the Secretary-General of the Royal Academy of Sweden. 'The Academy of Sweden has this morning awarded you the Nobel Prize for Literature. . . .' Journalists and photographers invaded his study. He had been preferred to Paul Valéry and G. K. Chesterton, the other candidates of that year, and, when the photographers and cameramen asked him to pose, Pirandello sat down at his little table and typed out repeatedly the word *'pagliacciate'* ('buffooneries').[41] Judging by the number of times he repeated the word it must have been a long session. But Pirandello was greatly comforted by this last recognition of his merit, even though he confronted this new triumph prudently, feeling that life was slipping from him. He did not care about the lack of official honours given him in Italy. On 10 December he was in Stockholm and he received from the hands of the King of Sweden the parchment, the medal, and the sum of money.

Everybody was jubilant and so, it would appear, was Pirandello. In his speech to the Swedish Academy, he said: 'I have been a good pupil. A good pupil not at school but in life, a good pupil who started by assembling with absolute faith all that he learnt. . . . The determination with which I followed this doctrine . . . was absolutely necessary for meeting the bitter disappointments, cruel experiences, terrible words, and all the errors of naiveté which have made of me a being (as an artist should be) totally unequipped for life and equipped only for thinking and feeling.'

From Stockholm Pirandello went to Prague to attend the first night of *No One Knows How*. The Bohemian producer had used a set loaded with abstract symbols in an attempt to lend metaphysical profundities to the drama ('skies full of symbolic circles, an idea of the infinite with pilasters and parapets, sinister lights').[42] But Pirandello did not want any complaints to be made to the young producer. 'No, no, don't say anything to him. He might take offence, and even if he didn't take offence he might be upset, poor chap. . . . He sees my things like that. What can one do about it? Let him see them like that. . . .'

In Prague Pirandello went readily to all appointments, ceremonies, and speeches. But a 'great inner anxiety' appeared in him 'even when he tried to keep up his morale or distract himself with irony. He looked as though he had only just arrived, arrived from nobody knew where.'[43] Once again it was Paris which filled Pirandello with joy. George Pitoëff produced *Tonight We Improvise* for the first time in France and Pirandello, having arrived in Paris in December 1934, became the object of festivities and homage. *Le Figaro*, *Paris-Soir*, the Société des Auteurs, the Société des Gens de Lettres, organized dinners, tea-parties, and meetings in his honour. On 17 January, in *Comoedia*, his portrait appeared in the column entitled 'la figure du jour', with, printed beneath it, 'Luigi Pirandello, whom Paris is proud of having introduced to the world.' On that same 17 January, at the Théâtre des Mathurins, Pitoëff's production opened. Silvio D'Amico described the event:[44]

From Rome, where Mussolini invited him to a cordial meeting, Pirandello went back to Paris . . . for the great gala performance at the Théâtre des Mathurins where Pitoëff had produced *Tonight We Improvise*. It was followed by an unusual, bizarre, and enthusiastic act of homage by all the Paris actors of his plays, and by the presentation of the Légion d'honneur to the guest by the Minister of Education, Mallarmé. [Pirandello had never bothered to collect the first rosette given to him many years earlier.] On Gaston Baty's announcement, the characters filed past, one by one, each wearing the make-up of his part and pronouncing the appropriate words: the Mother (Marie Kalff) and the Producer (Michel Simon) from *Six Characters in Search of an Author*, Baldovino (Dullin) from *The Pleasure of Honesty*, Signora Frola (Madame Dullin) from *Right You Are (If You Think So)*, Ersilia (Madame Simon) and her fellow actors from *Naked*, Fulvia (Paulette Pax) and Mauri (Clariond) from *As Before, Better than Before*, the Mother and the Nun (Rivorin and Bing) from *The Life I Gave You*, Frida (Ludmilla Pitoëff) from *Henry IV*, the Unknown Woman (Marguerite Jamois) from *As You Desire Me*, and finally, our Marta

Abba who performed in Paris, in French, *Man*, *Beast and Virtue*, dressed as Signora Perella, with Paolino and Captain Perella (Lefour and Pauley). . . . The festivities in Pirandello's honour were more than an act of friendship, more than a political gesture.

In *L'Italia Letteraria*[45] Ivan Goll commented: 'It is the triumph, the apotheosis of Pirandello. It is the height of worldly success. The other night Pirandello was happy. All Paris had come to render homage to him: ambassadors, politicians, writers, poets, the most beautiful women in Paris had assembled to witness . . . the apotheosis of Pirandello's entire career as a dramatist.' The Pirandello who had been decorated in Stockholm acquired a very different fame from the controversial notoriety of twelve years earlier. In the eyes of his contemporaries he really had been transformed into the 'Somebody' of his play.

Now that he was surrounded by an aura of conventional fame gossip columnists, writers, and journalists started to regard him with new curiosity, ready to record his most picturesque characteristics and idio-syncracies. At times this gave rise to almost hagiographic anecdotes, but at others, to acute and illuminating observations. Pirandello's face became the object of every sort of interpretation. Marco Ramperti referred to his 'symmetrical Pythagorean face and the half-closed eyes from which memories seemed to be sailing towards different shores . . .' and Guglielmo Lo Curzio to 'his eye which gleams as if with an absorbed irony and fades out, as though out of indifference. But his smile is kindly and it quivers almost with pain on the weak, satirical mouth. His broad, hard brow dominates his heavy nose, his cavernous cheeks, his sensual lips, his pointed chin; in that face, you see contra-riety and indulgence, secretiveness and passion, spirit and sense, lines and curves.' His qualities were exalted—'a good, just and generous man'. In Prague, 'on his way back from Stockholm, his main concern was with a waiter who was about to be sacked for being impolite to him. . . . Pirandello cabled twice that he should be forgiven.'[46]

He was superstitious. He was interviewed by a journalist-fortune-teller.[47] 'The interviewer stared at a knot between the lines of his palm. A death? No, something worse. Pirandello was very excited and wanted to know all that palmistry said and did not say.' In 1936 Bontempelli told Ugo Ojetti that, three years earlier, in Brazil, 'Pirandello had said that he was going to die in 1933. Thirty-three years in the nineteenth century and thirty-three in the twentieth. He liked these calcula-tions. . . .'[48] He was candid. 'One night he was furious with a famous actor who had re-elaborated one of Pirandello's texts in his own way.

Shut in the dressing-room Pirandello hurled the most terrible curses at him: "If I had a gun I would have shot him." Then his anger passed and he calmed down.' 'He was as happy as a child on the day when the lift boy in Paris had been asked who that gentleman with the white beard and the expressive face was and had answered: *Le plus grand écrivain d'Italie.*'[49]

People were also told how Pirandello travelled and how he dressed. He only took 'indispensable objects with him: the suit he has on, his overcoat, a pair of strange shirts which also serve as waistcoats, socks, vests, pyjamas, a few books to read.'[50] He smoked Xantia cigarettes, as many as three or four packets a day. He only ate *pain carré*, and he typed with one finger on a red type-writer. Before he started typing his hand-writing was 'honest, precise, nineteenth-century. He liked certain very beautiful and spacious capital letters, like the P of his surname.'[51]

In the last period of his life his house became ever more anonymous and, according to Alvaro,[52] more like 'some hotel room, like the ones he had seen and lived in over the last twenty years. . . . It was no good searching for signs of a particular habit or preference. Everything was casual and everything was alien to him. When he wanted to embellish his bedroom he turned that, too, into a hotel room: a copper bed and turquoise wallpaper. I never heard him talk about furniture or decorative objects (the only object he liked was a Greek vase), but he talked a great deal about people. . . .'

Pirandello had now become very untidy. His books piled up messily during his provisional stays in Rome. On the shelves along the walls a volume of Petrarch would stand next to a propaganda brochure, a multi-volume history of Venice next to a bibliophile's edition of Boccaccio. Even his own books were not all there: there might be thirty copies of one and none of others. In a corner, between a cupboard and the wall, there would be a huge pile of reviews, books, and newspapers. The spines of the dictionaries were falling off and the books he had used years earlier as a young teacher and an essayist were broken and scattered about the place. On one shelf the translation of his works into every language in the world had replaced, or stood between, worn editions of the classics. The same untidiness was to be found in his drawers. His correspondence piled up on his desk, and there were letters of twenty years earlier which were still awaiting an answer.[53]

The observations of his contemporaries could be still more perceptive. Here we have an account of Pirandello's chastity. 'Once, when he came to Paris,' said Juliette Bertrand,[54] 'he brought with him his faith-

ful secretary Saul Colin, Nardelli, and Marta Abba. Colin was talking
about the Swede who had changed sex. Frivolous words were uttered
which were meant to be witty. Pirandello was not interested in the
subject. To one question he barely answered a word. The austerity of
what he said filled me with respect. . . .' And Corrado Alvaro wrote:[55]

I remember one evening when we were walking home along Via Ludo-
visi in Rome with Pirandello and his sons. . . . Pirandello walked along
ahead of us, his hands in his pockets. It was a beautiful spring evening
and we breathed in the scent of the trees and the roses of Villa Malta.
The sound of our steps was enough to make us happy. Pirandello was
alone with himself and his daemon. At one point we started talking
about women because the air had something feminine about it. Pirandello listened for a second and then started walking faster, clenching his
fists in his pockets and raising his face in one of the typical expressions
of his solitude.

Other people were struck by the remoteness of his inner thoughts.
'He turned inspiration on and off like the tap of a fountain.'[56] 'He had
no need of any external stimulus'.[57] Alvaro tells us that Pirandello
never sought inspiration in literature and never read new books, unless
they happened to be sent to him. 'When he read he was always on the
look-out for some true revelation of the artist in the author.' He had
recently returned to the great writers, to Boccaccio and Shakespeare.
To Giulio Caprin he said that he felt himself related to Dante, Machia-
velli, Leopardi, Manzoni; that he had read and meditated on Manzoni;
that he would reread *Orlando Furioso* to satisfy his imagination; that he
admired Anatole France among foreign writers and that the greatest
impression he had received was from the Russians, above all from
Dostoyevsky.[58] And he added: 'I'm not a bibliophile. What counts in a
book is the spirit. The rest is just paper that gets in the way. I don't
want to keep my own books. I don't particularly want to keep anything!'

The Nobel Prize was far from re-establishing a direct contact between Pirandello and the new generation of writers. Not until twenty
years after his death did the young rediscover him—and they did so in
their own way. The men who were closest to him, Bontempelli,
Frateili, and Alvaro, regarded him with admiration and respect, but
these same friends, like so many others, had for some time been following a different artistic current. In the end Pirandello tried to approach
the young himself. He wrote his last short stories with a new literary
polish, as if he had learnt a lesson from some of Bontempelli's sur-

realist tales and from Cecchi of *The Red Fish* (*I pesci rossi*). Thus
Bontempelli, who had for so long been influenced by Pirandello, had a
certain influence on the last of the master's writings.[59] 'It was the time,'
noted Corrado Alvaro,[60] 'when a man in his decline bends down to
pick up the torch from the uncertain hands of the young and writes his
last works with a tinge of regret and with the illusory bloom of
autumn. . . .'

About *Oneself*, a work written in 1932, Tyyni Tuulio, a young
Finnish writer, commented:[61] 'On 1 November 1933 *Oneself* was performed in Pirandello's presence in Helsinki. Pirandello's celebrity
electrified both the theatre and the performance, but it was hardly a
success. We had the impression, rather, that Pirandello was no longer
a contemporary of ours . . . that we had *found* Pirandello, and had no
need to go on looking for him.' In October 1935 Camillo Pellizzi
wrote from London:[62] 'It now seems that young writers and critics
have agreed that Pirandello should no longer be discussed. Despite the
protests of his youth he is now regarded as a character on whom to
write a thesis or a monograph for university examinations.'

When, at the end of 1935, Pirandello found a company ready to
perform *No One Knows How* in Italy, it was hissed—not at the first
night, in the author's presence, but at the repeat performances when he
listened from the wings. 'He smiled delightedly as he stood in the
wings . . . and exclaimed: "They're hissing me! I'm still young".'[63]
Corrado Alvaro says that the first performance before an unconvinced
but reverent audience filled him with unease: 'The spectators felt that
they should show some emotion at the passage when a lizard is described, a fine piece of prose and bravura, and they applauded him.'[64]
The audience were as attentive as if they were at a ceremonial and they
clapped where previously they would have booed.

During Pirandello's last years Raoul Radice frequently came across
him in the evening in restaurants or cafés. 'Calm and courteous, he
spoke about himself and others as though he were not even aware of
the world around him. . . . Argument seemed to be banned from his
circle, even when he was seated next to young men who admired his
intelligence but not his art, which seemed too closed and sterile to
them. And he knew it.'[65] 'He had already entered the grey season of the
artist,' said Alvaro,[66] 'the season in which great men find themselves
holding a fistful of ashes, when, in their lifetime, they are already being
pushed towards history. . . . This is the time when a man can no longer
rely on any judgement passed on him. He has been discussed too much.

The die has been cast. Whatever has been written has been written. I felt that such a moment was being lived by Pirandello.'

Yet the official and, in a sense, the definitive recognition accorded to his work by the Nobel Prize, ended by reassuring him, by relieving his anxiety, even his despair. He no longer uttered those disconsolate words he had written to his daughter Lietta as late as 1933: 'I don't know whether I am fleeing from life or whether life is fleeing from me. I know that I feel almost completely "detached". I see the earth in the distance. . . . From my present vantage point in life, I am very, very distant. And I do not need to go to the stratosphere with Professor Piccard.' Now, as he looked into himself in this year of 1935, he rediscovered his former sense of possessing a truth of his own. 'The only impression I receive from the world, however new and varied it may appear, is something like a pleasant memory: almost a sense of re-awakened memories. It is merely a moment: . . . [an impression] through the senses of a fleeting rebirth in which the new life of things seen consumes in a flash what we had imagined. . . . And we immediately feel nostalgia for the things we had imagined. . . . Sometimes new men and countries look to me like portraits and landscapes in a gallery I must have visited many years ago, who knows when. . . . I have always *recognized* everything'.[67] We find this same tone in Pirandello's last short stories.

Premonitions of death became continuous towards the end. From the cruel reality of illness (the attacks of *angina pectoris*) they turned into parables, like the short story 'A Geranium in the Evening' ('Di sera, un geranio'), in which the end of life is compared to a geranium which suddenly comes to flower at night in a garden. Death seems to have lost the semblance of a barrier which had once obsessed him. The wall fell without any resistance. Pirandello stuck to the line of conduct he had planned in the distant days of 1911 when he wrote his 'last wishes which must be respected': 'Nothing, not even my ashes, must remain.' This desire for liberation from all things physical, this dispersion of the senses, now became a recurrent theme.

Shortly before he died, Pirandello ordered a register for those who visited his body and wrote his own name at the head of the page.[68] For him death was to have been very different from the rigid survival of his corpse: 'As soon as one is freed from all the illusions of the senses it will be like that imperceptible, sudden spray which punctures a bubble of soap. Light and colour, movement, everything will be as nothing. And silence.'[69] In the meantime his body was going to be cremated;

the wind was to free the ashes. It was not a desire for a lyrical death, but a search for the absolute in non-literary symbols, which involved both body and soul. Though Pirandello frequently repeated that he wanted to write life and not to live it, he seemed to want to live it in death.

He had had continual attacks of *angina pectoris* of late. When, in 1935, he had such attacks in Paris where he stayed on his own in a flat in the Avenue Victor-Emmanuel he would call a friend to his bedside and say: 'Death can come'. 'I heard him formulate this faith in death, this authorization of death,' said Benjamin Crémieux,[70] 'not on a day of health but after a sudden attack which made him writhe with pain in front of me, as though he were about to succumb.'

At times Pirandello now thought that his old frustration about his need to communicate had been overcome. 'In some places,' he wrote in 1935,[71] 'and I am thinking of my last stay in the Argentine, my communication with others was so affectionate and moving, so human, that I could give it as a prize to that ingenuous and trusting child who still lives inside me. And so I finally satisfied him.'

Raoul Radice remembered him at Viareggio one evening in August. Friends were sitting at his table on the terrace of a restaurant in the harbour. They were all facing the sea and only Pirandello had his back to it. 'I can still see him immobile and silent, staring at the wine in his glass with a beatific smile on his thin lips.'[72] The last images we have of Pirandello are of an absent-minded man absorbed in his own limbo. For the most part he was quietly submissive to others, to an official, conventional political life, to commitments, to contracts.

He would suddenly break out into solemn utterances, and quote the Greeks or some great name, drawing a comparison with himself.[73] 'Nietzsche said that the Greeks raised white statues against the black abyss, to hide it. Those times are over. I push the statues away in order to reveal the abyss.' But he added immediately afterwards, almost intimidated by his own audacity: '"In this nothingness I hope to find all," said Faust, entering the infernal regions. In order to plunge deeper into the abyss there must at least be the hope of finding Helen. . . . We must get used to seeing in the dark.' But, from the role of a prophet he could pass on to the 'vocabulary' session of the Literature Class in the Italian Academy, to which he had been elected in 1929. Ugo Ojetti has given us the last description of Pirandello as an academician.[74] 'Between Bontempelli and Novaro the chair . . . of Luigi Pirandello. On this side of the table, opposite that chair, myself, between Panzini and

Bertoni. Formichi presided. . . . Pirandello was always punctual. He arrived, smiled at us with a broad smile, spreading his lips but not opening them, and he suddenly raised his brows and looked for a second like a Chinaman. From between his wrinkles his clear eyes flashed like a spark. He sat down, put his cigarettes next to the inkwell . . . passed them round, lit one, opened the pages which were already annotated, waited for Bertoni to start reading.'

In his last months Pirandello found more and more serenity with his family, especially with his grandchildren. He directed them in a production of *Hamlet* to be performed on the terrace, and on this occasion Frateili found that 'he had no more anxiety. . . . He seemed to be reconciled with life, content with the familiar reality which surrounded him and gave him a visible happiness'.[75]

But there was no question of real happiness. His health deteriorated. He suffered from constipation and further heart pains. On the last occasion when he read a work of his to some friends Corrado Alvaro recalled that the page trembled in his hands, that the clear and expert diction was no longer what it used to be: it had become slurred and confused. In November Pirandello was working at a new cinema adaptation of *The Late Mattia Pascal*. One day he returned home with a temperature. 'He was shivering,' said Alvaro, 'and he paced his study impatiently as he did whenever something went wrong, while he waited for his bed to be prepared.'

During his illness he joked, made fun of the doctor and of medicine in general. At dawn on 10 December, he said to the doctor who had taken some blood and was trying to encourage him:[76] 'No need to be so scared of words, doctor. This is called dying.' The day before he died he was thinking of the third act of *The Giants of the Mountain* (*I giganti della montagna*), his unfinished work whose title was probably influenced by Dunsany's *Gods of the Mountain*. To his son Stefano, who was at his bedside, he said: 'There is an olive tree in the middle of the stage; it has solved everything for me.' He said this with a smile. 'My father's imagination,' recalls Stefano,[77] 'was occupied with these phantoms throughout the last night of his life; the next morning he told me that it had been terribly tiring to compose the third act and that now, having solved all the problems, he hoped to get a little bit of rest. He said that he was looking forward to writing down in a few days' time, as soon as he was better, all he had imagined in those few hours.'

At his death a priest was called to grant him absolution and two nuns kept vigil over him all night on their knees, intimidated by a corpse without any flowers or candles. 'They covered his face with a sheet,' remembers Ojetti.[78] 'I put a hand on his brow. Through the shroud I thought it still felt warm. Then I squeezed his folded hands. Other hands must have touched those hands before me, caressed that face; the linen clinging to the round skull, the nose, the cheek bones, the tip of the beard, the wrist, the knuckles, modelled the slender body, presented a sort of rough sketch of it.'

The page with his last wishes was read out—a page of that cheap writing paper which used to be sold for a farthing, including the envelope. The ink was faded, the handwriting that of twenty-five years earlier. On the sheet was written:

My last wishes which must be respected.
1. My death must be passed over in silence. My friends and my enemies are begged not only not to write about it in the papers but not even to mention it. No announcements or invitations to the funeral.
2. Do not dress my corpse. Let me be wrapped naked in a winding sheet. And no flowers on the bed or lighted candles.
3. A pauper's hearse. Bare. No one to accompany me, neither friends nor relations. The hearse, the horse, the driver—that is all.
4. Burn me. And as soon as my body has been burnt the ashes must be thrown to the winds, for I want nothing, not even my ashes, to remain. But if this cannot be done the funeral urn must be taken to Sicily and walled into some rough stone near Agrigento, where I was born.

Alvaro relates:[79]

The next day the mist drenched the last parched flowers in the little garden behind the gate in Via Antonio Bosio. An old jade pulling a pauper's hearse stood in the wet street, craning forward so as not to fall. We saw everything as dear Pirandello would have seen it. The coffin of fir wood, recently dyed with a coat of brown paint, was placed on the hearse and the few friends stood at the gate to watch it fade away between the misty trees at the end of the street.

Once it had turned the corner, the horse broke into a trot.

The ashes, taken to the Verano cemetery and forgotten, were found with the greatest difficulty ten years later when, after a number of problems with the clergy, they were transferred to Agrigento. For fifteen years they were preserved in Pirandello's favourite Greek vase, first in the Museo Comunale where they passed unnoticed amongst all the archeological material, then, at Il Caos, where they were at last buried under 'Pirandello's pine-tree', next to the house where he was born. By a presidential decree of 8 December 1949 and thanks to the good will of a few inhabitants of Agrigento the house was turned into a 'national monument'. The ashes were never thrown to the winds since nobody had the courage to do so. Yet that was exactly what Pirandello had wanted—to be set free, not imprisoned in a funerary monument.

Once Pirandello's life was over the commotion that it had aroused gradually died down—yet the perplexity of those who judge him as a man and as an artist still remains: we are still too close to him and to the 10,000 pages he wrote. But perhaps we are beginning to distinguish which of his works stand up best to time. And so the prophecy the playwright made shortly before his death is coming true:

The commotion aroused almost everywhere [by my work] is not the ideal environment for it. For me it is no more than a pledge for the future. Before it is attacked, as every human creation inevitably is, the meaningless clamour around it must be silenced; and there will be a moment when, in the first lull it will come to life . . . clear as it once was in my mind when I contemplated it in its finished form and, for an instant, thought it perfect.[80]

NOTES

CHAPTER ONE: SICILY

1. L. Pirandello, *Quaderni di Serafino Gubbio Operatore*, in *Tutti i romanzi*, Milan, 1941.

2. Stefano Landi (i.e. Stefano Pirandello), 'La vita ardente di Luigi Pirandello', *Quadrivio*, 13 December 1936.

3. L. Pirandello, 'L'informazione sul mio involontario soggiorno sulla terra' in *Almanacco Letterario Bompiani 1938*, Milan, 1938.

4. F. V. Nardelli, *L'uomo segreto*, Milan, 1932, p. 33-4.

5. *L'Illustrazione Italiana*, 23 June 1935.

6. S. Landi, art. cit.; F. V. Nardelli, op. cit.; Cappa, *Almanacco Letterario Bompiani 1938*, Milan, 1938.

7. *Il Giornale di Sicilia*, 11-12 September 1915.

8. F. V. Nardelli, op. cit.

9. *Galleria*, January-April 1961.

10. S. Landi, art. cit.

11. L. Pirandello, *Saggi, poesie e scritti vari*, ed. by Manlio Lo Vecchio-Musti, Milan, 1960, p. 1241.

12. S. Landi, art. cit.

13. *L'Ora*, 11 December 1936.

14. *La Gazzetta d'Italia*, 4 May 1874.

15. L. Pirandello, *I vecchi e i giovani* in *Tutti i romanzi*.

16. Innocenzo Pirandello, 'Appunti sulla vita di Pirandello', *Retroscena*, 15 February 1937.

17. S. Landi, art. cit.

18. S. Landi, art. cit.; F. V. Nardelli, op. cit.

19. L. Pirandello, 'Prosa moderna', *Vita Nuova*, 5 October 1890.

20. A. Frateili, 'Pirandello, uno e due', *Almanacco Letterario Bompiani 1938*.

21. 'Lettere ai famigliari' published by Sandro D'Amico, *Terzo Programma*, No. 3, 1961.

22. S. Landi, art. cit.

23. L. Pirandello, 'Between Two Shadows'.
24. S. F. Romano, *Storia dei Fasci Siciliani*, Bari, 1959.
25. L. Pirandello, 'Fumes'.
26. L. Pirandello, 'The Quick and the Dead' ('La morta e la viva').
27. Sebastiano Aglianò, *Cos'è questa Sicilia*, Siracuse, 1945, p. 39.

CHAPTER TWO: UNIVERSITY

1. Letter from Palermo, dated 31 October 1886. Pirandello's letters to his sister are in the possession of his children and grandchildren. The correspondence is described by Elio Providenti in *Terzo Programma*, No. 3, 1961, where Sandro D'Amico published eight of the letters.
2. An administrative post in the government offices.
3. Letter dated 18 December 1893, published in *Omnibus*, 18 October 1946.
4. The five letters from Pirandello to Ernesto Monaci were published by L. Finazzi Agrò in *Nuova Antologia*, 1 April 1943. The letters themselves are kept at the Società filologica romana, founded by Monaci in 1902.
5. Letter to Rosalina, dated 26 October 1889.
6. S. Landi, art. cit., *Quadrivio*, 13 December 1936.
7. He even wrote a short thesis on Tieck.
8. 'Taccuini di Bonn' in *Saggi, poesie e scritti vari*, p. 1194.
9. *Vita Nuova*, 8 December 1889.
10. Letter from Bonn, dated 24 June 1890.
11. 'Taccuini di Bonn' in *Saggi, poesie e scritti vari*, p. 1190–1.
12. F. V. Nardelli, *L'uomo segreto*, 1932.
13. Letter to Monaci of 7 September 1890.
14. Undated letter to Monaci.
15. The articles in *Vita Nuova* appeared on 29 June, 6 July, and 5 October 1890.
16. L. Pirandello, 'Prosa moderna', *Vita Nuova*, 5 October 1890.
17. *Vita Nuova*, 23 November 1890.
18. See Pirandello's autobiographical letter as a preface to Benjamin Crémieux, *Vieille Sicile*, Paris, 1928.
19. Information from Professor Franz Rahut, professor of Provençal at the University of Würzburg, who has done detailed research on the period Pirandello spent at the University of Bonn.
20. The thesis, a volume of about 100 closely printed pages, was printed in Halle a.S. (Druck der Buchdruckerei des Waisenhauses), 1891.
21. F. V. Nardelli, op. cit.
22. The letter has not been published yet. But see E. Providenti, *Terzo Programma*, No. 3, 1961.

CHAPTER THREE: ROME
1. Letter to Giuseppe . . . of 23 May 1891, kept at the Museo del Caos.
2. Letter of May 1890 kept at the Museo del Caos.
3. *L'Ora*, 11 December 1936.
4. *L'Ora*, 4–5 August 1901.
5. 'L'esposizione di belle arti in Roma 1895–96'. The articles appeared in *Il Giornale di Sicilia* between 20 September and 1 December 1895.
6. F. V. Nardelli, *L'uomo segreto*, p. 127.
7. Corrado Di Blasi, *Luigi Capuana*, Mineo, 1954.
8. Tomaso Gnoli, 'Un cenacolo letterario: Fleres, Pirandello e C.', *Leonardo*, March 1935.
9. Mario Corsi, 'Come Pirandello si accostò al teatro', *L'Illustrazione Italiana*, 12 December 1937.
10. *Ariel*, 20 March 1898.
11. *Terzo Programma*, No. 3, 1961.
12. Ibid. Also in 1893 (17 April) Pirandello told Angiolo Orvieto, who had asked him to contribute to his paper, that he had 'so much material that he did not know what to choose', poems and short stories, 'long, very long ones', which might be published in instalments. In the same letter Pirandello said he was staying in Agrigento where he had had an unpleasant operation on his groin. The letter is reproduced by R. O. J. Van Nuffel in 'Luigi Pirandello', *Le Flambeau*, No. 9–10, 1961.
13. Corrado Alvaro, Preface to L. Pirandello, *Novelle per un anno*, Milan, 1956.
14. Lucio D'Ambra, *Trent'anni di vita letteraria*, Milan, 1928, vol. II.
15. F. V. Nardelli, op. cit.
16. *L'Ora*, 11 December 1936.
17. The twelve letters to Antonietta, from 15 December 1893 to 7 January 1894, were published in *Omnibus*, 18 October 1946 and 25 October 1946.
18. The letter, dated 15 January 1904, is reproduced by R. O. J. Van Nuffel, art. cit.
19. F. V. Nardelli, op. cit., p. 145.
20. See n. 18.
21. *Il Giornale d'Italia*, 8 May 1924.

CHAPTER FOUR: POLITICS AND WAR
1. See Pirandello's article 'Arte e coscienza d'oggi', *La Nazione Letteraria*, September 1893; and his speech at the Convegno Volta in 1934 in *Saggi, poesie e scritti vari*.
2. The letter is at the Museo del Caos.
3. *I Mattaccini* (Naples), 29 December 1901.

4. A close friend of Pirandello's states that he found Corradini 'odious', that he had no respect for him, and that he considered him 'ambitious, substantially insincere' and 'dishonest'.

5. Paola Boni-Fellini has recounted the episode in lectures and articles.

6. Paola Boni-Fellini, *I segreti della fama*, Rome, 1955.

7. *Il Giornale d'Italia*, 8 May 1924.

8. *Quadrivio*, 20 December 1936. Pirandello had signed the pro-fascist Gentile Manifesto in 1925.

9. Letter dated 3 January 1908.

10. Pirandello gave a favourable review to a poem by Costanzo and, on several occasions, asked him for small loans.

11. Private communication.

12. The letter is dated 29 March 1908 and has been published in *Il Contemporaneo*, 26 January 1957. Pirandello was telling Bontempelli about the Magistero since Bontempelli was hoping to obtain the chair of stylistics.

13. A broadcast produced by Aldo Scimè. The typescript of Maria Alaimo's text is at the Museo del Caos. Maria Alaimo's book on Pirandello is *Luigi Pirandello e il suo mondo*, Girgenti, 1926.

14. Private communication.

15. The text of this lecture is at the Ente per il Turismo di Agrigento.

16. Lucio D'Ambra, op. cit., p. 91f.

17. Information from a niece of Antonietta Portulano, Signorina Rosalia Portulano, the daughter of Antonietta's brother. But which is the short story?

18. Tomaso Gnoli, art. cit. Apparently Pirandello's friends really did tease him about this.

19. See n. 13.

20. In a note he wrote on reading the manuscript of the present study.

21. A. Gramsci, *Letteratura e vita nazionale*, Turin, 1950, p. 47.

22. See n. 20.

23. All the letters to Pirandello's son Stefano are in *Almanacco Letterario Bompiani 1938*.

24. See n. 20.

25. See n. 20.

CHAPTER FIVE: THE THEATRE

1. L. D'Ambra, *Trent'anni*; M. Corsi, in *L'Illustrazione Italiana*, 13 December 1937; Ugo Fleres, *L'Urbe*, January 1937.

2. L. D'Ambra, op. cit.

3. *Saggi, poesie e scritti vari*, p. 875.

4. M. Corsi, art. cit.

5. Pirandello made similar statements in his article entitled 'Illustratori, attori e traduttori', *Nuova Antologia*, 16 January 1908.

6. Angelo Musco, *Cerca che trovi*, Bologna, 1930, p. 309.

7. N. Zuccarello, an actor in Musco's company, wrote in *Il Giornale di Sicilia*, 22 February 1957: 'At one point Pirandello quarrelled with Musco because he did not appreciate him enough. Pirandello had little respect for us and value us still less.'

8. *Il Messaggero*, 1 April 1918.

9. A. G. Bragaglia, 'Pirandello, l'uomo', *Almanacco Letterario Bompiani 1938*; Jia Ruskaia, 'Intervista da Roma', *Nostro Tempo*, December 1961.

10. *Almanacco Letterario Bompiani 1938*.

11. Ibid.

12. Orio Vergani, 'L'ora dei *Sei personaggi*', *Il Corriere della Sera*, 15 December 1936. See also L. Antonelli, *Maschera nuda di Pirandello*, Rome, 1937; F. V. Nardelli, op. cit.; C. Strada, 'Marta e Luigi', *L'Europeo*, 19 February 1952.

13. Biblioteca Comunale di Palermo, 2 Qq. c. 249, no. 5.

14. Marcello Gallian, 'Intimo Dissidio', *Quadrivio*, 18 November 1934.

15. *Il Giornale d'Italia*, 8 May 1924.

16. *Terzo Programma*, No. 3, 1961.

17. *La Concordia*, 12 July 1916.

18. *L'Avanti*, 5 October 1917.

CHAPTER SIX: SUCCESS

1. In 1936, shortly before he died, when Enrico Roma told Pirandello that a life ended after its various aims had been fulfilled, the playwright answered: 'I used to think that too. But since poor Tozzi, who had a great literary future, was killed by a stupid accident, I no longer believe it.' *Almanacco Letterario Bompiani 1938*.

2. All Pirandello's letters quoted here were published by Sandro D'Amico, *Terzo Programma*, No. 3, 1961.

3. See Frederick May's communication at the Congresso Internazionale di Studi Pirandelliani, Venice, 1961.

4. *Sipario*, No. 80, 1952.

5. George Pitoëff, *Notre Théâtre—Textes et documents de Pitoëff, réunis par Jean de Rigault*, Paris, n.d. An article by George Pitoëff on the occasion of Pirandello's death has been partially reproduced in *Quadrivio*, 20 December 1936.

6. All these comments are quoted in Aniouta Pitoëff, *Ludmilla, ma mère*, Paris, 1955.

7. 'This time,' wrote Pitoëff in op. cit., 'Pirandello could not come and he only saw the performance when we staged it in Milan.'

8. F. V. Nardelli, *L'uomo segreto*, p. 257.

9. *L'Impero*, 11–12 November 1924.
10. *Almanacco Letterario Bompiani 1938*.
11. Charles Oulmont, 'Le vrai visage de Pirandello', *Revue Théâtrale*, No. 9–10, 1949.
12. But on other occasions he said that he preferred *Henry IV*. See Camardella-Carelli, 'Pirandello va in America', *Retroscena*, 15 February 1937; Aniouta Pitoëff, op. cit.
13. See Camardella-Carelli, art. cit.
14. Information from Signora Lietta Pirandello.
15. *Il Giornale di Sicilia*, 10 April 1924.
16. Ibid.
17. *Il Giornale d'Italia*, 8 May 1924.
18. For a description of events accompanying the performance see Lucio Ridenti, 'Contributi pirandelliani, Ciascuno a suo modo 1924', *Il Dramma*, August–September 1961.
19. *Almanacco Letterario Mondadori 1927*.
20. A. Tilgher, *Studi sul teatro contemporaneo*, Rome, 1928, p. 262.
21. *L'Epoca*, 5 July 1922.
22. See his letter to Lietta, dated 5 April 1923.
23. *Raccolta*, January 1940.
24. *Saggi, poesie e scritti vari*, p. 987.
25. *L'Illustrazione Italiana*, 7 October 1934.
26. *Raccolta*, January 1940.
27. The letter has been lost.
28. Undated letter written shortly after Amendola's article in *Il Mondo*.
29. This, and all the other letters quoted, are in L. Sciascia, *Pirandello e la Sicilia*, Caltanissetta, 1961.
30. Letters of 17 October 1924, 6 April 1925, and 19 November 1925.
31. A. Tilgher, op. cit., pp. 254 and 257.
32. L. Sciascia, op. cit., p. 101.
33. *Il Tempo del lunedi*, 8 March 1948.
34. *Almanacco Letterario Bompiani 1938*.
35. *Quadrivio*, 20 December 1936.
36. *Stampa Sera*, 4 September 1956.
37. *L'Epoca*, 5 July 1922.
38. *Sipario*, No. 80, 1952.

CHAPTER SEVEN: FASCISM

1. Nino Valeri, *Da Giolitti a Mussolini*, Florence, 1958, p. 48.
2. *Almanacco Letterario Bompiani 1938*.
3. *Il Giornale d'Italia*, 8 May 1924.

4. Reported in *L'Impero*, 23 September 1924.

5. Ibid.

6. L. Sciascia, *Pirandello e la Sicilia*, p. 86.

7. N. Valeri, op. cit., p. 209. Pirandello's enemy, Benedetto Croce, also continued to support the fascist government after the murder of Matteoti.

8. F. V. Nardelli, op. cit., pp. 263–4.

9. Preface to *Novelle per un anno*.

10. Luigi Ferrante, *Pirandello*, Florence, 1958, p. 229.

11. Preface to *Novelle per un anno*.

12. *Quadrivio*, 18 March 1934.

13. Luigi Chiarini, 'Perchè è stata proibita in Germania *La favola del figlio cambiato*', *Quadrivio*, 18 March 1934.

14. Published by Emilio Mariano in *L'Osservatore Politico Letterario*, March 1958. D'Annunzio's first letter is dated 9 September 1934 and Pirandello's 18 September. D'Annunzio's third missive to Pirandello seems to have been a telegram.

15. Preface to *Novelle per un anno*.

16. *Saggi, poesie e scritti vari*, pp. 918, 1027. See also Pirandello's article 'Il neo-idealismo' in *La Domenica Italiana*, 27 December 1896.

17. According to Signor Nino Bertoletti, during a broadcast on the Italian radio produced by Fernaldo di Giammatteo on 10 December 1961.

18. F. Pasini, *Luigi Pirandello (come mi pare)*, Trieste, 1927. See also Pasini's article in *L'Italia*, March 1926.

19. *Il Corriere della Sera*, 18 February 1962.

20. Ibid.

21. Preface to *Novelle per un anno*.

22. *Quadrivio*, 3 November 1935.

23. Preface to *Novelle per un anno*.

CHAPTER EIGHT: THE ARTS THEATRE

1. A. Camilleri, *I teatri stabili in Italia 1898–1918*, Bologna, 1959.

2. C. Strada, 'Marta e Luigi', *L'Europeo*, 19 February 1952.

3. *Almanacco Letterario Bompiani 1938*, p. 93.

4. C. Strada, art. cit.

5. L. Antonelli, *Maschera nuda di Pirandello*.

6. C. Strada, art. cit.

7. See L. Baldacci, 'Il teatro di Bontempelli e l'esempio di Pirandello', *Paragone*, December 1961.

8. G. Lo Curzio, 'Serata con Pirandello', *Il Mattino*, 17 December 1939.

9. *Saggi, poesie e scritti vari*, p. 989. The article originally appeared in *Il Messaggero della Domenica*, 30 July 1918.

10. Vito Pandolfi, *Regìa e registi nel teatro moderno*, Rocca di San Casciano, 1961, p. 64.

11. In a broadcast on the Italian radio produced by Sandro D'Amico on 2 June 1961. The programme was entitled 'Pirandello rinnovatore del teatro drammatico'.

12. *La Voce dell'Isola*, 13 December 1946.

13. A. G. Bragaglia, art. cit., *Almanacco Letterario Bompiani 1938*.

14. Dario Niccodemi, *Tempo Passato*, Milan, 1929, p. 81f.

15. *Quadrivio*, 20 December 1936.

16. *Il Corriere della Sera*, 16 June 1929.

17. D. Niccodemi, op. cit.

18. Ibid.

19. G. Lo Curzio, art. cit.

20. See n. 11.

21. *La Lettura*, February 1937.

22. D. Niccodemi, op. cit.

23. Guy Dumur, *Pirandello*, Paris, 1955, p. 150.

24. Oscar Büdel, 'Pirandello sulla scena tedesca', *Quaderni del Piccolo Teatro*, No. 1, Milan, 1961.

25. Ibid.

26. *La Lettura*, 1 March 1927.

27. Silvio D'Amico, *Storia del teatro drammatico*, Milan, 1960.

28. *La Lettura*, 1 March 1927.

29. Ibid.

30. A. Frateili, art. cit., *Almanacco Letterario Bompiani 1938*.

31. See Aniouta Pitoëff, op. cit.; Oscar Büdel, art. cit.

32. *La Lettura*, 1 March 1927.

33. *Almanacco Letterario Bompiani 1938*.

34. Lucio D'Ambra, *Trent'anni*, vol. III, p. 255.

CHAPTER NINE: THE LAST SEASON

1. *Il Tevere*, 16 March 1928.

2. Lucio D'Ambra, loc. cit.

3. P. Solari, 'Giornate a Berlino', *Almanacco Letterario Bompiani 1938*, p. 78.

4. O. Büdel, 'Pirandello sulla scena tedesca', *Quaderni del Piccolo Teatro*, No. 1, Milan, 1961, p. 103.

5. Ibid., p. 101.

6. *L'Italia Letteraria*, 3 July 1932.

7. O. Büdel, art. cit.

8. *Terzo Programma*, No. 3, 1961.

9. Ibid. Letter dated 30 July 1931. Pirandello now lived at 37, Rue La Pérouse.

10. Preface to *Novelle per un anno.*

11. Ibid.

12. The text of the will was published in *Il Giorno*, 20 February 1962.

13. Ibid.

14. Preface to *Novelle per un anno.*

15. See Delfina Pettinato's interview with Lietta Pirandello, *Stampa Sera*, 6–7 September, 1956.

16. *L'Illustrazione Italiana*, 27 May 1934.

17. A. Frateili, 'Pirandello e il cinema', *Cinema*, 25 December 1936.

18. This and the following letters were published in *Cinema*, 25 December 1936.

19. Lucio D'Ambra, 'Sette anni di cinema', *Cinema*, 25 January 1937.

20. Orio Vergani, 'Ritratto di Pirandello', *Rivista d'Italia*. 28 February 1919.

21. Lucio D'Ambra, art. cit.

22. A. Frateili, art. cit.

23. Ibid.

24. Published in *Scenario*, January 1933.

25. *La Lettura*, February 1937.

26. *La Lettura*, 1 March 1927.

27. Alberto Rossi, 'Pirandello e il cinematografo', *Il Dramma*, 1 January 1937.

28. *L'Italia Letteraria*, 27 October 1935.

29. Corrado Alvaro, 'Pirandello e gli sceneggiatori', *Cinema*, 10 November 1938. The film was completed in 1939.

30. *Il Tevere*, 7–8 October 1936.

31. *Saggi, poesie e scritti vari*. See also G. C. Castello, 'Filmografia ragionata di L. Pirandello', *Cinema*, No. 135, 1954.

32. Only two acts of Pirandello's unfinished play *The Giants of the Mountain* were published in his lifetime—the first act, entitled 'The Ghosts' ('I fantasmi') in *Nuova Antologia*, 16 December 1931, and the second act in *Quadrante*, November 1934.

33. Pirandello always denied any knowledge of Freud or of psychoanalysis, just as he refused to acknowledge any other influence on his work.

34. *L'Illustrazione Italiana*, 7 October 1934.

35. P. Mignosi, *Il segreto di Pirandello*, Milan, 1937, 2nd. edition.

36. In an interview with G. Cavicchioli in *Termini* (Fiume), October 1936 and *Quadrivio*, 15 November 1936.

37. *Almanacco Letterario Bompiani 1938*.

38. Ibid., p. 69.

39. *Civiltà Cattolica*, 19 May 1923.

40. *La Vie intellectuelle*, 10 May 1937.
41. The sheet of paper is reproduced in *Almanacco Letterario Bompiani 1938*.
42. G. B. Angioletti, 'Pirandello a Praga', *Emporium*, August 1937.
43. Ibid.
44. *La Lettura*, 1 March 1935.
45. *L'Italia Letteraria*, 2 February 1935.
46. G. B. Angioletti, art. cit.
47. *La Lettura*, February 1937.
48. U. Ojetti, *Cose viste*, Milan, 1939, p. 141.
49. A. Franci, 'Pirandello aneddotico', *Almanacco Letterario Bompiani 1938*, p. 93.
50. E. Roma, 'Intimità del maestro', ibid.
51. C. Alvaro, Preface to *Novelle per un anno*.
52. Ibid.
53. For a description of Pirandello's rooms see A. Frateili, *Almanacco Letterario Bompiani 1938*, p. 84; C. Alvaro, *Nuova Antologia*, 16 November 1934, p. 196.
54. *Les Nouvelles littéraires*, December 1936. See also *Quadrivio*, 20 December 1936.
55. *Nuova Antologia*, 16 November 1934.
56. P. Solari in *Almanacco Letterario Bompiani 1938*.
57. C. Alvaro, Preface to *Novelle per un anno*.
58. *La Lettura*, 1 March 1927.
59. See L. Baldacci, in *Paragone*, 1961.
60. Preface to *Novelle per un anno*.
61. *Almanacco Letterario Bompiani 1938*, p. 70.
62. *Leonardo*, October 1935.
63. A. G. Bragaglia, art. cit.
64. Preface to *Novelle per un anno*.
65. R. Radice, 'Pirandello al caffè', *Almanacco Letterario Bompiani 1938*.
66. Preface to *Novelle per un anno*.
67. *L'Illustrazione Italiana*, 23 June 1935. Forty-six years earlier, on 26 October 1889, he wrote in a letter from Bonn to his sister Rosalina: 'I have seen very many things; but I had seen nearly everything before in my imagination.'
68. R. Cristaldi in *Retroscena*, 15 February 1937.
69. 'Informazioni sul mio involontario soggiorno sulla terra' (1936) in *Saggi, poesie e scritti vari*.
70. *Quadrivio*, 20 December 1936.
71. *L'Illustrazione Italiana*, 23 June 1935.
72. R. Radice, art. cit.

73. *Quadrivio*, 15 November 1936.
74. U. Ojetti, *Cose viste*, p. 142.
75. *Almanacco Letterario Bompiani 1938*.
76. U. Ojetti, op. cit.
77. In a note at the end of the second act of L. Pirandello, *I giganti della montagna*, Milan, 1951, p. 191.
78. U. Ojetti, op. cit.
79. Preface to *Novelle per un anno*.
80. *L'Illustrazione Italiana*, 23 June 1935.

BIBLIOGRAPHICAL NOTE

My bibliographical sources are indicated in the notes, so I shall not repeat them here. I would simply like to mention the texts which were of greatest use to me. To start with there is *Saggi, poesie e scritti vari di Pirandello* (Milan, 1960) edited by Manlio Lo Vecchio-Musti, a collection that is well furnished with bibliographical and chronological notes in addition to information concerning translations, theatrical premières, film adaptations, and so on. Another and very different book which I have had to consult and from which I have quoted extensively is Federico Vittore Nardelli's *L'uomo segreto* (Milan, 1932), the only good biography of Pirandello which has hitherto been published. Though one may object to certain errors and inaccuracies and to the adulatory tone of the book, it tells us about some of the most important episodes in Pirandello's childhood. Nardelli's biography, which was written around 1930, has an authenticity all of its own since it was the consequence of direct conversations with the playwright who sanctioned its publication, and it was published by Pirandello's publisher.

Of the more useful recent books on Pirandello I should mention: Leonardo Sciascia's *Pirandello e la Sicilia* (Caltanissetta, 1961) which contains illuminating comments on Pirandello's work as well as interesting information about Pirandello's relationship with Adriano Tilgher and about his attitude towards fascism; and Luigi Ferrante's *Pirandello* (Florence, 1958), which provides a collection of reviews of Pirandello's plays and contains a good chapter on 'Pirandello and Catholicism'. L. Antonelli's book *Maschera nuda di Pirandello* (Rome, 1937) is of less interest.

The following works contain recollections of Pirandello: U. Ojetti, *Cose viste*, vols. I, III, VII, Milan, 1925, 1926, 1939; D. Niccodemi, *Tempo passato*, Milan, 1929; Lucio D'Ambra, *Trent'anni di vita letteraria*, Milan, 1928–9; A. Musco, *Cerca che trovi*, Bologna, 1930;

A. Casella, *I segreti della Giara*, Florence, 1941; A. Pitoëff, *Ludmilla, ma mère*, Paris, 1955; P. Boni-Fellini, *I segreti della fama*, Rome, 1955; G. Longo, *La Sicilia è un'isola*, Milan, 1962.

One of the best pieces written about Pirandello as a man is, to my mind, C. Alvaro, Preface to *Novelle per un anno* (Milan, 1956). Silvio D'Amico's many studies on Pirandello are more concerned with literary criticism.

There are some extremely useful articles in *Almanacco Letterario Bompiani 1938* which is devoted to Pirandello, and of these Arnaldo Frateili's article, entitled 'Pirandello, uno e due' is of particular interest from the biographical point of view. Other reviews have devoted special numbers to Pirandello: *Quadrivio* (18 November 1934 and 13 December 1936—the latter number contains an article by the playwright's son Stefano, 'La vita ardente di Luigi Pirandello'); *Retroscena* (15 February 1937, with a biographical article by the playwright's brother Innocenzo, 'Appunti sulla vita di Pirandello'); *Sipario* (No. 80, 1952); *Quaderni del Piccolo Teatro* (No. 1, Milan, 1961, entitled 'Pirandello ieri e oggi' and edited by Sandro D'Amico).

There is also the collection of documents concerning the first night of *Each In His Own Way* published in *Il Dramma*, August–September 1961, by Lucio Ridenti.

The other books and pamphlets about Pirandello seem to me to be of less value. I have found further important information and impressions in newspaper and review articles, and I have noted them in the course of this study.

Only a small part of Pirandello's correspondence has been published, and that not in full. I have given the references of what letters I have been able to consult. The most important collections of letters have been published in *Almanacco Letterario Bompiani 1938* (letters to Pirandello's son Stefano); in *Omnibus* (18 October 1946 and 25 October 1946—letters to Antonietta at the time of their engagement); in *La Nuova Antologia* (1 April 1943—letters to Ernesto Monaci); in *Terzo Programma* (No. 3, 1961—letters to Pirandello's sister Rosalina and his daughter Lietta).

I would finally like to say that my main source has been Pirandello's own work. It was by reading his writings and finding in them countless autobiographical indications that I decided on the direction my research was going to take. Some areas obviously still remain unexplored, but I feel that this is inevitable and probably even desirable.

WORKS OF PIRANDELLO [1]

POETRY

Mal giocondo, Palermo, 1889.
Pasqua di Gea, Milan, 1891.
Pier Gudrò, Rome, 1894.
Elegie renane, Rome, 1895.
Elegie romane, Leghorn, 1896 (translation from Goethe's *Römische Elegien*).
Zampogna, Rome, 1901.
Scamandro, Rome 1909 (verse play).
Fuori di chiave, Genoa, 1912.

Pirandello's poetry is available in Manlio Lo Vecchio-Musti's edition of the *Saggi, poesie, e scritti vari*, Milan, 1960. This is the sixth and final volume of Mondadori's definitive edition of the works of Pirandello in the series *I Classici Contemporanei Italiani* (1956–60).

CRITICISM AND ESSAYS

Laute und Lautentwickelung der Mundart von Girgenti, Halle a. S., 1891 (Pirandello's doctorate thesis).
Arte e Scienza, Rome, 1908.
L'umorismo, Lanciano, 1908; second edition, Florence, 1920.

These critical writings and other essays are to be found in Lo Vecchio-Musti's edition of the *Saggi, poesie, e scritti vari*, op. cit.

SHORT STORIES

The short stories were for the most part first published in newspapers and periodicals, many of them in the *Corriere della Sera*. They first appeared in book form in fifteen volumes between the years 1894 and 1919:

Amori senza amore, Rome, 1894.
Beffe della morte e della vita, Florence, 1902.
Quand'ero matto . . ., Turin, 1902.

[1] Compiled by Felicity Firth.

Beffe della morte e della vita. Seconda serie, Florence, 1903.
Bianche e nere, Turin, 1904.
Erma bifronte, Milan, 1906.
La vita nuda, Milan, 1910.
Terzetti, Milan, 1912.
Le due maschere, Florence, 1914.
La trappola, Milan, 1915.
Erba del nostro orto, Milan, 1915.
E domani, lunedì..., Milan, 1917.
Un cavallo nella luna, Milan, 1918.
Berecche e la guerra, Milan, 1919.
Il carnevale dei morti, Florence, 1919.

Later Pirandello rearranged his short stories into a totally different fifteen-volume collection under the title *Novelle per un anno,* which is available today in the *Biblioteca Moderna Mondadori* series (most recent edition 1960). The two volumes of short stories (1956 and 1957), edited by Corrado Alvaro, in Mondadori's definitive edition of the works cit. include in addition some titles previously rejected by Pirandello.

For a complete list of the individual stories, see the appendix of Luigi Pirandello, *Short Stories,* selected and translated by Frederick May, Oxford University Press, 1965.

NOVELS
Dates refer to the year of publication in book form. Some of the novels first appeared in instalments in periodicals.

L'esclusa, Milan, 1908 (written in 1894).
Il turno, Catania, 1902.
Il fu Mattia Pascal, Rome, 1904.
Suo marito, Florence, 1911 (later published as *Giustino Roncella nato Boggiòlo*).
I vecchi e i giovani, Milan, 1913.
Si gira . . ., Milan, 1916 (later published as *Quaderni di Serafino Gubbio, operatore*).
Uno, nessuno e centomila, Florence, 1926.

The novels are available as single volumes in the *Biblioteca Moderna Mondadori* series, and as the third volume (1957), edited by Corrado Alvaro, of Mondadori's definitive edition cit.

PLAYS
Dates given refer to year of first publication.

La Morsa, 1898 (under title *L'epilogo*).
Lumìe di Sicilia, 1911.

Il dovere del medico, 1912.
Liolà, 1917 (Sicilian text. Italian text 1928).
Pensaci, Giacomino!, 1917.
Il berretto a sonagli, 1918.
Il piacere dell'onestà, 1918.
La patente, 1918.
Così è (se vi pare), 1918.
Ma non è una cosa seria, 1919.
Il giuoco delle parti, 1919.
Tutto per bene, 1920.
La ragione degli altri, 1921.
Come prima, meglio di prima, 1921.
L'innesto, 1921.
Sei personaggi in cerca d'autore, 1921.
Enrico IV, 1922.
L'uomo, la bestia, e la virtú, 1922.
La signora Morli, una e due, 1922.
Vestire gli ignudi, 1923.
La vita che ti diedi, 1924.
Ciascuno a suo modo, 1924.
La giara, 1925.
L'altro figlio, 1925.
Sagra del Signore della Nave, 1925.
Cecè, 1926.
All'uscita, 1926.
L'imbecille, 1926.
L'uomo dal fiore in bocca, 1926.
Diana e la Tuda, 1927.
L'amica delle mogli, 1927.
La nuova colonia, 1928.
O di uno o di nessuno, 1929.
Lazzaro, 1929.
Come tu mi vuoi, 1930.
Questa sera si recita a soggetto, 1930.
Trovarsi, 1932.
Quando si è qualcuno, 1933.
Non si sa come, 1935.
Sogno (ma forse no), 1936.
Bellavita, 1937.
La favola del figlio cambiato, 1938.
I giganti della montagna, 1938 (First act with title *I fantasmi*, 1931; second
    act, 1934).

Pirandello's plays have been published in various editions under the collective title of *Maschere nude*. The most easily obtainable editions are the *Biblioteca Moderna Mondadori* one in seventeen volumes (1948–51) and the two volumes of the plays, edited by Silvio d'Amico (1958) in the Mondadori definitive edition cit.

SOME RECOMMENDED CRITICAL WORKS IN ENGLISH ON PIRANDELLO

BISHOP, T., *Pirandello and the French Theatre*, London, 1960.

BUDEL, O., *Pirandello*, London, 1966.

CAMBON, G. (ed.), *Pirandello, a collection of critical essays*, in the series *Twentieth Century Views*, Englewood Cliffs, New Jersey, 1967.

MACLINTOCK, L., *The Age of Pirandello*, Indiana University Press, 1951.

STARKIE, W., *Luigi Pirandello*, University of California Press, 1965 (first published 1926).

VITTORINI, D., *The Drama of Luigi Pirandello*, New York, 1957 (first published 1935).

GENERAL WORKS WITH INTERESTING SECTIONS ON PIRANDELLO

BENTLEY, E., *In Search of Theatre*, New York, 1953; Vintage Books, 1957.

BRUSTEIN, R., *The Theatre of Revolt: An Approach to Modern Drama*, London, 1965.

NICOLL, A., *World Drama from Aeschylus to Anouilh*, London, 1949.

STYAN, J. L., *The Dark Comedy: The Development of Modern Comic Tragedy*, Cambridge University Press, 1962.

STYAN, J. L., *The Elements of Drama*, Cambridge University Press, 1969.

WILLIAMS, R., *Drama from Ibsen to Eliot*, London: Penguin Books, 1964 (first published 1952).

WILLIAMS, R., *Modern Tragedy*, London, 1966.

INDEX

(The abbreviation P stands for Luigi Pirandello throughout)